A GRIM ALMANAC OF THE
WORKHOUSE

A GRIM ALMANAC OF THE
WORKHOUSE

PETER HIGGINBOTHAM

Also by the Author

Voices from the Workhouse

The Workhouse Encyclopedia

Life in a Victorian Workhouse

The Workhouse Cookbook

The Prison Cookbook

Workhouses of the North

Workhouses of the Midlands

First published in 2013

The History Press
The Mill, Brimscombe Port
Stroud, Gloucestershire, GL5 2QG
www.thehistorypress.co.uk

British Library Cataloguing in Publication Data.
A catalogue record for this book is available from the British Library.

ISBN 978 0 7524 8739 7

Typesetting and origination by The History Press
Printed in Great Britain

CONTENTS

INTRODUCTION   7

A WORKHOUSE TIMELINE   9

JANUARY   11

FEBRUARY   34

MARCH   52

APRIL   70

MAY   88

JUNE   106

JULY   125

AUGUST   143

SEPTEMBER   162

OCTOBER   178

NOVEMBER   198

DECEMBER   215

BIBLIOGRAPHY   234

INDEX OF WORKHOUSE LOCATIONS   236

INTRODUCTION

Workhouses never had a good image. From the seventeenth century, when the earliest such institutions appeared, until the inauguration of Britain's National Health Service in 1948, which is often taken as the date of their final demise, workhouses were regularly painted as places of shame, abuse, degradation, slavery, cruelty, disease, squalor, and – due in no small part to a certain Oliver Twist – of starvation.

For most decent people, the possibility of ending up in a workhouse carried an enormous stigma. For one thing, it would be a very public humiliation – everyone would be aware of where they had gone. On top of that, there was the sheer unpleasantness of the whole experience – the separation of families, the monotony of the food, the uniform and, for the able-bodied at least, the daily grind of workhouse labour. For the elderly, the prospect of dying in a workhouse held out the grim possibility of a pauper's funeral in an unmarked grave or, even worse, being despatched for anatomical dissection.

But were things really that bad? From the 1870s onwards, many aspects of workhouse life materially improved. Inmates increasingly benefited from better medical care, more varied and better quality food, and better recreational facilities in the shape of books, newspapers, entertainments, and outings to the country or seaside. The elderly, in particular, received extra 'indulgences' such as weekly allowances of tea, tobacco and snuff.

Despite such changes, the workhouse remained a place that many people would rather die than go into. Over the years, as illustrated in the pages of this book, numerous examples can be found of individuals taking their own life rather than enter the workhouse. (In one case at least, though, a suicide resulted from an individual *not* being allowed entry to a workhouse.) Suicides also regularly took place amongst those who were already workhouse inmates, the most favoured methods being throat-cutting, hanging, taking poison, or jumping from a high window.

Even for those who reconciled themselves to institutional life, the workhouse could be a dangerous place. There could be violence – sometimes with fatal consequences – between inmate and inmate, inmates and staff, or between members of staff themselves. Some of the most disturbing events in the history of the workhouse, though, occurred where those in positions of authority and control inflicted abuse or neglect on those in their care, sometimes for years on end before being discovered. Some of these individuals, most notably the tyrannical workhouse masters George Catch and Colin McDougal, and the sadistic children's nurse Ella Gillespie, have now become infamous for the vileness of their activities.

For all workhouse inmates, though, life could hold unexpected perils. As this almanac reveals, even apparently innocuous activities such as eating dinner, having a bath, paying a visit to the toilet, sitting in front of the fire, or even lying asleep in bed could all turn into life-threatening situations. The medical care provided to inmates, too, could sometimes have perilous consequences. The accidental or inept administering of injurious treatments to workhouse patients was the cause of a number of deaths, including that of a workhouse master who had devised and himself tried out a particularly poisonous concoction. The occasional mind-numbing foolishness of staff is also evidenced in more than one instance when the investigation of a gas leak was conducted with a lighted candle or lantern.

The outbreak of fire was a danger in all large institutions, especially ones such as workhouses where children, the elderly, and the mentally impaired formed a large proportion of the inmates. Some of the most harrowing scenes described in this volume were the devastating results of fires which proved too intense for the facilities available to fight them or where defects in the buildings prevented the evacuation of those inside.

Despite such hazards, longevity was surprisingly common amongst workhouse inmates, with the remarkable age of 136 years being claimed in one instance. Romance, too, was not unknown in the workhouse. Despite the enforced separation between male and female inmates, love could find a way – as proved in a number of instances. Given the constrained lives imposed on workhouse employees, it is also not surprising that relationships between staff blossomed from time to time. There are even instances of staff and inmates falling for one another.

Workhouse inmates were not, of course, just passive recipients of poor relief. They knew how to play the system. Whether it was harbouring secret stashes of money, illicitly consorting with the opposite sex, smuggling alcohol or drugs into the premises via visitors or the informally appointed inmates' 'messenger', or even – in the case of at least one elderly couple – getting married in order to benefit, it was alleged, from the provision of their own private room.

Although most of the events related in this book took place in the British Isles, a few are included from other countries around the world which operated workhouse-style institutions, including the United States, Russia, Sweden and Czechoslovakia. Inevitably, to rate as newsworthy in Britain, such incidents were generally major disasters such as devastating fires. An index of all the workhouse locations mentioned is included at the end of the book.

Finally, to keep the many grim events presented here in perspective, it must be remembered that under the new poor relief system established in 1834, there were more than 600 union workhouses set up in England and Wales. For most of these establishments, scandal or catastrophe was a rarity – perhaps occurring just once or twice over the century or so of their existence. For the vast majority of their lifetime, they just got on and did their job.

A WORKHOUSE TIMELINE

This book does not aim to be a comprehensive history of the workhouse system. However, for those not familiar with its development, here is a timeline of some major events:

1601   The Poor Relief Act is the basis of what becomes known as the Old Poor Law. Parishes become responsible for relieving their own poor funded by a local property tax – the poor rate. The poor rate can be spent on 'out-relief' (handouts to individuals) or accommodation for the 'impotent' poor – the elderly, lame or blind.

1630s   Workhouses gradually evolve to house the poor, with labour required from the able-bodied. Prototype workhouses include Reading, Abingdon, Sheffield, Newark and Newbury.

1698   Bristol's parishes promote a local Act of Parliament allowing them to jointly administer poor relief and run workhouses.

1723   Knatchbull's Act allows parishes to establish workhouses. Parishes can dispense with out-relief and offer relief claimants only the workhouse – a 'test' that they are truly destitute. Workhouse operation can be handed over to private contractors, the practice becoming known as 'farming the poor'.

1777   Around 2,000 workhouses are in operation, covering about 14 per cent of parishes. Out-relief is still the dominant form of provision, however.

1782   Gilbert's Act allows groups of parishes to form 'unions' and run joint workhouses to house non-able-bodied paupers.

1818   The national poor relief bill reaches an all-time high, having risen fivefold over the previous forty years.

1834   The Poor Law Amendment Act (the New Poor Law) establishes a new national system of poor relief administration, run by the central Poor Law Commissioners, based on groupings of parishes called Poor Law Unions. Each union is run by a locally elected Board of Guardians and has to provide a central union workhouse.

1837   Charles Dickens' *Oliver Twist* begins publication.

1838   A total of 584 Poor Law Unions are now operative in England and Wales. The Poor Relief (Ireland) Act establishes a union workhouse system in Ireland.

1845   The Poor Law (Scotland) Act introduces a new poor relief system in Scotland, with poorhouse provision as an option.

1847   The Poor Law Board replaces the Poor Law Commissioners.

1867   The Metropolitan Poor Act improves medical care for London's poor, with the new Metropolitan Asylums Board to deal with infectious and mental conditions.

1872   The Local Government Board replaces the Poor Law Board.

1900   A major overhaul of workhouse food allows more varied and flexible menus.

1905   A Royal Commission begins a major review of the poor relief system. Its report, published in 1909, recommends abolition of Boards of Guardians, replacement of workhouses by more specialised institutions, removal of children from workhouses, and the provision of old age pensions, health insurance and unemployment support.

1913   Updated official regulations now refer to 'poor law institutions' rather than 'workhouses', and 'poor persons' rather than 'paupers'. Inmate uniforms are now described as 'suitable and sufficient clothing'.

1915   Children aged over three are no longer allowed to reside in workhouses.

1930   Boards of Guardians are abolished. The administration of poor relief, now known as 'public assistance', passes to county and borough councils.

1948   The National Health Service is inaugurated.

JANUARY

The horrific scene at the Wigan workhouse where
a nine-month-old child was fatally scalded at the
hands of Catherine Dawber, a pauper nurse who was
officially classified as an 'imbecile'. (*See* 9 January)

1   JANUARY **1890**   In the early minutes of the New Year, a disastrous fire broke out at the Forest Gate Industrial School in East London, home to about 650 pauper children from the Whitechapel and Poplar Unions. The blaze, which devastated the north wing of the building, originated in a clothes storage cupboard through which a stove pipe passed. An assistant mistress raised the alarm after smelling smoke, but the building was soon engulfed in flames. Fifty-eight boys were sleeping in two dormitories on the floors above. Twenty-six died. The recovered bodies were wrapped in blankets and placed on the floor of the school's infirmary, with identifying numbers marked in big figures, or the names chalked over those which had been identified. Many of the survivors had jumped from the lower dormitory, or had been dragged out by their friends or brothers. Others were not so lucky. The younger brother of a boy called Jones had insisted on putting on his socks before leaving the dormitory but had fallen down on the floor, never to rise again.

2   JANUARY **1857**   Henry Taylor, a pauper in the Harrogate workhouse, was passing over the line at a level crossing at Starbeck station when the five o'clock passenger train for Leeds knocked him down, severed his head from his body, and smashed his skull to a pulp.

1868   An inquest was held at Preston following the death of a boy named Patrick Burke, an inmate of the Walton-le-Dale workhouse, and also the son of Stephen Burke, executed in 1866 for murdering his wife. Two days before Christmas, the governor had decided to make the workhouse boys more presentable for inspection by visitors, and obtained from the surgery a pot of 'blue ointment', which contained a considerable quantity of mercury. He rubbed half a tablespoonful of the ointment on the head of each of the eighty or so boys in his charge and, a few hours later, washed them and sent them to bed. Next morning, they all felt unwell, and the following day, the doctor was called and salivated four of them. Burke died shortly afterwards, and the governor then revealed what he had done, with forty of the boys being confined to bed for treatment. The inquest was told that Burke would have been buried without an inquest had it not been for an anonymous letter sent to the authorities. The jury returned a verdict of accidental death, but cautioned the governor to be more careful in future.

3   JANUARY **1881**   At the Leeds workhouse, a fire was discovered just before noon in a new hospital block. The blaze began in a storeroom on the fourth floor of the building in which 216 inmates were accommodated. The workhouse steward, Mr Strain, was summoned and rapidly organised a body of twenty men to use fire buckets

in dashing water into the room. Water from the building's main storage tanks, located in the vicinity of the fire, was also deployed, literally flooding the place and rapidly quelling the fire.

1894 An aged inmate of the Retford workhouse named Elizabeth Blenkhorn was found dead today in suspicious circumstances. The woman was a confirmed opium eater, and when she was visited by friends, precautions were taken to prevent anything illicit being introduced into the workhouse. On the day prior to her death she had received visitors, and the master, being suspicious, examined her bed and found a bottle containing laudanum. An inquest revealed that Blenkhorn had been a large-scale consumer of narcotics for more than twenty years. A woman who visited her recently had been sent to buy her half an ounce of laudanum, together with twopence-halfpenny worth of gin. The same person had seen Mrs Blenkhorn regularly drink a 'basinful of beer and laudanum'. On a recent occasion, while out on leave for four hours, Blenkhorn had swallowed 2 ounces of laudanum, and smuggled back a large amount of the same drug. The master stated that a quantity of opium had been found concealed in her stockings.

4   JANUARY **1839** A letter to the editor of the *Essex Standard*, from a ratepayer living in the Essex union of Tendring, claimed that workhouse inmates were now being treated worse than felons. It was, he asserted, 'the first time within the memory of any man living, that the poor in our workhouse were, on a Christmas, without roast beef and plum pudding, tea, sugar, snuff, and tobacco, with a little good porter to wash it down.' He hoped that some kindhearted guardian would join him in declaring that it was 'not too late even now to cheer the heart of the aged pauper.'

1850 Hannah Boothby, a poor woman in an advanced state of pregnancy, together with her two children, was taken to the Hull Charity Hall workhouse to ask for assistance. She was accompanied by an Irishwoman named Kitty. They arrived at about 9 a.m. and Kitty knocked at the workhouse door which was opened by the porter, Robert Peacock. Kitty told him, 'Here is a poor woman bad in labour.' Peacock refused them entry saying, 'We cannot take you in until ten o'clock, until the Governor comes. Go away.' He then shut the door. Kitty and another woman then tried several times more, saying that Hannah was in a dying state. On each occasion, Peacock told them to go away. At about ten o'clock, Hannah gave birth on the street in front of the workhouse. The workhouse door was then opened and the mother and child wrapped in blankets and taken inside. The child at first appeared to be dead, but on being warmed, it quickly revived. At a subsequent inquiry, Peacock denied having been told that Hannah Boothby was in labour. This may have had something to do with his being extremely deaf – a fact that, strangely, appeared to be unknown to his employers. Described by one guardian as being 'a most improper person to be the doorkeeper of this establishment', Peacock was ultimately given the blame for Hannah Boothby not having been taken into the workhouse. As soon as her situation became known to the workhouse authorities, she had been properly attended to.

5   JANUARY   1825   Today's *Morning Chronicle* reported the melancholy events following the birth of a child to a young mother at St Martin's workhouse, just before Christmas. Within a few days, the woman was seized with an inflammation of the bowels. She was attended by Messrs Simmons and Gosna, the parish surgeons, but despite their best efforts she died on Christmas Eve. On the morning of Christmas Day, the two gentlemen visited the workhouse to conduct a post-mortem on the body. Mr Simmons, while removing the intestines, slightly lacerated one of his fingers, but paid no attention to the incident. A little later, Mr Gosna wiped his hands upon a cloth in which a pin was sticking, and scratched his finger. The following day, Mr Simmons had a violent pain in the arm, extending to the shoulder, and two tumours were found near to the armpit. Fomentations were applied, resulting in some relief from the pain and a reduction of the tumours. But, reluctant to take any medicine, he soon had a relapse and died a few days afterwards. Mr Gosna had been similarly attacked and was now dangerously ill.

1856   An inquest was held today on the body of William Jones, an old man who had been admitted to the Hereford workhouse after being found at midnight standing in the Gloucester & Hereford Canal. From the time of his admission, he had sometimes been very violent and had also briefly escaped from the workhouse. On the night of his death, he was more than usually violent, and struck and kicked at several men in the sick ward. He fell backwards and hurt his head a little, from which he appeared stunned for a minute or so. It later proved necessary to restrain him by means of a straitjacket, in which he died at about half past eight. It was stated that death was probably due to a long-standing affliction of the brain and not from the fall which had only caused a mild abrasion to the back of the head. A verdict was returned of death from natural causes.

6   JANUARY   1736   On this day, it was reported that the governor of a workhouse in the Liberty of Westminster had been committed to the Gatehouse for ravishing a girl of about nine years of age.

1858   Alfred Feist, the former master of the Newington workhouse, was today charged with the illicit sale of pauper bodies to Guy's Hospital medical school. Although the disposal of unclaimed bodies for such purposes was permitted by the 1832 Anatomy Act, Feist's activities fell far outside the provisions of that statute. His scheme, which was said to have extended to more than twenty corpses, involved a cunning act of deception. On the day of an inmate's funeral, any relatives present were allowed to view the body, but after they had departed to await its transfer to the hearse, the coffin was secretly switched. The fresh corpse was then sent off for use at Guy's, while the funeral proceeded with a coffin which contained the dissected remains of a different person that had been returned by the medical school. At his subsequent trial, Feist was initially found guilty, but the verdict was later quashed by the Court of Appeal. The court decided that because the relatives of the deceased had not explicitly stated their objection to the medical disposal of the bodies – even though the question had not been raised with them – Feist had acted within the law.

7   JANUARY **1850**   A riot took place today at Barham workhouse in Suffolk. Around fifty able-bodied inmates got out of their ward and demanded more food. After the governor told them that he had no power to alter their diet, they tore up the seats and flooring in their dayrooms. With the arrival of a policeman, the men remained quiet during the night but their rioting was resumed the next morning and the governor was struck and injured. Eventually a detachment of Lancers was sent from Ipswich but, by the time they arrived, the riot had been quelled by the police and six of the ringleaders put into prison.

  1924   It was reported that a tramp sheltering for the night at a workhouse at Eastry, near Canterbury, had had an encounter with a ghost. The tramp, who was the sole occupant of the vagrant ward, was found in the middle of the night trembling from head to foot. He related how 'something white', uttering dreadful, guttural sounds, approached with long, thin, bony fingers spread out as though to throttle him. It disappeared when he screamed. The guardians were making it known that a ghost had been seen in the vagrant ward, and the master reported that as a result there had been a falling off in the number of vagrants.

8   JANUARY **1834**   At London's Marlborough Street magistrates' court, Sarah Corney, 'a rawboned Irishwoman' with an infant, was charged with having behaved in a disorderly manner in the parish workhouse of St George, Hanover Square, and with having broken nine squares of glass. Mr Randford, the workhouse master, said the woman had been in receipt of parish relief for many years. She was one of the most violent, vicious and drunken women in the house, and had on several occasions been brought before the Bench on account of her conduct. The previous Monday, she had

gone out and got drunk and so was barred from leaving the workhouse. She became very violent, and when brought before the Bench, the magistrates recommended that she be re-admitted to the workhouse but not allowed to go out. When she got back to the workhouse, she demanded her dinner and a pint of beer. When this was not immediately brought, she seized a pint pot and smashed windows to the value of £3. She then fought and resisted until overpowered. The woman said she admitted breaking the windows. She had asked for her dinner and beer, but she did not get it. The overseer, she considered, promoted bad conduct amongst the paupers by not giving them as much 'wittles' as they could eat. The woman was sentenced to six weeks' imprisonment.

1925 An inquest today heard allegations that an inmate of Barnsley workhouse was placed in a bath that was too hot. The deceased, Elizabeth Preston, sixty-nine, was said by Edith Pearson, a probationer nurse, to be unable to walk and had been taken in a chair to the bath. When her supervisor Nurse Prentice started to bathe the deceased, she found that the water was too hot, and they lifted her out of the bath. Dr Collings, the workhouse medical officer, attributed death to heart disease accelerated by the shock of scalds, although it did not appear the water had been excessively hot. Nurse Prentice had been at the institution for six years and was considered to be most competent. The coroner returned a verdict of death from misadventure.

Nottingham workhouse staff pose outside the institution's entrance block.

9   JANUARY **1839**   *The Times* today reproduced a letter to the editor of the *Berkshire Chronicle* signed by seven inmates of the St Lawrence's workhouse, Reading:

> Jany 3rd, 1839. – Mr Edetor, – Sir, we should be very glad if you put these few words in Press. We saw in the Reading Mercury that the Workhouses in Reading had Puding, meat, and Beer, which we all can contrydict—our Allowance was six ounces of Bread and two ounces of Chees for Cristmas Diner in Saint Lawrences Workhous.

     1868   At Wigan workhouse, an inquest was held on the body of Ruth Bannister, an illegitimate child aged nine months, who had been scalded to death in a bucket of hot water. The body was said to present a shocking appearance, the lower extremities having been dreadfully burned. The child had been placed in the infant ward in the care of two pauper nurses, assisted by a girl of seventeen named Catherine Dawber, who was described as an imbecile. On the morning of the incident, Dawber brought the child to a nurse named Margaret Gaskell, saying it was dirty, and was told to take off its napkin. The girl took the child into another room, and a few minutes later another pauper ran in to inform Gaskell that the child was scalded. Gaskell went to see what the matter was, and found the child on Dawber's knee, near to a bucket containing eight or nine quarts of scalding water. Its feet and legs were so badly scalded that the skin was peeling off and blood was coming from the wounds. Although previously being a healthy child, it had died the same evening. Mary Finch, another inmate, said she saw Dawber place the child in the water, and it gave a piercing cry. She then took it out and began to wipe it with a coarse towel. Finch saw she was doing this roughly and took the towel, in which she found a piece of skin 3in long. The inquest jury decided that the child had died from being negligently and carelessly scalded whilst being nursed by Dawber, a verdict the coroner considered amounted to one of manslaughter. At her subsequent trial, however, Dawber was found not guilty of the charge.

10   JANUARY **1894**   At a meeting of the North Dublin guardians, the chairman gave details of a letter written to the board by a man named Hayes, whose aunt, Mary Hayes, was an inmate of the workhouse. Mr Hayes had been informed by the officials that she had died, and he came and identified a woman in a coffin in the mortuary as his aunt. He then went away, had a grave dug at Glasnevin Cemetery, bought a coffin, and brought it in a hearse to the workhouse to hold the funeral. But it was then discovered that the dead woman was not his aunt at all but another inmate of

the same name, and that his aunt was alive and well. He had now written a letter of complaint, and asked the guardians to refund him the money he had expended in preparing for the funeral. The guardians declined to comply with the request.

1895 Following a recent explosion in a steam pipe at Liverpool workhouse which led to the deaths of three men, a new theory emerged as to the cause of the catastrophe. The blast had occurred when steam was being blown off from the main boiler into an underground tank. Subsequent inspection of the tank revealed the body of cat which, from its appearance, had not been there long. It was believed that the cat had somehow got into the tank and blocked an overflow pipe, causing a build-up of pressure and eventual explosion. The three fatalities, all resulting from the horrific scalding injuries they received, were the workhouse engineer, Richard Long, and two inmates who acted as stokers.

11   JANUARY

1854 A child of sixteen months was murdered by its mother, Isabella Thompson, at the Bishop Auckland workhouse. On her admission to the workhouse, it had been noticed that the child had a black eye, which the mother accounted for by saying that it had fallen on the ground. Later the nurse, hearing that the infant was ill, went to the ward and found it dead. Its arms, face and the left side of its head were swollen and black, and there was fresh blood on its hair. The stone fireplace was spattered with blood and it was evident that the poor child had been dashed against the mantelpiece. The mother left the workhouse, saying she did not wish to stay until the child was buried. While in the workhouse, she had been seen to throw the child in a rough careless manner on the bed. Thompson denied having injured her child in any way, and said the blows had been inflicted by the child having thrown itself, whilst in a fit, against an iron plate at the head of the bed.

It was subsequently discovered that, six months earlier, the child had been kidnapped by its killer, real name Isabella Crosier, from a woman named Thompson who, being ill, had engaged her from the workhouse at Sunderland. Mrs Thompson identified Crosier as her absconding servant and, after the disinterment of the infant's body, confirmed it as her lost child.

1839 On this day a report in *The Times* alleged that smallpox was rife at the Wimborne and Cranborne Union workhouse in Dorset. Mothers and their children were said to be sleeping three to a bed and, in one very small room, five beds were being shared by thirteen inmates, five of whom had gone down with the disease. It was also claimed that little was being done to halt the spread of the infection through the ward. No nurse had been appointed to attend the patients and the workhouse surgeon was receiving only £10 a year to attend the workhouse's 195 inmates. The report, subsequently revealed to have originated from one of the union's medical officers, George Place, provoked a robust rebuttal from the Wimborne guardians who claimed it had contained 'unfounded and exaggerated statements'. The smallpox outbreak had originated, it was said, with a newly admitted mother and child who had been isolated from other inmates once the disease had been confirmed on 28 December. Vaccination of all previously unvaccinated inmates had been carried out as soon as it could be arranged and no further instances had been diagnosed until 8 January. The following day, the workhouse school, a large and well-ventilated room, had been adapted for use as an isolation ward. Thirteen inmates were then placed there, attended by three nurses. It was conceded, however, that for a short period, thirteen persons did, without the knowledge of the guardians, sleep in five beds in the same room which measured just 18ft by 16ft. Finally, there was no specific salary for the medical officer attending the workhouse since it formed part of one of the union's medical districts. In the preceding year, the total salaries of the union's four medical officers had amounted to £151.

12 JANUARY 1866 Today's *Pall Mall Gazette* carried the first instalment of a remarkable account of the grim conditions inside the Lambeth workhouse tramps' ward. The article was written by journalist James Greenwood who, a few days earlier, had garbed himself in a ragged and ill-fitting overcoat, battered billycock hat, and the boots of a tramp, and shuffled into the establishment to apply for a night's shelter. Greenwood's colourful account of his experiences caused a sensation and also provoked an immediate visit to the premises by a Poor Law Inspector, Mr Henry Farnall. Typical of Greenwood's revelations was his encounter with the tramps' bath, to which he was introduced by an old-timer known as 'Daddy':

The porter went his way, and I followed Daddy into another apartment where there were three great baths, each one containing a liquid so disgustingly like weak mutton broth that my worst apprehensions crowded back. 'Come on, there's a dry place to stand on up at this end,' said Daddy, kindly. 'Take off your clothes, tie 'em up in your hank'sher, and I'll lock 'em up till the morning.'

Accordingly, I took off my coat and waistcoat, and was about to tie them together when Daddy cried, 'That ain't enough, I mean everything.'

'Not my shirt, Sir, I suppose?'

'Yes, shirt and all; but there, I'll lend you a shirt,' said Daddy. 'Whatever you take in of your own will be nailed, you know. You might take in your boots, though – they'd be handy if you happened to want to leave the shed for anything; but don't blame me if you lose 'em.'

STARTLING PARTICULARS!

A NIGHT

IN A

WORKHOUSE.

From the PALL MALL GAZETTE.

HOW THE POOR ARE TREATED IN LAMBETH!

THE CASUAL PAUPER!

"OLD DADDY," THE NURSE!

THE BATH!

The Conversation of the Casuals!

THE STRIPED SHIRT!

THE SWEARING CLUB!!

"Skilley" and "Toke" by Act of Parliament!

The Adventures of a Young Thief!

&c. &c. &c.

F. BOWERING, 211, BLACKFRIARS ROAD,
MANSELL & SON, King Street, Borough, and all Newsagents.

PRICE ONE PENNY.

The cover of James Greenwood's *A Night in a Workhouse*, articles reprinted in pamphlet form.

James Greenwood, who became known as the 'amateur casual'.

The other inmates in the ward were a very rough crowd:

> Towzled, dirty, villainous, they squatted up in their beds, and smoked foul pipes, and sang snatches of horrible songs, and bandied jokes so obscene as to be absolutely appalling. Eight or ten were so enjoying themselves – the majority with the check shirt on and the frowsy rug pulled about their legs; but two or three wore no shirts at all, squatting naked to the waist, their bodies fully exposed in the light of the single flaring jet of gas fixed high upon the wall.

1871 A fire broke out in the tailors' workshop at Stockport workhouse but was extinguished by the inmates before the arrival of the fire brigade.

13 JANUARY **1826** Today's *Cambridge Chronicle* reported the proceedings of a vestry meeting in the town's Trinity parish to examine the conduct of its workhouse governor, John Allum. It appeared that Robert Silk, of about twenty-five years of age, had been in the workhouse some years. Silk was a distressing and unfortunate case, being dumb and an idiot. The charge against Allum was that, for a long period, and during the worst of weathers, he had confined Silk to an unheated outhouse where, with no chair or stool to sit on, he was penned up on a board in one corner. Silk had no shoes or stockings, bare arms, and only some coarse covering for the upper part of his body. He remained there all day, trampling in his filth, until being put into a crib with a small portion of straw. Eventually, news of this state of affairs reached the ears of a magistrate, Mr Alderman Coe, who went to the workhouse. Finding Silk in his cage, he instantly ordered him to be taken into the house, clothed with shoes and stockings, placed near the fire, and properly taken care of. On a return visit two days afterwards, the magistrate was astonished to find that the poor young man had been returned to his former condition, with the very water and dirt he stood in gushing up between his toes. Allum was subsequently dismissed for his acts of cruelty.

14 JANUARY **1842** A tragedy occurred today after Thomas and Sarah Brunt, their four-year-old son Thomas, and two younger children were admitted to the Rugby Union workhouse. At 5 p.m., the children were taken to the kitchen to be fed bread and cheese and then let out to play. At bedtime, Thomas could not be found. After some searching, the kitchen's cellar door was found to be open. The cellar was never used as it was undrained and always had several feet of water standing in it, although the top of the steps was used for storage. After a lamp was brought, bread was seen floating on the water and Thomas's body was then recovered by one of the paupers but he could not be revived. A bruise was found on his right temple, assumed to be caused by falling down the stairs after he had gone through the wrong door.

1850 Also on this day a disastrous fire resulted in the loss of more than thirty lives in two auxiliary premises of the Killarney workhouse in County Kerry. The fire broke out at about 10 p.m. in a building known as the College which was being used as a hospital for more than 160 patients. After the blaze took hold, the cries of the wretched inmates from the windows were truly appalling. So fierce was the fire that within two hours, the building was a blackened heap of ruins. The immediate death toll was said to be three, although the number unaccounted for the following morning was fifteen. The most dreadful part of the events, however, took place a few hundred yards away in a branch workhouse known as the Brewery, housing pauper girls and their nurses. The cries of 'fire' and the livid glare of the flames from the burning College building awoke the children. After shouting in vain for the doors of their dormitories to be unlocked, they sought an alternative means of exit through an unused loft. Under their weight, the rotten planks of its floor gave way with twenty-seven girls and two nurses being killed in the collapse, and a similar number being frightfully mutilated.

15 JANUARY 1887 Elizabeth Berry, a nurse at the Oldham workhouse infirmary, was charged with poisoning her eleven-year-old daughter Edith Annie Berry. Edith, who usually lived with her aunt and uncle, had come for a stay with her mother at the workhouse on 29 December and become ill on 1 January. Despite receiving treatment from the workhouse medical officer, Dr Thomas Patterson, Edith had died three days later. An inquest on the child, whose life was insured by Mrs Berry for £13, had returned a verdict of 'wilful murder' after a post-mortem by Dr Patterson indicated the cause of death to be corrosive poison. Following her trial, Berry was found guilty of 'a murder, cold-blooded, merciless, and cruel upon her poor little child' and sentenced to be hanged.

Berry's trial also raised suspicions over the sudden death in the previous year of her mother, Mrs Mary Ann Finley, whose life had been insured for over £100. Her body was exhumed and was found to contain traces of poison. Berry was found guilty of the wilful murder of her mother and received a second death sentence, her execution being the first to take place at Liverpool's Walton Gaol. Berry, who had always blamed her daughter's death on the workhouse medical officer, protested her innocence to the end, her last words being 'God forgive Dr Patterson.'

The hangman, coincidentally also named Berry, operated a lever to open the floor-level trap. The drop was 6ft 6in and the rope was ¾in, government made. To those on the scaffold, no movement was perceptible and death appeared to be instantaneous. The gaol surgeons, Dr Beamish and Dr Hammond, descended into the pit by means of a ladder and, having examined the body, pronounced life extinct, and that the executioner had done his work effectively.

1839 Mary Matthews, the schoolmistress, and Samuel Hewitt, the porter of the Greenwich Union workhouse, were today convicted of a number of offences. They had embezzled a considerable amount of butter, meat and bread intended for the children in their care, much of it being smuggled out to Matthews' mother's house by the children themselves, who had been threatened with punishment if they told anyone. Matthews had pocketed a 10s donation from the guardians which had been intended to buy the children cake and fruit at Christmas. Children had also been used to transport bottles of gin into the workhouse. Finally, Matthews was found guilty of various assaults on the children in the workhouse by beating them with an iron bar and a heavy ruler, and making them stand all night with their hands above their heads. Both were sentenced to terms of imprisonment in Maidstone Gaol.

1867 On this day George Edward Douglas, master of the St Marylebone workhouse, was walking in Regent's Park when ice on the frozen lake gave way. Two hundred skaters were instantly plunged into the freezing water. Douglas immediately organised the transport of the survivors back to the workhouse for medical attention. Forty bodies were subsequently recovered and taken to the workhouse mortuary where relatives later came to identify them.

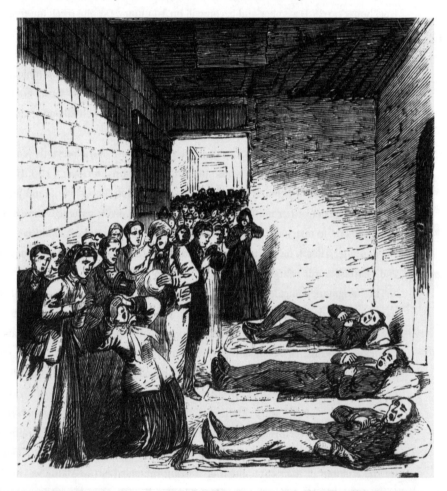

Relatives queue up to identify bodies at the Marylebone workhouse mortuary.

1871 This day a fire broke out in the roof of the Clerkenwell workhouse. The master, Mr Roe, ascended the roof and, following his instruction, able-bodied inmates passed him fire buckets from which he tried to douse the burning rafters. The fire brigade arrived and the fire was extinguished in about twenty minutes. It was most fortunate that the fire did not occur at night as the house contained about 200 aged and sick persons confined to their beds, together with many mothers with infants, and a number of lunatics.

16 **JANUARY 1834** The *London Standard* reported riot and confusion around Orchard Street, Westminster, following the appearance of four teenage girls at the windows of an empty house there. They told the passers-by that they had been confined in a dungeon at St Margaret's workhouse, stripped naked and, after fourteen days' unmerciful beating, had just escaped. A seething mob of more than 500 soon gathered, screaming abuse against the parish authorities. Fortunately, two parish officers happened to be passing and quickly revealed that the girls were notorious characters who, because of their repeated misdeeds, had frequently been sentenced by the magistrates to hard labour. The master of the workhouse had put them into solitary confinement from which they had escaped by a window 20ft above the ground. They had then scaled a wall and entered the back of the house which adjoined the workhouse. Amongst the riot and confusion, two of the girls were taken back from the officers by the mob, and it was only with great difficulty and danger that they were finally secured.

According to the report, the frequent disturbances amongst the juvenile paupers in the workhouse were entirely understandable. There was no classification amongst them, with orphaned and abandoned youngsters being placed in the same wards as young prostitutes. It was no wonder that their minds were soon corrupted like those who had incited the riot.

17 **JANUARY 1880** It was reported today that at Horsham, Sussex, a complaint of a somewhat unusual nature had been laid against the workhouse chaplain, the Revd J.F. Cole. The master of the workhouse had discovered a young female inmate with a large hole in her apron. The girl revealed that during a recent communion service the chaplain had accidentally spilt a quantity of wine on the apron. He had told her that the affected area had become consecrated and that he would have to cut it out and deposit in a box at a local church. At their next meeting, the Horsham guardians reprimanded the chaplain for mutilating workhouse property in such a manner. If the girl had committed the same act herself, she would have been liable to punishment.

In his defence, the chaplain later stated that he had ascertained that the apron had been worn out and worthless but would gladly pay for its replacement.

1891 On this day the *Illustrated London News* revealed that an old woman named Henley had been buried at Gosport after living more than ninety years in the workhouse there. Her early history was unknown but parish records showed that in 1801, when the new workhouse was built, Henley, who was then six years of age, had been transferred from the old to the new premises. The last forty years of her life were spent in the workhouse infirmary. Twelve years previously, she had fallen into a trance, in which she remained so long that she was regarded as dead, and was actually placed in her coffin before the mistake was discovered.

18 JANUARY **1859** An inquest began today at Drogheda, County Louth, following the death of Patrick Kenny at the workhouse fever hospital where he had been admitted the previous Wednesday. At about 2 a.m. on Friday, he rose from his bed and began running about the wards raving. He managed to enter the female patients' ward where, being very boisterous, he was accosted by two nurses, one of whom he knocked down. He then entered the water closet, climbed through its open window and jumped into a paved garden, some 30ft below. He was subsequently brought into the house by the nurses but, remarkably, did not complain of having received any injury. He died in the evening of the following day.

1868 A wealthy farmer, Joseph Hankins, and his wife, of Almely, Herefordshire, were today reported to have been heavily fined for assaulting and beating Sarah Ann Baker, twelve years old, whom they had taken out of the Weobley workhouse the previous March. The girl testified that during haymaking time Hankins beat her with a horsewhip and left severe marks. At apple picking, he again beat her with a riding whip, cut her head against the stair post, and made her nose bleed. She had run away from him six times through his cruelty. On another day he had pulled her hair, kicked her on the hip, and knocked her over the pump trough. At haymaking, Mrs Hankins had struck her on the head with a shoe-brush causing blood to flow, then cut her across the shoulders with a holly stick. The Hankins's son, Charles, under his mother's directions, had beaten her with a birch in an indecent manner.

19 JANUARY **1884** At Braintree, Essex, a resident living near to the workhouse raised the alarm after observing flames in the stable at the east of the premises which contained a load of straw. On receiving the news, the master, Mr Nowell, at once summoned assistance and organised a band of workers from among the inmates to pump and carry water. The Braintree fire engine soon arrived and the fire was soon

fully extinguished. The blaze was believed to have been instigated by an evil person breaking a pane in the stable window and dropping in a lighted match. A tramp who had presented himself for admission shortly before the outbreak departed during the confusion and had not been heard of since.

20 JANUARY 1881 Details were given today of an extraordinary blunder at Devonport. An inmate of the workhouse who had just died was removed to the mortuary to be placed in a coffin. By some error, when the bearers came to take it away and bury it, they removed an empty coffin instead of that containing the corpse and it was taken to the cemetery and buried with the usual rites. The mistake was not discovered until another death caused the mortuary to be visited again, when olfactory evidence indicated that something was amiss, and further investigation revealed what had happened.

1900 On this day it was reported that a meeting of the Colchester guardians had agreed to advertise for a new superintendent nurse for the workhouse infirmary. A member of the board suggested that a postscript be added that there were 'still a few widowers left'. This remark provoked much merriment – the explanation being that the last two ladies who had filled the position of superintendent nurse had abandoned the post for the purpose of marrying widowers who were members of the board. At a previous meeting it had been proposed that in engaging ordinary nurses they should be told as an inducement that the women so employed at the workhouse usually left to get married.

Sarah Ann Baker being beaten by the Hankins, who had 'rescued' her from the workhouse.

21 JANUARY 1882 A young man named John Wood, who was in the last stage of consumption, was today admitted to Sheffield workhouse, and died a few minutes after his admission. The body was removed to the workhouse mortuary and Wood's wife arranged that the funeral should take place on the following Tuesday. Some relatives from Manchester attended with her on that day, and on their going to the mortuary they found that the coffin which bore his name and age was screwed down. There was some reluctance on the part of the officials to have the coffin unscrewed, but on Mrs Wood insisting that she wished to take a last look at her husband, the lid was taken off. She was then horrified to find that the body was not her husband's, but that of a seventy-five-year-old man named Ellis. A search was then made for the body amongst a number of others, but it could not be found. It eventually occurred to one of the officials that it might have been taken to the School of Medicine. A messenger was despatched and Wood's body was found in the dissecting-room, whence it was promptly returned.

22 JANUARY 1830 Between five and six o'clock in the morning, a daring burglary took place at the Mile End Old Town workhouse, where 500 residents were asleep. The thieves forced open a window and headed to the Committee Room where cash for relieving the outdoor poor was usually kept. They were disappointed, however, as the previous night it had been removed for safekeeping to the room of the mistress, Miss Mudge. They then proceeded to Miss Mudge's bedchamber, passing several doors where workhouse servants slept. To guard against interruption, they fastened these doors from the outside using the bolts fitted there. The intruders told inmates who threatened them that they would receive immediate vengeance if they interfered. The men burst open Miss Mudge's locked door, approached her bedside and, putting a dark lantern close to her face, asked her where the gold was stored. When she answered that there was none in the house, they demanded her keys, threatening to blow her brains out if she made a sound. The keys were given to them by a young girl who also slept in the apartment and, after remaining some time, they noticed a tea board on which was piled £125 in silver, provided for the payment of the poor. They tipped the money into a sack and made their escape. A £40 reward was later offered for their discovery.

23 JANUARY 1860 At Thames magistrates' court, Elizabeth Pinners and Elizabeth Regan, inmates of the workhouse at Wapping, were charged with violently assaulting fellow pauper Frances McDonald. The workhouse porter stated that the two were guilty of gross insubordination and misconduct, and their language was extremely bad. McDonald, whose head was cut, and who had lost a good deal of blood, said that the prisoners had assaulted and beaten her, and had accused her of kicking

up a row for which they had sworn to be avenged, with Pinners striking her on the head with a saucepan lid. The prisoners claimed that McDonald had provoked them and struck them first with the lid, and they were only in court because they had offended the master, matron and porter. They both entered into a long harangue, and almost tired out the patience of the magistrate. Elizabeth Wood, a wards-woman, said that McDonald had been in a lunatic asylum, and was a very irritating and irritable person, and had threatened to 'rip up the bowels' of the defendants. There had been a row and a fight, and the shrieks and shouts were awful. The magistrate, Mr Selfe, said that a most disgraceful state of affairs existed in Wapping workhouse, which was the worst regulated in the district. There was no classification, with the good and the bad, the sane and the lunatic, decent married women and prostitutes, all huddled together. It was shocking that such a state of things should exist in a civilised country.

As a result of this incident, Charles Dickens made a visit to the Wapping workhouse. His generally favourable account appeared in his volume *The Uncommercial Traveller*.

24 JANUARY **1839** At about eight-thirty this evening a fire broke out at London's Saffron Hill workhouse. Inmates witnessed a sudden eruption of flames in a workroom in the lower part of the building. At the time, the pauper children were undressing and some were already in bed. The master, Mr Mantiman, ordered them all instantly to dress themselves, whence they were placed in the yard. Great efforts to suppress the fire was made by many of the elderly paupers who poured water onto the flames from pails and buckets. The hand engine from the Farringdon fire station arrived within a few minutes followed by another small engine belonging to Clerkenwell. The success of these two engines was such that a larger engine which arrived from the Farringdon station was not required.

1856 At Leicester magistrates, James Rodwell pleaded guilty to breaking windows at the workhouse and doing damage to the value of 10s. He was ordered to pay for the damage and costs, and in default, a month's imprisonment with hard labour.

1886 The poorhouse in Jackson, Michigan, was burnt down in the early hours. The fire broke out in the kitchen and, no fire extinguishing appliances being available, the whole of the interior of the building was quickly destroyed. Forty of the inmates, five of them insane, blind or deaf and dumb, were literally roasted to death. The others rushed out half-naked into the snow where the temperature was ten degrees below zero. It was feared that many would die from exposure. The survivors were taken for treatment into Jackson, some six miles distant.

25 JANUARY 1823 The funeral was held today of Clerkenwell workhouse inmate Thomas Drisdell, aged fifty-eight, whose story was a remarkable one. A lifelong bachelor, Drisdell had been a scale-maker by trade, always highly industrious, but disliked by most of his acquaintances for his reluctance to part with money. In later life, he became an itinerant, cleaning and servicing shopkeepers' scales, but always casting himself on the charity of others and claiming to be penniless.

A week before his death, it became known that Drisdell was perishing for want of food, and without immediate assistance would not survive many hours. The parish beadle, with a chair and two carriers, was despatched to bring the dying man to the workhouse. The beadle found Drisdell's room a wretched sight. The floor had not been cleaned for years, and in one corner of the hovel Drisdell was stretched on a few old rags, covered with a piece of filthy blanket. The only furniture was an old deal table, two bottomless chairs, and a small deal box containing filthy old garments. Drisdell, who could not speak, and the box were taken to the workhouse where he expired the next day.

When Drisdell's box was examined, amongst the filthy rags were found three silver watches, thirteen sovereigns, and an old stocking half-filled with silver, crowns, half crowns, shillings and sixpences. A bundle of papers tied round with string turned out to contain a large sum of Navy 5 per cent bonds, together with his will bequeathing all his property, valued at about £1,700, to his natural daughter, thirteen-year-old Mary Ann Thompson. The girl was eventually located, living with a poor woman who sold watercress on the street. She became the chief mourner at Drisdell's funeral, which was attended by a vast throng. Remarkably, the child had never received the least assistance from Drisdell, although she was wandering the streets barefoot.

26 JANUARY 1820 Four sturdy vagrants, inmates of the Bishopsgate workhouse, were brought before the Lord Mayor of London, charged with refusing to work. The Bishopsgate overseers stated that the men had been given the task of clearing away rubbish from the pavement in front of the workhouse. They had been supplied with spades and pickaxes but would not pick up a tool unless supervised by the workhouse master. The pathways ended up in an even worse condition because of their laziness. They had consequently been dismissed from the workhouse so that their example would not have a bad effect on the other inmates. The Lord Mayor told the vagrants that they were guilty of great ingratitude, and if they chose not to submit to the regulations they must take the consequences. Upon hearing this, the men suddenly changed their tone, said they were willing to work, and hoped the overseers would reconsider their exclusion from the workhouse. The overseers agreed to do so, and the Lord Mayor requested that if they were again guilty, they should be brought back before him for exemplary punishment.

27 JANUARY **1850** *Lloyd's Weekly Newspaper* reported that a fire had broken out at the Kenmare Union workhouse in County Kerry. It originated at the rear of the infirmary in a store containing 10 tons of straw used for bedding. The room was accessible to paupers at all hours and often used by them to take refuge from the cold. A spark from one of their pipes may have led to the conflagration. Still suffering from the effects of the Irish famine, the workhouse, originally built to hold 500, together with two auxiliary premises, now housed 2,800 paupers with staff unable to cope. Eight or nine sharing a bed was not uncommon. One of the auxiliaries contained 1,000 children who had little supervision at night. The previous week, a child got out of bed, somehow missed its way, and walked out of a window which was on a level with the floor. Its body was found the following morning, having fallen from the third floor.

1876 An inmate of the Parsonstown Union workhouse at Birr, County Offaly, committed suicide by cutting his throat from ear to ear. He was subsequently discovered in a pool of blood, but life was extinct. No cause could be assigned for his action.

28 JANUARY **1875** A fatal boiler explosion occurred today at the Preston Union workhouse, Fulwood. At about 8 a.m., the boiler fire for the boys' and girls' schoolrooms was lit as usual by eleven-year-old John Longley. Just before ten o'clock the children began to enter the school. Suddenly the boiler exploded into a hundred pieces, with bricks and stones hurled in all directions and the thick plate-glass windows smashed or cracked. The unfortunate Longley was found in the ash-pit under a mass of bricks, iron and stone, in a dreadful state of mutilation, his body having been fearfully scalded – or, as it appeared in some places, literally parboiled. He was quite dead and bleeding from the mouth, ears and back of the head. Two other small boys were severely scalded but expected to recover. The screams and terror of the rest of the children were considerable, but apart from the shock they largely escaped unhurt. Had the accident occurred a few minutes later, the schoolmaster would have been killed as his desk was immediately above the boiler. The cause of the disaster was a freezing of water in the boiler's pipes which prevented the steam escaping. The boiler had no safety valve, being of a type considered not to require such devices.

1899 At the Bromsgrove Union workhouse, Sarah Jane Ward, aged six, died from horrific burns after playing with a piece of lighted paper. An inquest jury recommended that the fireguard in the children's quarters be moved further back from the fire and that children be better supervised. The Local Government Board, who should have been informed of the incident by the workhouse medical officer, Dr Kidd, were none too pleased that their first knowledge of it had been in an article in the *Birmingham Daily Post*.

29 **JANUARY** **1924** It emerged today that the Visiting Committee at St Marylebone workhouse had been asked to protect the inmates against some of the appalling concerts which were given in the institution from time to time by amateur entertainers. One of the guardians, Mr F.W. Dean, suggested that while these troupes no doubt had the best possible motives, it had to be admitted that they were often not worth the coffee which was provided for their refreshment. Their performances really inflicted cruelty on the poor old folk who had to listen to them. Councillor Vincent, chairman of the Visiting Committee, accepted that some of the concerts were of a questionable standard but, however bad an entertainment might be, it usually had the great advantage, from the inmates' point of view, of postponing bedtime for an hour or two.

30 **JANUARY** **1837** Today's *Morning Post* carried a 'sketch from an amusing paper, entitled *Oliver Twist, or, The Parish Boy's Progress*, from the forthcoming number of *Bentley's Miscellany*.' The recently launched magazine, whose second issue appeared two days later, was edited by 'Boz', the pen-name of Charles Dickens and author of the new story. However, the *Morning Post* extract probably marked the very first public appearance in print of the boy whose experiences of the workhouse were to create an indelible image of such establishments in the minds of all its readers:

> Scene — the workhouse. Time — Oliver's introduction into the world. As Oliver gave this first proof of the free and proper action of his lungs, the patchwork coverlet which was carelessly flung over the iron bedstead rustled; the pale face of a young woman was raised feebly from the pillow; and a faint voice imperfectly articulated the words, 'Let me see the child, and die.'

1896 On this day the *Huddersfield Chronicle* published revelations as to the former status of various inmates of London workhouses. In one workhouse was a man aged forty-seven who, at the age of twenty-one, had inherited a fortune of over £30,000 a year. Over a period of fifteen years, he had squandered the money in the wildest excesses, eventually becoming a beggar and tramp. In the same workhouse was a former lieutenant-colonel in the British army. In both these cases, the persons concerned had expressed the belief that since being in the workhouse they had enjoyed a degree of peace and quiet they had not known for years.

31 **JANUARY** **1883** An inquest was held at the Sunderland workhouse on the body of inmate James Coyne, aged eighty-three, who had choked on a piece of meat

two days before. Eleanor Hall, the workhouse cook, said that she was in the dining hall at five past twelve, when she saw Coyne's head drooping towards his plate. She went to him and found a piece of corned beef sticking in his mouth. She tried to get it out, but only a piece broke off, and then she patted him on the back. He snored a little, became slightly discoloured in the face, and died in her hands. The doctor was sent for the moment she saw what was happening. Dr Low said that Coyne was dead when he saw him. He put his fingers down his throat, but did not find any meat in it. There was a good deal of corned beef in the mouth, which had evidently come forward from the throat. The food the deceased had eaten was proper for a man of his age. Coyne, a former schoolmaster, was said to be addicted to drink, and was known in the workhouse as 'the poet' and 'the doctor'. The jury returned a verdict that Coyne had died from suffocation by choking.

FEBRUARY

The Mayor of London on an unannounced visit to the West London
Union's casual ward in 1857. The men were sleeping on the floor of a
stable with no straw or bedding provided. (*See* 20 February)

1 **FEBRUARY** 1865 On this day, Richard Gibson, aged forty, a patient in the St Giles's workhouse infirmary, asked fellow inmate Felix John Magee to write a letter on his behalf to local magistrate Sir Thomas Henry:

> Sir, I wish to bring under your notice the case of a pauper named Richard Gibson, at present an inmate of St. Giles's Workhouse, 47 Ward. His disease is scurvy, and through weakness he has been unable to wait on himself, and therefore has been inhumanly neglected. On Sunday morning he asked me to wash his face, and he would give me twopence, I took it, for it enabled me to write. I washed him, and such a sight of suffering may I never see again. He was covered from the crown of the head to the soles of the feet with scabs and sores. He had sores on the back, and his legs are in a shocking state from neglect. I have never seen them dressed since I have been in the ward, and I can say on oath that they have not, and so will others. The bed he lies on has not been made for five nights. It is an iron bedstead, with wood laths for the bottom, with no mattress, in a dark corner of this underground ward, and it is only through part of the day that you can discern his features. On Sunday when I washed him I took out of his head a half-pint of scabs. His hair is unusually long, and was matted from constantly lying in bed, and his hands were as it were enamelled with his own soil. It was an eighth of an inch thick on the palm of his hand and fingers, for I see no night-stool and bed-pan in this ward. Sir, I hope you will send an officer as soon as you can, for should he die, the ends of justice would be evaded. If the officer keeps the object of his visit a secret I will be able to get the under nurse and helper to own to it themselves. He is now delirious, and cannot last long, and if he dies the proof of guilt will be removed.
>
> I remain, your obedient servant, Felix John Magee.

Gibson died two days later. A post-mortem examination found his body to be extremely emaciated, with the hair of his head matted together, his nostrils closed up with dirt, his beard a mass of filth, and vermin swarming over his face, chest and neck.

At the end of a lengthy inquest, the jury essentially concurred with the claims in Magee's letter. Their verdict was that Gibson's death from 'serum on the brain' had been greatly accelerated by the neglect of all the officials in the workhouse, and that the ward in which he had died should be closed as improper for the reception of sick paupers. They also considered that the neglect of the nurses to change the linen of the deceased 'was highly reprehensible'.

2 FEBRUARY 1866 At the Great Yarmouth workhouse, Hannah Francis, aged about fifty-three years and an inmate of the imbecile ward, committed suicide by hanging herself with a handkerchief from the top of the doorframe of a water closet.

1873 On this day *Reynolds's Newspaper* gave details of an action for false imprisonment brought by an eighty-six-year-old woman named Wilding against Dr J.R. Hill, the medical officer of St Pancras workhouse. On 23 October, the woman had met with an accident in the street and was taken to the workhouse for treatment. She was visited there the next day by her foster daughter, Jane Wilding, who was anxious that her mother return home. However, Dr Hill did not consider she was in a fit state to leave and declined to let her go. The daughter contacted one of guardians who, after seeing the old woman, agreed she could be safely taken home. Dr Hill stood firm, however, and at the guardians' meeting on 4 November, stated that the patient was of unsound mind. The case was referred to a meeting of the Visiting Committee on 12 November. On the 11th, however, Dr Hill found his patient sufficiently recovered to be allowed home. The action now being brought was for Wilding's alleged illegal detention between the 4th and 11th November. Wilding was herself called as a witness but it was plain she was mentally confused and could not say what day of the week it was. Little could be extracted from her beyond the fact that she was glad to leave the workhouse, although she had been kindly treated while there. The jury decided that Dr Hill had acted conscientiously and the case was dismissed.

3 FEBRUARY 1832 At London Guildhall magistrates, the constable of Cripplegate ward, John Anderson, reported that he had not succeeded in tracing the bodies of an aged man and a woman, stolen from the mortuary at Cripplegate workhouse. Two women, relatives of the deceased, came forward in tears to learn if there was any hope of recovering the bodies. They were told by Sir Peter Laurie that this was now unlikely. The best consolation he could offer was that a member of the royal family, the Duke of Sussex, had made provision in his will for his body to be surgically examined after his death. A few months after this incident, the 1832 Anatomy Act attempted to end the illegal trade in bodies by giving surgeons and their students legal access to corpses that were unclaimed after death, with workhouses and prisons becoming the main sources.

1912 On this date it was reported that a woman named Sarah Payne had appeared before Coventry magistrates charged with wandering abroad, after being turned out of the room where she had been living with five cats, one dog and a hedgehog. She had refused to enter the workhouse without the animals but eventually agreed to do so after being assured they would be looked after until she found work.

1911 Also on this day, Robert Tressell, author of *The Ragged-Trousered Philanthropist*, died in poverty in the Liverpool workhouse.

4 FEBRUARY **1842** An inquest was concluded at Bromsgrove, Worcestershire, into the death of Henry Cartwright, aged five, at the Bromsgrove Union workhouse. Cartwright had entered the workhouse three months earlier, along with his mother who could not afford to support the family. The boy, along with several other pauper children, had contracted 'the itch', or scabies, a contagious skin disease caused by a small mite. The treatment prescribed by the medical officer, Thomas Fletcher, was a bath of potassium sulphate. However, the bath was made so strong that Cartwright died from its effects three days later, and several other children were badly affected. Although Fletcher was severely reprimanded, his previous good record and loyal service resulted in his retaining his post.

5 FEBRUARY **1832** The *Kentish Gazette* revealed that an extraordinary robbery had taken place at an unidentified location in the county when a lad was sent to the workhouse to get the weekly allowance for his own family and one or two others. While returning, he was attacked by a person who demanded his money. The lad called out, 'Murder! Thieves!' and upon assistance coming up, they succeeded in taking the supposed highwayman – who turned out to be the lad's own mother, disguised in male apparel. The affair had apparently been hushed up.

6 FEBRUARY **1837** An inquest was held at Hertford's All Saints workhouse into the death of James Breacher, aged eighty-one years, who had died there the previous Saturday. Earlier on that day, officers of the Welwyn Union had sent the man to Hertford, as his home parish of Aston fell within the Hertford Union. Breacher was said to have been in a most unfit state to be removed at all, and was not accompanied by the usual removal order. It was only from being noticed by one of the guardians leaving the boardroom that he was immediately taken into the workhouse. He was in a most deplorable condition and apparently in a dying state. One witness said he had been so covered with vermin that they were 'clustered like bees' under his clothes. He was immediately taken into the yard and put into a warm bath to be cleansed, and while he was being wiped dry he died. A post-mortem examination indicated that the cause of death was the inflammation of a rupture. The inquest jury decided that Breacher had 'died by the visitation of God' but his death had been accelerated by exposure to cold while being conveyed to Hertford in an open cart.

7 **FEBRUARY 1838** In a letter to *The Times* written on this day, John Bowen of Bridgwater, Somerset, made a number of serious complaints about the management of the Bridgwater workhouse and the treatment of its inmates. Bowen, an opponent of much of the New Poor Law, had been a member of the Bridgwater guardians until resigning in protest at what had taken place. Many of Bowen's grievances related to the union's adoption of the 'No. 3 Dietary' – one of the six menu plans devised by the central Poor Law Commissioners for use in the country's union workhouses – in which the daily breakfast for adults included 1½ pints of gruel. Oatmeal did not commonly feature in the labourers' diet in the area, and it was widely held locally that gruel was unhealthy. Not long after its introduction, there had been a serious and sustained outbreak of diarrhoea and dysentery amongst workhouse inmates, which Bowen's letter graphically described:

> A large proportion of the inmates became reduced to mere skeletons by this loathsome disease. The sufferers, however cleanly in their former habits, involuntarily voided their faeces. The governor, in describing the effect of the gruel, said that, 'It did not affect the poor people so much at first, but after the use of it for a few days they became terribly bad; it ran away from them while they were standing upright as they took it. It affected them upwards and downwards. All the

No. 3.—DIETARY for ABLE-BODIED PAUPERS.

		BREAKFAST.		DINNER.					SUPPER.	
		Bread.	Gruel.	Cooked Meat.	Potatoes or other Vegetables.	Soup.	Bread.	Cheese.	Bread.	Cheese.
		oz.	pints.	oz.	lb.	pints.	oz.	oz.	oz.	oz.
Sunday	Men	8	1½	. .	. .	. .	7	2	6	1½
	Women	6	1½	. .	. .	. .	6	1½	5	1½
Monday	Men	8	1½	. .	. .	. .	7	2	6	1½
	Women	6	1½	. .	. .	. .	6	1½	5	1½
Tuesday	Men	8	1½	8	¾	. .	. .	.	6	1½
	Women	6	1½	6	¾	. .	. .	.	5	1½
Wednesday	Men	8	1½	. .	. .	. .	7	2	6	1½
	Women	6	1½	. .	. .	. .	6	1½	5	1½
Thursday	Men	8	1½	. .	. .	1½	6	.	6	1½
	Women	6	1½	. .	. .	1½	5	.	5	1½
Friday	Men	8	1½	. .	. .	. .	7	2	6	1½
	Women	6	1½	. .	. .	. .	6	1½	5	1½
				Bacon.						
Saturday	Men	8	1½	5	¾	. .	. .	. .	6	1½
	Women	6	1½	4	¾	.	. .	. .	5	1½

Old people, of sixty years of age and upwards, may be allowed one ounce of tea, five ounces of butter, and seven ounces of sugar per week, in lieu of gruel for breakfast, if deemed expedient to make this change.

Children under nine years of age, to be dieted at discretion; above nine, to be allowed the same quantities as women.

Sick to be dieted as directed by the medical officer.

The 'No. 3 Dietary' – one of the six menu plans issued by the Poor Law Commissioners in 1835 for the use of union workhouses.

way down the stairs, across the hall, and down the garden path, was all covered every morning, and the stench was horrible all through the house; making the people ill and sick who had not got the diarrhoea.'

Thus a nauseous pestilence appears to have pervaded the whole house, not confined to those who took the gruel, but infecting others who were obliged to breathe an atmosphere saturated with foetid exhalations. The family of the governor were attacked; the governor himself, although previously a healthy and a powerful man, became unable to go into the paupers' apartments without being violently affected, and the medical attendant, after repeated attacks of diarrhoea, and temporary respites, was at length obliged to relinquish his post to another.

Whether gruel was indeed the source of all the illness in the workhouse was never fully resolved. However, despite strenuous agitation by the workhouse medical officer, supported by Bowen, the Bridgwater guardians appear to have largely been indifferent to the crisis that was happening under their noses.

8 FEBRUARY 1837 The *Morning Post* reported the trial at Newington of nine young men, all paupers in the Guildford Union workhouse. Thomas Aimes, the workhouse master, stated that on 4 January the defendants had complained that their food was so dirty that they could not eat it, and that the cook was a dirty person and should be discharged. Aimes made the protests known to the visiting magistrates who, on learning that the master and matron had no complaints against the cook, said they would not remove him. On learning this, the paupers started kicking the door of the room where the magistrates were meeting, and repeated their claims. After an order was given for the men to be put on bread and water for three days, they began shouting, throwing stones and breaking down the fence between them and the female paupers. When constables arrived to take the ringleaders into custody, several of them were struck with violent blows.

On being questioned as to the paupers' diet, the master stated that inmates received 1½ pints of gruel for breakfast, and three times a week they had 14 ounces of soup made from 4 ounces of meat and vegetables, this being the only meat given to them. Neither he nor his wife lived on the same food as the paupers, nor was their food prepared by the same cook.

The defendants were all sentenced to imprisonment with hard labour. The Chairman of the Bench observed that the men would find that the gaol allowance was not superior to that in the workhouse.

9 FEBRUARY 1863 William Atkins, an inmate of the Nottingham Union workhouse, cut his throat with a pocket knife. At the subsequent inquest, Atkins, who was thirty-five years of age, was said by the house surgeon, Mr Forbes Watson, to be suffering from a 'loathsome disease' – presumably syphilis – and consumption. He would have died in a day or two in any case, but the wounds to his throat had hastened his death.

1893 Late on this evening, a devastating fire broke out in the lunatic asylum of the Strafford County workhouse at Dover, New Hampshire. The two-storey wooden building was completely destroyed, with more than fifty inmates burned to death and only three rescued. After the alarm was raised, the keeper and attendants rushed to the lunatics' sleeping cells on the first floor. They burst open the locks and tried to rouse the occupants, who began running wildly about. When the building finally collapsed, one witness reported seeing a group of six lunatics in their nightclothes, fighting furiously together, disappear. Whether the inmates understood the danger, or simply could not find their way out, was unclear. One woman, who appeared to be entirely unaware of her danger, came to one of the windows nursing a pillow in her arms as if it were a baby and apparently delighted at all the commotion and glare of the flames. She was still carrying on her strange performance when part of the roof fell in on her. The fire was believed to have been started by a female inmate inside her cell. Two months prior to the disaster, the lack of fire-escape facilities in the building had been a subject of discussion in the local press. However, the authorities had replied that there was no danger of fire.

10 FEBRUARY 1865 At Tadcaster this evening, a torch-lit procession was held following the funeral of Elizabeth Daniel, former inmate of the West Tadcaster workhouse. In a field in front of the workhouse, an effigy of a woman, with a poker in her hand and striking a figure of a little boy, was set on fire. The effigy represented the workhouse matron, Mrs Catherine Levers, against whom a long series of allegations of cruelty and misconduct had arisen.

A few weeks later, an inquiry into the matter was opened by the Poor Law Board's Assistant Commissioner Andrew Doyle. The charges against Levers were that she was habitually drunk, had ill-treated inmates including Elizabeth Daniel and Hannah Buck, and had used excessive punishments on the children in the workhouse.

Former inmate Christiana Standeven, thirteen, said that Levers had regularly beaten her with a strap and a stick, sometimes resulting in bleeding, and that her head had been 'jowled' against a bedpost. She had been locked in a windowless cellar for half a day at a time. Levers was also said to have fixed a cord to a boy's leg and tied it to the ceiling, forcing him to remain standing on one leg for ten minutes. Another ex-inmate, Bridget McCormack, testified that Levers had children stripped naked at bedtime and beat them with a rolling pin. She also made them stick their tongues out and then 'chucked' them under the chin, making their tongues bleed and forcing them to swallow the blood. The workhouse milkman, William Boniface, said that on one morning he had seen a boy facing the wall holding aloft a stone in one hand and a piece of brick in another. When he had returned to the workhouse that evening, the boy was in the same position. He had also seen Levers kicking children and beating them with a hand-brush and a poker. One day, while Elizabeth Daniel was ironing, Levers had said the irons were not hot. She had put one on Mrs Daniel's arm and taken the skin off. He had also seen her knock Daniel to the floor with a large bunch of keys and subsequently seen her head swollen through being washed with ammonia. Innkeeper Joseph Sykes stated that on one occasion when he was at the workhouse, Levers had told him that one of the children had dirtied its bed but that she had cured it. When asked how, she said, 'I took a spoon up and put some of its own dirt in its mouth.' Jane Trinity, Elizabeth Daniel's niece, said that her aunt had been a stout, healthy woman before entering the workhouse. When visiting her aunt, a few days before her death, she had been shocked to see her face and head swollen to nearly double their size. On speaking to Levers after the woman had died, she had found her drunk. Levers had also claimed to have caused the old woman's death by rubbing her face with ammonia, and would do the same again. A number of witnesses described Levers' frequent ill-treatment of Hannah Buck who was said to have been beaten at various times with sticks, a wet floor cloth, a poker, a lading-can, and a cat-of-nine-tails.

Despite the overwhelming evidence against Levers, the case was effectively buried when, after consulting with the guardians, Assistant Commissioner Doyle stated that the workhouse building was not fit for use and that he would recommend its closure forthwith. This would effectively end Levers' employment and so it was not necessary for her to present a defence. Doyle also felt sure that the guardians' professed ignorance of the claimed abuses was due to their having been kept in the dark by the inmates.

11 FEBRUARY 1858 In the early morning, a fierce and destructive fire broke out at the Athy Union workhouse, County Kildare, resulting in the loss of eight lives. The fire was discovered in the matron's storehouse at 4 a.m. and in less than an hour almost the entire right wing of the building was a sheet of flame engulfing the schoolroom, warehouse, cook's and schoolmaster's apartments, and the boys' dormitory. The ringing of the alarm bell brought a gathering of townspeople to the scene, who assisted in subduing the blaze. A fire engine played water on the rear of

the building while copious water was poured from a ladder placed at the front. After the pumps failed from being overworked, water had to be carried from a canal some distance off. During these exertions, a loud cry arose that several persons were still in the building. A rush was immediately made round to the place indicated and several men ascended a staircase down which rolled dense volumes of smoke. They brought down, one after another, eight bodies, all dead – five adults who were suffocated by smoke, and three small children charred to cinders. The scene in the yard was heartrending. The shrieks of women tearing their hair in grief, the cries of children, and the general lamentation heard amidst the falling ruins and blazing timbers, constituted a spectacle that few would wish to witness.

12 **FEBRUARY** **1866** At London's Thames police court, Mary Bernard, aged twenty, Margaret Sullivan, twenty-six, Ann Briant, twenty-five, and Elizabeth Macarthy, twenty-one, appeared before Mr Partridge charged with refractory conduct in the Poplar workhouse. The first three were also charged with violently assaulting Mrs Marian Speed, the matron, and the fourth with wilful damage. The prisoners had all been inmates of the workhouse for upwards of five years. Although Briant was blind, and Sullivan had only one leg, they were all classed as able-bodied. On the previous Saturday, they had refused to work in the oakum shed and were summoned to the office of the master, Mr Joseph Speed. When they refused to go, Mrs Speed went to fetch the four, who directed threats and foul language towards her. Three of them attacked her and the fourth, Macarthy, smashed the shed windows.

In court, the prisoners claimed they had been threatened and abused by Mr and Mrs Speed who had called them lazy, dirty beasts. They had not struck Mrs Speed, only pushed her. They then claimed that a poor female lunatic had entered the workhouse a week earlier and, because of inadequate care, had committed suicide by jumping from a third-floor window. The matron had called down to two men to wash the dead woman's brains down the sink. In reply, Mrs Speed said that the woman in question was named Susan Davis, who had been admitted with her seven-week-old baby. After spending the night in the sick ward, both were pronounced fit by the workhouse surgeon but the master had said that, as the birth was so recent, they had better stay a day or two longer so that inquiries could be made. At five the following morning, the woman dashed herself headlong from a small circular window in a water closet at the top of the building into the yard below. Her body was horribly mutilated and she had died half an hour later. Mrs Speed said that Davis had received the best of attention and was shocked at the suggestion that she ordered the men to do anything as inhuman or indecent as sweep brains down the sink.

Mr Partridge described the prisoners' conduct as disgraceful and sentenced them each to two months' imprisonment and hard labour.

13 FEBRUARY 1887 A shocking incident took place at the Guiltcross Union workhouse in Kenninghall, Norfolk. In the night, an inmate of the establishment, Jonas Revelt, aged seventy-two, rose from his bed. He then approached the sleeping figure of Henry Baker, fifty, who acted as sick nurse, and stabbed him three times with a knife. One of the stabs severed Baker's windpipe and jugular vein, causing almost instant death. Revelt was said to have shown previous signs of insanity.

14 FEBRUARY 1890 An inquest took place on the body of John Haynes, an inmate of Chertsey workhouse infirmary, who had cut his throat at the end of January. Mr Cooper, the relieving officer who had given the order admitting Haynes to the house, stated that a few days before the man's death, he had brought him, at his request, a razor. At about the same time, Haynes, who was a former Metropolitan police sergeant with a £30 a year pension, and whose life was insured, signed a will in Cooper's favour. The jury returned a verdict of suicide whilst temporarily insane, and added a rider that death was accelerated by Cooper's act in supplying the razor, and they considered he should be severely censured.

15 FEBRUARY 1911 William Hennen, aged ninety-four, and Fanny Wadhams, eighty, took their marriage vows after taking their leave of the Medway Union workhouse at Chatham, where they had fallen in love while inmates. Each of the two had been married three times before. The couple were one of a number of such matches that had come about following the introduction of the old-age pension which offered the possibility of independent living to some of the elderly who previously would have had no other option than the workhouse.

The happy couple – William Hennen and Fanny Wadhams.

16 **FEBRUARY 1867** The *Illustrated London News* gave details of an entertainment provided for the inmates of the Bethnal Green workhouse by the 'Delaware Minstrels'. The troupe, with faces blacked-up in the style of the popular 'Christy Minstrels', were an amateur company of bank clerks from an establishment on Lombard Street. As well as music and songs, the show included a stump speech, an eccentric dance, comic dialogue, and the 'Grand Plantation Walk Round' – all given with admirable spirit, and set off by appropriate costumes and gesticulation.

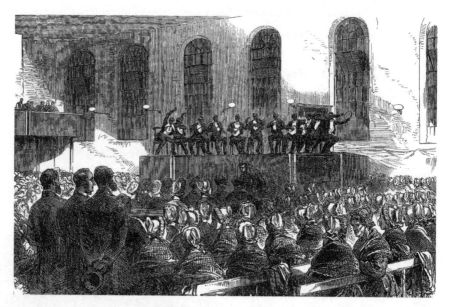

The Delaware Minstrels on stage.

17 **FEBRUARY 1887** A riot was started by inmates of the New Ross workhouse in County Wexford. The disturbance marked an escalation in the Irish National League's 'Plan of Campaign' to support agricultural tenants who were being charged excessive rents and evicted from their land. At New Ross, the board of guardians welcomed evicted families into the union workhouse, giving them separate quarters (known as the 'Ward of Honour') and allowing them to stay together in their family groups. They were also able to keep their own clothing and to receive food and visitors from outside. In response, the Local Government Board dissolved the board of guardians and appointed two paid vice-guardians to run the union and its workhouse. Things came to the boil today when the inmates revolted and began searching for the vice-guardians, with the intention of wreaking vengeance upon them. A marauding mob descended on the workshop containing the officials, who immediately locked the door and prepared to defend

themselves. Some of the 400 or so mutineers were armed with crowbars and quickly smashed down the door. One of the vice-guardians was savagely beaten, with his head cut and his clothing torn almost to rags. His colleague and the workhouse master were also badly beaten. A force of police eventually arrived and restored order. The female rioters later barricaded themselves into their quarters. When police broke in they found that the women had stripped themselves naked, defying the officers to arrest them.

18 FEBRUARY 1909 Charles Saunders, aged nine years, an inmate of the Shoreditch Union's cottage homes at Hornchurch, died today from the burns he received by falling into a bath of hot water while playing with another boy. An inquest later heard from William Radley, aged fourteen, that he and Saunders had been playing in the washroom in 'Ivy Cottage'. Saunders had run into him and then fallen against a tub of hot water, with his right arm going right into it. Chrissie Pipe, an assistant in the house, said that the water had been placed in a wooden trough prior to washing the children. She had immediately treated the boy's arm with Vaseline and a clean rag. The arm was not blistered, only slightly red, and she had not reported the matter to the house mother until the next day as she had not considered it was serious. A day later, according to the homes' medical officer, the boy had become highly feverish and was in a state of stupor. He was given special treatment, but it became clear that part of the skin on his arm had been destroyed. He sank into a coma and died after having a convulsive fit. Death had been due to shock following the scalding, and the doctor did not consider the Vaseline and rag treatment a proper one. In returning a verdict of accidental death, the jury recommended that the rule that cold water should be placed in the bath first should be strictly adhered to, and that assistants should be supplied with a book of rules.

19 FEBRUARY 1825 A poor woman named Hannah Metcalfe died in the seventieth year of her life at the Horbury workhouse, West Yorkshire. She had taken to her bed some forty-five years earlier, owing to a disappointment in love, and never rose from it to the day of her death. It was calculated that, over this period, the woman had cost the parish in the region of £500.

1881 Today it was reported that an inquest had been held at the Walton workhouse, Liverpool, on the body of inmate Ellen Coleman. It was stated that she had asked for a cup of tea, which was given to her by a nurse. She was also supplied with her weekly half-ounce allowance of snuff. By some means, the old woman got the snuff into her mouth. One of the other inmates observed her choking and raised the alarm, but she died about an hour afterwards. The jury expressed a hope that this case would not affect the supply of snuff to the poor old people in the workhouse.

1843 Also on this day, following claims that lax supervision at Liverpool workhouse had resulted in it becoming the largest brothel in England, today's *Satirist* published statements made at a recent meeting into the matter by stipendiary magistrate Mr Rushton. He alleged that in the classification ward, abandoned profligates were living with decent people and there was indiscriminate prostitution going on; an access route had been created over the wall between the male and female wards by knocking off the glass bottles from the top, and women wearing only shifts were going over to the men during the night. It was also claimed that the governor was afraid to go into some parts of the workhouse at night.

20 **FEBRUARY 1857** London's Lord Mayor and other City officers this evening paid a surprise visit to the West London Union casual ward at King's Cross. They discovered that the premises consisted of a large stable, containing fourteen horse-stalls, with a few men being huddled together round a fire. The place was completely devoid of any straw or bedding. The inmates stated that, on admission, they received a small portion of bread, but in the morning were turned out without anything to eat, unless they first broke a certain quantity of stone. The party next entered an adjoining cattle-shed, where they found two destitute females huddled together on a rug, lying on the bare ground, almost perished with cold, and without either fire or food.

Female casuals at the West London Union workhouse.

1883 On this day an inquest was held at Stroud workhouse on elderly inmate Robert Cowley. A few nights previously, Cowley had got out of bed and gone wandering about the ward. Edward Bennett, the attendant, awoke and asked him what he was doing, and he said he wanted to go home. Bennett told him it was night and not day, and to get back into bed. The old man went feeling about the beds, apparently not knowing which was his, and got to the bed of a blind old man named Drake, and was feeling him over. Drake awoke in fright, and being blind, gave a sharp push, knocking over Cowley, who fell with considerable force against an iron bedstead. The wardsman got out and put him to bed, and he made no particular complaint, except of his hand, which appeared to be swollen. In the morning, the workhouse surgeon found a slight wound on his hand, to which a poultice was applied. An infection of erysipelas set in, however, and the man died. The coroner and jury agreed that no fault was attributable to Drake, and the old man – who seemed in a terrible state of mental torment – was told that he was not to blame.

21 FEBRUARY 1868 An inquiry was held at the Aston Union workhouse, Birmingham, following the death of two inmates – Mary Pritchett, sixty, and her daughter, Mary Ann Pritchett, twenty-three. Both had been suffering from 'the itch' and had been placed in a ward for such cases, along with another similarly afflicted pauper named Mary Baker. In the absence of the regular nurse, her inmate assistant, a girl named Louisa Bosworth, went to the surgery and brought a quantity of carbolic acid, which she mistook for a solution of sulphur and lime – the dressing usually employed for the itch. The girl smeared this over the three women, who were soon seized with dreadful pains, and Mary Ann Pritchett then suffered a fit. The nurse was then called and the fatal mistake discovered. Despite all possible medical aid, the mother expired five hours later. After lingering in great pain, the daughter also died two days afterwards, while Baker slowly recovered. The inquiry was told that there had previously been two paid nurses in the workhouse, but after one was dismissed, the board of guardians had dispensed with the services of a second nurse. On the day of the accident, the nurse had directed Bosworth to get the three women undressed, and then she herself would administer the lotion. The nurse, however, had not come immediately, and the girl herself went to the surgery, returning with the wrong preparation. The jury returned a verdict of accidental death, and censured the guardians for not providing sufficient nurses for the establishment.

22 FEBRUARY 1838 A dreadful case of death by burning occurred on this day at the Wallingford workhouse. A female inmate, aged forty-six, who was employed in washing for the establishment, approached too near to the fire grate and part of her dress caught light. A bedridden female pauper lying nearby tried to extinguish the flames, but without effect. The woman, in great agony and fright, ran into another room and threw herself upon a bed, which immediately caught fire (though the blaze

was soon extinguished). She then rolled off the bed onto the floor, and so powerful were the flames which by now enveloped her, that the boards were charred where she lay. Assistance eventually arrived and the flames were subdued, but her injuries were so extensive that she never rallied. Up until the time of her death, some two days later, she never suffered the slightest pain, although one of her hands and a great portion of her body were literally toasted.

23 FEBRUARY **1858** Reports appeared today of what was described as a fatal hoax that had taken place at the Northampton workhouse. Because of some misconduct, the master had put a boy, by way of punishment, into the workhouse mortuary where a corpse of a recently deceased inmate was lying in a coffin. The boy took the corpse out of the coffin, dressed it in his own clothes, and propped it up against the wall of the room. He then got into the coffin, lay down, and covered himself over. Not long afterwards, the master came, looked in at the door, and saw what he took to be a sulky lad standing against the wall. 'Now,' said the master, 'do you want any supper?' There was no answer. The question was repeated with the same result. The boy looked out from the coffin and said, 'If he won't have any, I will.' The master fled under terror, and received such a shock that it was said that he had died from the effects. The story, an early 'urban myth', was later exposed as being completely without foundation.

1895 On this day, at a meeting of the Pontefract guardians, a member stated that on a surprise visit to the workhouse he found the inmates eating potatoes he would not have given to his pigs. They were absolutely unfit for food. Another member said he discovered butter fit for nothing save greasing cart wheels, and calculated to poison anybody. The workhouse master, on being called before the guardians, promised to be more careful in future, and to send improper supplies back to contractors.

1907 A court at Newport, Monmouthshire, today heard that a former workhouse medical officer was himself to become a workhouse inmate. Walter Dixon had suffered a long period of ill-health and had been in and out of the Newport workhouse over the past two years. He was now being removed back to Eastry to face the prospect of entering the same institution where he had once served as doctor.

24 FEBRUARY **1767** At two o'clock in the morning a fire broke out in the Roodee workhouse at Chester. It was thought to have originated amongst the cotton which was spun by the child inmates. The building, which housed 200 boys and girls in addition to the adults, was totally destroyed. Seventy-seven perished, including sixty children, twelve men and five women. The workhouse clerk, Thomas Huxley, wrote:

It is impossible to express the horror and distress the poor people were in, some of them running out naked, others jumping out of windows and from the top of the building. In short, it was the most shocking sight that ever was seen. There are now upwards of thirty men employed in digging out the bones and dead bodies, but there is none found as yet, and it is supposed they are all burnt to ashes.

25 FEBRUARY 1836 At the Droxford Union workhouse at Bishop's Waltham, a sixty-six-year-old inmate named Honor Shawyer died today of 'mortification of the bowels'. At a subsequent coroner's inquest, accusations of neglect were made against the workhouse master and matron, Edmund and Elizabeth Privett, who it was said had failed to summon a doctor despite being repeatedly asked to do so. Although the coroner recommended that the Privetts be removed from their positions, they remained in post for a further seven weeks, with their eventual discharge due – it was said – to Mrs Privett's drunkenness. John Murphy was appointed as the new master but he, too, had to contend with unwelcome publicity when it was revealed that the inmates were being served 'pork-water' instead of soup, and puddings made of the skimmings of pork-water instead of suet. After Murphy had complained about the introduction of the diet, which had been imposed by the guardians, it was agreed that he should make the soup using half fresh meat and half salt meat. One of the guardians agreed to visit the workhouse to review the matter but, after he failed to appear, Murphy had reverted to the traditional way of making broth. Soon afterwards, Murphy was dismissed, for reasons which were somewhat unclear. The workhouse chaplain, the Revd Mr Brock, who had sent food from his own house for sick inmates, was censured by the guardians as being meddling and officious.

1884 In the early hours, a shocking event took place in Liverpool at the West Derby Union's workhouse infirmary on Mill Road after Adam Rutherford, a former inmate of the institution, somehow gained access to the premises. He found his way to the room where Ann Groves, a nurse, was sleeping, and with a razor cut her throat from ear to ear. He then attempted to kill himself by cutting his own throat. It seems that during the struggle Groves had with her assailant she screamed out, and her cries brought several other staff to her assistance. They found her lying in a pool of blood, and in the agonies of death. She could not speak, but pointed to a corner of the apartment, where they found Rutherford also lying in a pool of blood with his throat cut, and the razor beside him. Groves succumbed to her injuries shortly afterwards, but her killer survived for several weeks. Rutherford had just been released from prison after serving four months' imprisonment for breaking into the West Derby Infectious Diseases Hospital.

26 FEBRUARY 1877 George Catch, aged fifty, a man who had earned a reputation as the most tyrannical and heartless of workhouse masters, today threw himself in front of a Great Western express train at Southall. In 1855, Catch had been appointed master of the Strand Union workhouse on Cleveland Street, a post he held for three years – during which time his lying, cruelty and vindictiveness knew almost no bounds. He also took every opportunity to thwart the efforts of the medical officer, Dr Joseph Rogers, to improve the treatment of the sick at the workhouse. Eventually, after Catch unsuccessfully tried to frame Rogers for not attending to a patient in the workhouse sick wards, he was forced to take his leave. The Strand inmates celebrated his final departure from the workhouse by creating a cacophony of old kettles, shovels and penny trumpets.

Catch managed to secure a new post as master of the Newington workhouse where he again obstructed and abused the medical officer. Catch was finally forced to resign after falsely accusing a doctor and a nurse at the workhouse of having an improper relationship. Remarkably, Catch was then appointed as master of the Lambeth workhouse where he soon resumed his usual manner of cruelty to the inmates and quarrelling with the other officers. His downfall finally came when, in an effort to locate a female inmate whose behaviour had affronted him, he ordered hydrochloric acid to be added to a bowl of chloride of lime beneath a chimney where he believed she was hiding. Fortunately, the girl was elsewhere but the fumes created led to the collapse of sixteen pauper nurses with acute chlorine poisoning. Catch was forced to resign and was barred from ever again holding office in a workhouse. He spent the last few years of his life as a patent medicine manufacturer but prior to his death had become depressed after learning that his daughter had run away with an omnibus conductor and was living with him in Greenwich.

27 FEBRUARY 1894 William Davies, an inmate of the Bridgnorth workhouse, was today sentenced to three years' penal servitude for a murderous assault on Robert Mantel, another inmate, aged seventy-five years. The two had met in the workhouse garden on New Year's Day, when Mantel asked Davies why he had wheeled a barrow against him. Davies responded by striking Mantel on the head several times with a stone-breaking hammer and inflicting serious wounds.

1908 It was reported today that John Salisbury, aged sixty, had discharged himself from the Tiverton workhouse in order to marry Eliza Ellen Roberts, a fellow inmate of the institution, ten years his junior. Neither the master nor any of the other inmates knew of the courtship until the registrar had been consulted. It did not appear likely that the couple would be lonely in the little cottage that was being prepared for them, as they each had a family of young children.

28 FEBRUARY 1856 A number of today's papers reported the results of an investigation, carried out for the Poor Law Board by Dr Henry Bence Jones, into conditions at the St Pancras workhouse. Dr Jones had found that workhouse severely overcrowded with patients in the infirmary having to be placed on the floor. Ventilation throughout the building was deficient, with fetid air from privies, sinks, drains, urinals and foul patients permeating many of the wards and producing sickness, headaches and dysentery amongst the inmates. The staff also complained of nausea, giddiness, sickness and loss of appetite. A lying-in room, also used as a sleeping room by night nurses, had a smell that was 'enough to knock you down'. In the women's receiving wards, more than eighty women and children slept in two rooms which provided a mere 164 cubic feet of space per adult. Worst of all were the underground 'pens' where between 300 and 900 applicants for out-relief crowded each day, sometimes waiting until 7 p.m. without food. The smell in the pens was so poor as to cause women to faint and windows to be broken to obtain fresh air. The union's relieving officer reported that his predecessor had died of typhus, thought to be contracted from the foul air. Jones' heartfelt conclusion was that 'such a state of things ought not to be tolerated by the Government.'

29 FEBRUARY 1932 At daybreak, the Swerdsjo workhouse, near Falun, Sweden, was burned down. The twenty-seven inmates, who were all between seventy and eighty years in age, were asleep when the fire broke out. There were three floors to descend before they could reach safety and the building possessed only one staircase which was already blazing. The fire brigade was summoned but, owing to the distance the firemen had to travel, they arrived too late to rescue all the inmates, twelve of whom were burned to death and five seriously injured.

MARCH

The boys' training ship *Wellesley* ablaze on the Tyne at South Shields. (*See* 11 March)

1 MARCH **1766** A startling demonstration of the use of electricity was today performed by Mr Spence, 'operator of teeth to his Majesty', on a woman belonging to the workhouse in the parish of St Andrew's above the Bars. The woman had lost the power of speech some six weeks earlier following the onset of convulsive fits. After the electrical current was applied to several parts of her body, and then to her mouth, the convulsive fits left her and she recovered her speech. Mr Benjamin Franklin of Philadelphia was present at the proceedings and expressed his astonishment.

2 MARCH **1898** At the Blackburn workhouse this evening, one of the guardians, Mr M. Shorrock, entertained the inmates with a magic lantern show of the places he had seen in taking one of Cook's circular tours through Europe. The spacious dining hall had a crowded audience and the lecturer was carefully listened to as he described each place in turn. Starting at Dover, he took the audience in imagination to Ostend, Brussels, Lucerne, Genoa, Rome, Monte Carlo and Calais. Mr Shorrock told many anecdotes connected with the various places, and the pictures were much admired. During the interval, the ever-popular Mr Kisielowski sang a few songs in his own inimitable style. At the close Mr Wales, chaplain, proposed a vote of thanks to the lecturer for his very interesting and instructive entertainment. The vote was carried amid loud cheers.

3 MARCH **1829** An inquest took place today after tragedy struck Norwich's city workhouse. The drama had begun the previous afternoon when five inmates were struck down with symptoms that suggested they had been poisoned. John Burgess, his wife Rhoda, their child, and two other adults, all began vomiting violently after eating part of a dumpling. Burgess, who had made the dumpling himself, had eaten more heartily than the rest and was the most violently affected. Medical attendance was immediately obtained but Burgess steadily declined and he died at about 6.15 p.m.

Examination of the dumpling showed that it contained a considerable quantity of arsenic, as did the flour it had been made from. The flour came from a bag left at the workhouse three weeks earlier for an inmate named Thomas Briggs. Briggs, who was suffering from cancer in the face and confined to his bed, occasionally had parcels of flour sent in for him by his wife Jane. The bag in question had been received by a servant girl in the kitchen. Rhoda Burgess, who acted as Briggs' nurse, took the parcel to Briggs who told her to put it into a cupboard until he wanted it. There it had remained, untouched, until taken out by John Burgess who had thought it would spoil if not used. Further investigation revealed that the parcel had been delivered to the workhouse by a forty-two-year-old man named John Stratford. A druggist not far from where Stratford lived recalled having sold him some arsenic several months earlier.

At the inquest, Jane Briggs revealed that she had been having an affair with Stratford and had become pregnant by him. Stratford had begged her to keep her situation quiet as he did not want his wife to find out about it. The decision of the inquest jury was that John Stratford was guilty of wilful murder.

Throughout his subsequent trial, Stratford maintained his innocence, swearing he had never visited the workhouse premises. However, after being found guilty and sentenced to death, he made a full confession, claiming Jane Briggs had said it would be a blessing if God would release her husband from his sufferings. Stratford was hanged on 17 August, after which his body was put on public display in Norwich market hall, then taken to the Norfolk and Norwich Hospital for anatomical dissection.

4 **MARCH 1877** At the Belper workhouse today, the death occurred of inmate Jonathan Millward, aged seventy-three. Millward, who was being treated for heart disease in the workhouse infirmary, got out from his bed at about 4 a.m. to visit the water closet. A noise was heard and he was discovered to have fallen down some steps near a curve in the staircase. He had broken his neck, with death thought to have been instantaneous.

1897 On this day the journal *London* revealed that board meetings of the City of London Union were being conducted in a manner worthy of the pages of *Oliver Twist*. Proceedings began with a light luncheon of bread and cheese, beer,

An artist's impression of the 'banquet' that accompanied the City of London guardians' meetings as viewed by the diners and the workhouse inmates.

spirits etc. After the main business of the meeting, typically an hour or so later, the guardians were served a repast of fish (salmon for preference), fowl, roast mutton and beef, and sundry other dishes followed by a selection of puddings and sweets. The food was accompanied by champagne and other wines and spirits. Then came the important matter of a long series of well-lubricated toasts to the Queen and royal family, the chairman of the Board, the vice chairman of the Board, the chairman for the day, the vice chairman for the day, and so on, finally concluding with a toast for the oldest guardian and one for the youngest guardian. Finally, the members rounded off their meal with tea, coffee, biscuits, cakes, and other dainties and delicacies. As well as the unseemliness of such consumption and cork-popping taking place in earshot of the workhouse inmates, concerns were raised over whether such feasts were being subsidized by the ratepayers.

At a subsequent meeting of the guardians, board member Mr John Lobb proposed 'that the dining by the Guardians at the workhouse at Homerton and the infirmary at Bow after the business... be discontinued.' The motion, needless to say, was defeated.

5   MARCH 1902 At 4 a.m., the inmates of the Chorlton Union workhouse infirmary at Withington were woken, as usual, to be washed. One of their number, John Fletcher, rose from his bed, put on a dressing-gown, and walked to the lavatory. The nurse on duty, being suspicious, followed at a distance, and just as she entered the

An infirmary block at the Chorlton workhouse.

lavatory she heard a loud thud. The window was open and she realised that Fletcher must have thrown himself through. She immediately went out, and found him lying on the stones beneath the window, bleeding profusely from a fracture at the base of the skull and from injuries to the arm and thigh. He died an hour later.

An inquest heard that Fletcher, aged fifty-six, a gardener by trade, had been forced by ill-health to give up his work and, as a result, had become very depressed. He was referred by his doctor for treatment at the workhouse infirmary and had been admitted the day before his death. The jury returned a verdict of suicide whilst temporarily insane. They also recommended that the lavatory windows should be barred, and thought four o'clock was too early for sick patients to be disturbed.

6   MARCH 1892 Just after 1 a.m., a fire broke out in the City of London Union workhouse at Homerton. For a while, the blaze threatened a whole wing of the main building consisting of the cookhouse, kitchen, bread room, dining hall and the beautiful chapel on the floor above. The master and officers set to work with the hydrants and fire hoses and had extinguished the flames before the arrival of fire engines.

7   MARCH 1895 An inquest today heard that understaffing at the Atherstone Union workhouse had contributed to the death of an inmate, Joseph Hill. Hill, aged sixty-four, had gone missing from the workhouse and, following a search, his dead body was found in the River Anker at the nearby village of Witherley. The workhouse master, John Wainwright, said that Hill had been an inmate for about six months and was placed in the infirmary because of his weak state. After examining him, the medical officer reported that he was suffering from cerebral disease. The master noticed that Hill seemed 'a little bit soft' but not bad enough to be classed as a lunatic and had never shown any suicidal tendency. He also revealed that an inmate named Callis was in charge of the infirmary, under the direction of the workhouse matron. Although the medical officer had previously recommended that a nurse should be in charge of the hospital, the guardians had decided not to act upon this. The matron stated that she had many other duties and was obliged to leave the male patients in the charge of Callis and another inmate. There was nothing to prevent patients going into the garden whenever they pleased. It was from here that Hill had escaped by climbing over the garden wall. The jury concluded that Hill had drowned but there was insufficient evidence to show he had committed suicide. They also recommended that a nurse should be appointed to supervise the infirmary.

8   MARCH 1899 Today's sitting of the Warwickshire Winter Assizes considered the case of John Brewer, aged seventy-two, an inmate of the Coventry workhouse, who was

charged with the manslaughter of another pauper named John Mercer. The incident had happened in the workhouse dayroom when Mercer and two other men were sitting in front of the fire. Brewer came to the fire to pick up his tea tin, accidentally brushing against Mercer who said, 'Who the — are you shoving?' Brewer picked up his tin and, coming back, again touched Mercer, who then grabbed him and upset the tea. The two then starting fighting on the floor, with Mercer twice striking Brewer. They were pulled apart by other inmates and told to let the matter drop, but Mercer again grasped Brewer and another brief scuffle ensued. Mercer then sat down by the fire, and his mouth opened and eyes shut. He died a few minutes later. A post-mortem found no evidence of external injury and death had probably been caused by the effects of sudden shock and exertion on a weak heart.

9 MARCH 1875 The *Manchester Evening News* today reported the death of Charles Johnson, a sail-maker, about fifty-eight years of age, who for several years had been an inmate of Liverpool's Toxteth Park workhouse. While taking his tea, the unfortunate man got a piece of bread stuck in his throat which he was unable either to swallow or disgorge. Dr Rainford, the house surgeon, was called, but he was unable to render any assistance to the man until he had performed the operation of tracheotomy, when a tube was inserted into the windpipe After this Johnson seemed to get a little better, but on Thursday evening he became restless and bronchitis set in, with death ending his sufferings the following day.

10 MARCH 1890 An inquest was held at Bristol's Stapleton workhouse today following the death of seventy-eight-year-old inmate Matthew Wrankmore. He had been engaged in whitewashing a staircase and was up a ladder which was resting on a plank laid on top of two trestles. The ladder had evidently moved a little, throwing him off and resulting in a fatal fall to the ground. The workhouse master, Mr Richard Hughes, explained that elderly inmates generally liked to do a little work so as not to be thought incompetent and helpless. Wrankmore had been in the habit of doing whitewashing work ever since he had been in the workhouse and was a competent man. However, if it had been realised that he was going to whitewash the staircase he would have been stopped, as that part of the work was left to the younger men. The inquest jury returned a verdict of accidental death.

11 MARCH 1893 At Shropshire Assizes today, a charge of slander was brought against Walter Coleman, master of the Atcham Union workhouse, by Annie Brennan, the head nurse at the same establishment. According to Brennan, the master had told

The ship's company of the *Wellesley*, which sank a few years after this photograph was taken.

the workhouse medical officer that immoral behaviour had taken place between herself and the assistant master, Mr Eddin, on an occasion during the previous August. Brennan and Eddin had been out on the same evening and the porter's book had showed that they had returned at exactly the same time, namely 8.55 p.m. In his defence, the master said that he bore Brennan no malice, and was merely repeating information given to him by a schoolmaster at Berrington. He had not believed the story and had told the medical officer about it in professional confidence. He denied having said anything improper to Brennan and that he had a wife and four children living in the workhouse with him. The judge found in Brennan's favour and awarded her damages of £100 plus costs. Six months later, Coleman became bankrupt because of the fine.

1914 On this day in the harbour at South Shields, the training ship *Wellesley*, home to almost 300 boys, including many placed there by poor law authorities, caught fire and sank. Despite having to contend with thick black smoke, all those aboard were safely evacuated.

12 MARCH **1886** It was reported today that the body of a child, aged six months, which was supposed to have been buried four days previously, had been discovered in the mortuary of the Leicester workhouse. The body was found quite accidentally, and it was revealed that the mother had followed an empty coffin to the grave, where the burial service was read. A subsequent inquiry by the guardians found that the person responsible for removing the coffin, a man named Bryan, had been 'rather hurried'

and had not requested a nurse to accompany him into the mortuary as required by regulations. Nurse Adcock, who was supposed to have placed identifying labels on the body and coffin, had neglected to do so. The superintendent nurse, who was in a 'delicate state of health', had also made errors and was 'very much to blame'. All these, however, were let off and an under-nurse named Frisby was made the scapegoat and called upon to resign.

13 MARCH 1893 Eliza Mahony, an inmate of the Cork Union workhouse, was today arrested on suspicion of infanticide. Mahony, aged twenty-six, was a resident of the workhouse maternity ward along with her two children, one aged two-and-a-half years and the other two months. The previous morning, she had got up to go to early Mass and was seen making the children comfortable under covers. While she was away, no one had gone near the children. When she returned, she went to the baby's bed and took off the bedclothes. She was then heard to cry, 'Oh! What happened to the child since I went to Mass?' and the infant was discovered dead in her arms. Dr Murphy, the workhouse physician, had examined the body soon afterwards and found it cold and quite stiff, with large livid patches on its chest, arms and front of the legs. A post-mortem indicated that the child was quite healthy but had died of suffocation which, it was said, could have resulted from the mother lying on top of it. A court hearing later heard that Mahony's husband was shortly returning from a visit to America and that he was not the father of the dead child. Despite the suspicious circumstances, Mahony was released until any further evidence emerged.

14 MARCH 1899 At around midday, a bottle of ether exploded in the surgery of the male infirmary at the Rochdale Union workhouse. The blast resulted in the death of Superintendent Nurse Evans and horrendous burns to Nurse Barker who was alongside her. Great damage was done to the surgery, which was set on fire. Nurse Barker, who subsequently died from her injuries, briefly gained consciousness and was able to tell doctors that while replacing a bottle of ether on the shelves, it had accidentally knocked against another bottle and broken.

15 MARCH 1875 Local Government Inspector Mr Baldwin Fleming today concluded an inquiry into the death of a young woman named Mary Jane Rushworth, an inmate of the North Bierley Union workhouse, Bradford. When admitted to the workhouse she had been in an advanced state of pregnancy and was suffering from mania. Her mental state was said to have resulted from her having been seduced, a matter which had preyed heavily on her mind. She was put under the charge of a woman described by

witnesses as 'deaf as a post, and as silly as a boat-horse.' During this woman's absence, Rushworth went too close to a fire whose guard was faulty and either fell into the flames or set fire to her clothes. The severity of her burns brought about premature labour and she died ten days later. Without viewing the body, the medical officer had described the burns as slight and certified that her death had resulted from her confinement. The body was subsequently exhumed and an inquest held, with a verdict being returned that she had died from the burns. Mr Fleming expressed his belief that the head paid nurse was incompetent, and that the employment of imbeciles as under nurses was utterly indefensible. He also commented severely on the conduct of the medical officer.

16 MARCH 1858 At York Assizes, the trial began of John Sagar, master of the Keighley Union workhouse at Exley Head. Sagar was accused of the 'most cowardly and dastardly' murder of his wife Barbara, who had died the previous December after a week's illness. A coroner's inquest had showed that her death had appeared to have resulted from arsenic poisoning.

The Sagars had been married for nineteen years and had had nine children, all of whom were dead. At the time of Barbara's demise, the couple had been master and matron of the workhouse for six years, prior to which John had been a painter, a druggist for a short while, and then a publican for two years. Described by one newspaper report as 'a short, square-built fellow, of middle age, and with countenance "villainously low"', he was said to have once locked his wife in the workhouse mortuary, and had also handcuffed her to a bedstead for mistreating some children in the workhouse. The Sagars were also alleged to have been involved in a bizarre triangle with Ann Bland, the twenty-two-year-old daughter of one of the guardians. Bland claimed that Mrs Sagar had invited her to share the Sagars' bed, where she had lost her virtue.

The prosecution's case was largely based on evidence from the physicians who had conducted the post-mortem on Mrs Sagar's body which detailed the traces of arsenic they had found in her internal organs. There were also a number of allegations concerning Sagar's mistreatment of his wife. For the defence, a number of witnesses testified that he had invariably treated his wife kindly. The most decisive testimony came from Mr John Milligan, surgeon and medical officer at the Keighley workhouse, who had attended Mrs Sagar during her final days. He expressed great doubts about her death being caused by arsenic poisoning. The presence of the substance in her body was, he suggested, readily explicable by its absorption through the skin from various ointments she had previously used. Instead, he attributed her death to severe inflammation of the stomach which had arisen from natural causes. Following Milligan's evidence, the prosecution withdrew their case and Sagar was pronounced not guilty.

17 MARCH 1894 An extraordinary meeting of the Fareham board of guardians took place to consider the position of the workhouse master, Daniel Johnstone. It followed a much publicised court hearing into claims by workhouse inmate Fanny Vaughan, aged eighteen, that Johnstone was the father of her illegitimate son. Vaughan alleged that towards the end of January 1893, Johnstone had come into her room and, after turning out the gas, improper intercourse had taken place. A similar occurrence had taken place a few weeks later.

Following an earlier complaint to the board by the girl's stepmother, a committee appointed to investigate the matter was told by Vaughan that the master had not taken advantage of her. Vaughan had, however, later retracted this statement saying it had been made under fear and threats of violence. The workhouse nurse, Sarah Haggett, learned of the girl's condition in March 1893 and reported it to the master and matron. According to Haggett, the master had said that if it were true, 'I will shut her up and she shan't see daylight until it's over.' After the committee visited the workhouse to make inquiries, he had shaken his fists at the girl's window saying, 'My girl, you shall go as far as my money and the law will send you.' The matron had also threatened to wring the girl's neck if she repeated her claim.

Johnstone at first denied entering the girl's bedroom but later claimed he had seen the gas left burning and, while she was asleep, briefly entered to extinguish it. However, the workhouse cook, Eliza Roche, said she had seen him enter the girl's room on several occasions. Once, at around the time in question, he had stayed for about twenty minutes.

The magistrates decided that Johnstone was the father of the child and made an order that he should contribute 3s a week towards its support until it reached the age of fourteen. In the light of this verdict, the guardians agreed that Johnstone should be immediately dismissed.

18 MARCH 1865 It was reported today that the town of Brighton was in ecstasy. After four years of digging, a new well shaft at the Brighton Union's workhouse school site at Warren Farm had finally encountered water. The lack of a suitable natural supply in the area had delayed construction of an urgently needed new workhouse at nearby Race Hill because the guardians were reluctant to pay the cost of piped water to the elevated location. The Warren Farm well descended to a world record depth of 1,285ft, with reports showing that the water had risen to a depth of 700ft and was of good quality. Although the digging of the well had been entirely carried out by workhouse inmates, it was the engineers who were honoured with a parade, medals and a banquet, not the pauper labour force. The wife of a man who died during the digging work was given £6 in compensation.

19 MARCH **1834** A revolt took place today amongst the juvenile female paupers of St Margaret's workhouse, Dean Street, Westminster. A young man named Speed, appointed as their superintendent, had provoked their wrath by his allegedly tyrannical behaviour. He was unmercifully thrashed by the girls who tore his clothes nearly off his back and beat him until his cries raised the alarm. The arrival of the master had no effect and the police were sent for to quell the disturbance. After several skirmishes, six of the girls were secured in another part of the building. During the night, however, several of the juvenile male paupers stormed the prison and liberated the girls. The following morning a council of war was held, and the workhouse officers decided to convey the six girls, who were considered the ringleaders, into the country. They were taken away by the beadle amid the hisses and groans of the juveniles left behind. The girls themselves also made some resistance, and were only tamed by the beadle threatening to use force if they did not go quietly. The prisoners were left in pairs at different farmhouses in Camberwell and Peckham, but the following day two of them made their escape, and made their way to Westminster, where they had the audacity to send into the workhouse for their male companions, who shortly joined them, and they had not been heard of since.

1842 James Miles, the former master of the workhouse at Hoo St Werburgh, Kent, was today sentenced to six months' imprisonment for assaulting female children at the workhouse. The case had first come before magistrates in December 1840. A thirteen-year-old inmate named Jemima Danes said that she had been punished three times by Miles, who had laid her face down on a table, taken her clothes off, and beat her. Another time she was stripped, and received more than ten stripes. On a further occasion, he had pulled up her clothes, and beaten her until she had started to bleed – the beating had been because she did not clean out the corners of the room. Danes' evidence was corroborated by another female pauper, who said that the master fetched her to hold the girl down while he flogged her. The marks on the girl's flesh lasted for some considerable time. Another of Miles' victims was Eliza Screese who was twice flogged while standing up and on another occasion laid upon a table and beaten with a rod. A witness to the proceedings stated:

> She was very violently flogged, and I have seen spots of blood upon her chemise. When she was flogged the only clothes she had on was her chemise and under-petticoat, shoes and stockings. She took them off herself at the desire of the master, and laid them down by her. She also removed her things off her shoulders; and because her petticoats were not untied, Miles told her to strip. The Master stripped up her clothes, and it required two of us to hold her down, she struggled so violently.

Miles' defence was that it was part of his duty to chastise children under the age of sixteen and that he had only been acting in line with the workhouse regulations issued by the Poor Law Commissioners. As a result of the affair, the Commissioners banned the corporal punishment of female inmates in workhouses.

1911 In the evening of this day, a fire occurred at the Chipping Norton workhouse in Oxfordshire. The blaze broke out in a storeroom located at the centre of the main building which comprised four three-storey wings arranged in the form of a cross. Fortunately, no one was injured in the blaze.

20 MARCH **1891** This morning, a man named James Griffiths, aged fifty-nine, died in the Hartlepool workhouse in strange circumstances. Griffiths had been admitted about a month earlier, and acted as wardsman in the infirmary. He recently complained of pains in one of his knees, and the workhouse medical officer, Dr Ainsley, ordered him belladonna for external application. The next morning he was found in a room adjoining the infirmary unable to speak, and with the bottle containing the belladonna beside him. He pointed to his mouth, and also the bottle, from which it was presumed he had taken the poison. He died shortly afterwards.

1898 On this day details appeared of an amorous letter written by a sixty-year-old male inmate of the Edmonton workhouse to a rather younger female in the same institution who had taken his fancy from afar. His *billet doux* included a

Some of the damage caused by the fire at Chipping Norton workhouse.

proposal of marriage, which was not received with favour by its recipient. She had handed the letter to the matron, with its contents then being aired at a meeting of the guardians. 'I have taken a great liken to you,' wrote the suitor, 'although we have had no conversation with each other. But I have a great passion for you, and I cannot help it, for not a time that you enter that dining hall can I keep my eyes off you. What I want to know is if you are willing to keep in communication with me. If so, when you are coming into the dining hall let this be your sign – raise your right hand on the top of your head. I will be on the look-out when you have received this letter, or you may write to me if you like. If all is correct with you I will see what I can do to make you comfortable, also your children, if any. Whatever you do, keep as quiet as you can. I have kept off drink this last four months and left off smoking on purpose to gain your affections.' The master was instructed to see that discipline was maintained.

21 MARCH 1901 According to this day's *Manchester Courier*, the East Lancashire Coroner had been informed of the death in the Haslingden Union workhouse of Betty Smith, aged forty-five. The deceased had had an epileptic fit in early February, and when she recovered it was noticed that she was plucking at her right arm. The nurse in charge had apparently taken precautions to prevent the woman getting hurt during the seizure. However, after her death it was found that she had suffered for six weeks from a broken arm.

22 MARCH 1836 It was reported today that a very interesting and beautiful female child, thought to be between two and three years of age, was residing in the Liverpool workhouse. She had been found exposed on some steps in Ranelagh Street the previous May, dressed in an old lilac printed frock, a pink cotton bonnet, and a fine linen chemise, marked 'A'. The only words she could articulate clearly were 'papa' and 'mama'. Every inquiry was made, but in vain, to discover her parents. From the fineness of her linen, the mode in which it was marked, and the words she uttered, which were ones rarely used by the children of the humbler or working classes in that part of the country, it was suspected that she had been stolen, used for the purpose of begging, robbed of her better clothes, and then abandoned. As several instances had occurred in London and in other places of children being stolen, wider publicity was now being given to the case in hope of it leading to some discovery.

23 MARCH 1838 A deputation from the Kensington board of guardians today visited the workhouse at Chelsea to investigate complaints about the treatment of the paupers there. The matron of the establishment, Mrs Davis, gave a glowing account of how the

inmates were cared for. Of the 365 inmates, forty were allowed mutton chops, and twenty-six of those also received mutton broth. A total of 268 inmates were allowed tea and sugar, comprising 140 aged women, seventy-five sick, and fifty-three servants. The soup provided was made from 7 stones of legs and shins of beef, with three pecks of split peas and one peck of onions, boiled in a 57-gallon copper, each pauper being served a pint and a half. She also stated that if any of the paupers had money to purchase fish or anything else for themselves, she obtained and cooked it for them.

The only grievances voiced by the inmates themselves came from women employed in the laundry who complained of only receiving one pint of beer a day, and from some other women who objected to the small allowance of butter and cheese. The committee had some sympathy with the first of these complaints, but considered that the second was unjustified since the allowance was rather more than that enjoyed by many of the poor living outside the workhouse.

24 MARCH 1895 On this day, a Sunday, the death occurred of eleven-year-old Ernest Jarvis at the Barrow-upon-Soar workhouse at Mountsorrel. The boy and his parents had been staying in various workhouse casual wards while the father, Charles Jarvis, a bricklayer by trade, searched for work. The previous Thursday night, they had stayed at Oakham workhouse where, according to Mr Jarvis, he and his son were put in an outhouse having a brick floor, no fire, and no hot pipes. Prior to this, they had to take a hot bath then walk 10 yards along a passageway, which was open to the sky, wearing only their shirts. They were then locked in the outhouse, whose floor was wet, and given rugs, which were also wet. They had rung for help but no one came and they had to lie on the rugs until eight the next morning. They complained to the master but he just turned them out. Other inmates had refused to work because they were perished with cold and had been lying in wet rugs which 'stunk fit to knock you backwards'. Later that day, en route to Melton Mowbray workhouse, the boy complained of a bad head and aching chest, and wanted water to drink. He had been allowed to stay with his mother on the Friday night, before the family travelled to the Mountsorrel workhouse the next day.

The master of the Oakham workhouse, George Carter, later told an inquest into the boy's death that Jarvis's statement about the wet rugs was quite untrue. The ward where the father and son had stayed was dry and adjoined the bathroom where a large fire was kept going every day. The men were provided with slippers when walking along the connecting passageway. The Mountsorrel medical officer said he believed the boy's death was due to pneumonia, probably preceded by influenza, but would not have been caused by sleeping in a wet rug at Oakham. The jury returned a verdict that death was from natural causes.

25 MARCH 1896 The Hampstead board of guardians today discussed the case of two elderly workhouse inmates, Mr and Mrs James 'Pigeon' Hill, who had applied for an apartment in a newly completed block of the institution which was reserved for married couples aged over sixty. The request had come shortly after Mr Hill, sixty-six, and his bride, sixty-four, had left the workhouse for an hour or so and tied the knot at Christ Church, Hampstead. The two, who had each been married twice before, were said to have done their courting on Hampstead Heath during the weekly half-day outings allowed to inmates. The guardians, who clearly felt they were being manipulated, were unsympathetic to the application. One member of the board suggested that if the request were granted, dozens of paupers in the house would be getting married in order to benefit from the privilege. Another pointed out that the relevant official regulation stated only that elderly married inmates should not be 'separated', a condition that could surely not apply to a couple who had never lived together. A request to the Local Government Board to amend the regulations proved unsuccessful.

1903 On this day reports appeared of a tragic event at Ipswich workhouse. An inmate named Charles Freston, aged seventy, was alleged to have attempted to murder Ernest Grey, another pauper. Freston apparently had some grievance against Grey and waylaid him outside a dormitory, threw him to the ground and cut the man's throat from ear to ear. When the alarm was raised, Freston took another knife and stabbed himself in the throat. The two men were found lying side by side on the floor in a pool of blood.

26 MARCH 1833 An inquest today was told the extraordinary circumstances surrounding the death of Sarah Byrne who had died about two weeks earlier at the age of seventy-two. The woman was an inmate of the parish workhouse of All Saints, Poplar, and had been bedridden for some time. While crossing her room, carrying a small quantity of water in a pail, she fell and fractured her left thigh. She was immediately taken to the London Hospital, where she was discovered to be an extreme case of *fragilitas ossium* and that her bones were so brittle that they snapped with the slightest exertion. Evidence of the condition came at the hospital when, while being turned in bed, although great gentleness was used, the bone of her right arm snapped in two. It was said that the disorder was caused by the excessive absorption of animal matter which led the bones to contain too great a proportion of earthy substance.

1901 The *Councillor and Guardian* asked the masters of workhouses in England and Wales how many of their inmates had lived in the reigns of George III, George IV, William IV, Victoria, and Edward VII. Based on replies from 139 unions, there were 2,784 such inmates, giving an average of twenty per workhouse. The Camberwell workhouse headed the list with 133 five-reign inmates out of a total 916. Bethnal Green came next, with 109, out of 1,051 inmates; then Brighton, with 103 out of 1,260 inmates, and Hackney with 101 out of 1,407 inmates. The Liverpool workhouse, whose 3,624 inmates made it the largest in the country, had only eighty-five who had lived in the five reigns. Manchester came next, with 2,857, and of these fifty-eight had lived in the five reigns. The smallest number of inmates, seventeen, was at Aberayron in Cardiganshire. Of these, five had lived in the five reigns, giving it the largest percentage of five-reign inmates in its workhouse.

27 MARCH **1897** Details appeared today of the strange tale told to a visitor by a recently deceased female pauper at an unnamed London workhouse. At seventeen, the woman, who grew up in Norway, was informed by her parents that she was to be married, and although she had no say in the matter nothing could have been more satisfactory. Her husband was handsome, cultured and devoted. They lived in a charming country house, surrounded by every luxury, and four children were born to the couple. The only drawback to the perfect happiness of the young wife was the long and frequent absences of her husband, which he attributed to business, but would explain no further. At last there came a day when the man returned no more from his accustomed journey, but sent his lawyer instead, from whom the bewildered and heartbroken woman learned that her supposed husband was the King of —, and that owing to pressing reasons their marriage must end. An adequate sum was settled on her and the children, and wishing to break entirely with the past, she came to live in London. After some years she married an Englishman, and shortly afterwards the King died, leaving a lump sum to her. Her new husband took the money from her to invest, and ran off with the entire amount, leaving his wife penniless. She had never been trained in any sort of work, and things went from bad to worse until, utterly destitute and dying, she became an inmate of the workhouse.

28 MARCH **1881** Today's *Times* gave details of a murderous attack on William Prowse, the assistant master of the Greenwich workhouse. About a year earlier, a man named Howlett had broken into the workhouse and stolen tools from the carpenter's shop. Following a trial at the Old Bailey, at which Prowse was one of the main witnesses against him, Howlett was sentenced to twelve months' hard labour. On his recent release, Howlett took steps for a terrible vengeance on Prowse. During the night, he broke into the workhouse by climbing its high gates and entered the building through a window in the dining hall. As a former inmate of the workhouse, he quickly found his way to a cupboard where knives were kept, and with a butcher's chopper in his hand he went to Prowse's

bedroom and struck him several fearful blows on the head. Prowse sprang up and was then struck on the back, but by this time the noise had aroused the storekeeper, on whose appearance Howlett offered no further violence. Although his injuries were extremely grave, Prowse survived the attack. His assailant was later convicted of attempted murder and sentenced to penal servitude for life.

29 MARCH 1860 The Clifton Union workhouse at Bristol was in a state of great turmoil this evening following the sudden death of the matron, Mrs Phoebe Hunt, apparently at the hands of a lunatic inmate named Ann Richards. Richards, aged twenty-three, had been diagnosed as suffering from hysterical mania and had just been escorted to the workhouse by one of the union's relieving officers and placed in the receiving room under the charge of two female inmates. After about half an hour, she had become very violent and started banging on the door, the noise bringing Mrs Hunt and the assistant matron to the room. The assistant entered first, and Richards immediately flew upon her. A scuffle ensued between them, and Mrs Hunt was in the act of intervening when Richards was said to have struck her a blow behind the ear, knocking her to the ground. The porter and the union clerk then arrived and, finding the matron speechless, conveyed her to the kitchen. The workhouse surgeon was immediately sent for, but on his arrival he found her dead. Mrs Hunt, aged fifty-nine, was the widow of a former master of the workhouse who, coincidentally, had died on the same day nine years earlier. At a subsequent inquest, the evidence of witnesses proved inconsistent and the alleged blow had left no mark upon the deceased's body. After hearing medical evidence, the jury concluded that Mrs Hunt's death was caused by her heart stopping while under strong excitement.

30 MARCH 1925 It was revealed today that a sub-committee of the Bradford board of guardians had recommended that a portable cinematograph apparatus be installed for use at the union's Bowling, Odsal and Daisy Hill institutions. They also recommended acceptance of a tender from New Century Film Service Ltd to supply the equipment at a cost of £155, and that the offer by the firm to apply approximately 3,000ft per week of suitable films free of charge also be accepted. Such a provision was calculated to be cheaper than sending the inmates to outside picture shows or the installation of wirelesses.

31 MARCH 1911 A young woman and her two children were reported today to have left the Rugby workhouse in rather unusual circumstances. Over the previous Christmas, a young widower, hailing from a northern town, was admitted to the

casual wards. He was a painter, and stayed on at the workhouse for three weeks and did some painting. He saw the girl, and, taking a fancy to her, asked her to be his wife. She declined at first, but before he left in the middle of January he had so far been successful in his suit that he told the workhouse master he would return and marry her at the end of March. He then returned to his home, where he secured regular employment, and kept up a constant correspondence with the girl. Most of those who knew of the affair had been sceptical as to the man's sincerity, but the previous Friday, after travelling all night, he had presented himself at the workhouse soon after nine with an outfit for his intended bride. This she put on, was married by the Registrar at the union's offices, and before midday was travelling northward with her husband and children.

APRIL

A Holbeach workhouse inmate named Bingham enclosed in a sulphur fumigation box to treat his skin disease but which led to his death. (*See* 22 April)

1   APRIL, **1837** The new poor relief system introduced by the 1834 Poor Law Amendment Act received much opposition in the manufacturing areas of Lancashire and West Yorkshire. The angry local response to a visit to Keighley by Assistant Poor Law Commissioner Alfred Power was typical, as the *Yorkshire Gazette* today reported:

> [Mr Power] made his appearance in the Mechanics' Institute, when the doors were closed and locked; but owing to the pressure from without, the guardians and commissioner thought it expedient to yield to the public voice, and the doors were consequently thrown open, and the hall of the Institution was very soon crowded to excess. After a most boisterous scene, it was found that Mr Power was preparing to leave the room, but when the people saw it there were cries from all parts, 'stop him, stop him, no shuffling.' In the struggle Mr Power was minus his great coat which was torn in many places, and left in the reading room of the Institute to the mercy of an infuriated public Mr Power made the best of his way to the Devonshire Arms, followed by a great number of the people, amidst the shouts, groans and hisses of those around him. He left the town shortly afterwards and drove at a tremendous rate to meet his friends the guardians of Bradford.

     1910 The *Manchester Guardian* revealed how an aged pauper had saved a nurse from almost certain death at the Liverpool workhouse. The nurse had rushed into a ward with her dress on fire, her clothes from her feet to her waist being one mass of flames. She was on the point of hysterics and quite unable to save herself. As it was the middle of the night, no other staff were around, but Hudson had immediately jumped out of bed and, seizing his bedclothes, had wrapped them tightly around the unfortunate woman and so extinguished the flames.

2   APRIL, **1881** It was revealed today that a totally dark room known as the 'black hole' at the Leicester workhouse, used to confine ill-behaved or 'refractory' inmates, had been closed by order of the Local Government Board. The cell lacked any furnishing whatsoever, and the men and women who were cast into it for eight or ten hours at a time had to lie on the brick floor. The room was apparently constructed in defiance of Local Government Board regulations, which required that refractory wards should be properly lighted, ventilated, furnished with seats, and with a means of inspecting the occupants from the outside.

3   APRIL, **1902** An inquest took place at Rochdale workhouse today on the body of Michael Gorman, aged fifty-seven years. Gorman had been an attendant at the

workhouse infirmary but on the previous Monday night had absented himself without leave. Later that evening, the workhouse porter, Paul Widdup, had seen him drunk and being turned out of a local inn. At six the next morning, an inmate of the workhouse had found Gorman lying face down and unconscious in a field near the workhouse. Widdup said that he had been informed that Gorman had been found drunk and placed on some hay in a cowshed. He had been busy at the time and had not immediately gone to investigate. Gorman was later stretchered to the workhouse infirmary and was put to bed some two hours after he had first been found. He had died at around 2.30 p.m. A post-mortem revealed that Gorman had died of alcoholic poisoning and exposure. The coroner remarked that Widdup's having left the deceased in wet clothes for two hours might be the subject for further inquiry.

4 APRIL, **1863** Robert Mills, labourer, who had for ten weeks been an inmate of the Falkirk poorhouse, threw himself from a top-floor water closet window. He survived two and a half hours before he expired.

1906 Following recent publicity about a plague of enormous rats at the Eton Union workhouse, it was reported today that the master had received numerous letters from people offering advice. One was from the wife of one of the best-known English bishops, in which she stated that a mongoose had quite cleared the bishop's palace of a similar problem. Another remarkable suggestion was the employment of a guinea pig, which the writer said he had found most successful. Patent poison and trap vendors and professional rat-catchers galore had also offered their services.

5 APRIL, **1907** The *Gloucester Citizen* reported the case of Olive Hopkins who had appeared, with a child in her arms, at Gloucester police court. Having previously entered the workhouse at Gloucester, where she had no settlement or right to poor relief, she had been removed to the adjacent Stroud Union workhouse. She had, however, now returned to Gloucester and again entered the workhouse, an action that made her liable to a fine or a month's imprisonment. The woman eventually agreed to return to Stroud and left the court in the company of an officer who had instructions to supply her with a ticket. It later transpired that the workhouse master at Stroud had refused to admit the woman on the grounds that the proceedings were irregular.

6 APRIL, **1902** As a result of a nightmare, a tragic accident took place this morning at the workhouse in Northwich, Cheshire. An inoffensive inmate named Ralph Ellison, aged seventy-four, informed a companion that he had cut his own throat. His bed was covered in blood and there was a knife on the dormitory floor.

The workhouse surgeon, Dr Gough, was immediately summoned and found a jagged wound 3in long. Ellison explained that after reading a newspaper article, he had been dreaming about Boers, in the course of which he had leaped from his bed, taken a knife from his pocket, cut his throat, and then returned to bed. The injury, fortunately, was not fatal.

7 APRIL, 1928 Herbert Lawrence, an inmate of the Hatfield workhouse, aged thirty-eight, was today committed for trial at the Hertfordshire Assizes for the manslaughter of a fellow pauper, sixty-nine-year-old Charles Pales. The charge came two weeks after the two men had come to blows in the workhouse exercise yard. Lawrence had two wooden legs, having lost his limbs through being run over by a railway train, while Pales suffered from degeneration of the arteries. According to another inmate, the fight began with Pales saying to Lawrence, 'We had better have it out.' Pales took his coat off and the two were soon rolling on the ground striking at each other. They then got up and, having rested a while, resumed their fight. They again fell over and continued on the ground. After a few minutes, Lawrence got up, but Pales said that he could not rise. He was taken to the infirmary by the porter. Pales was diagnosed as having suffered a fracture of the right femur, and was bruised about the head and face. He died ten days later. Lawrence later told police that they had quarrelled over a needle.

8 APRIL, 1871 An inquest was held today following the death in mysterious circumstances of Richard Hollidge, a pauper at the Northampton workhouse. Hollidge, aged sixty-three, had the regular task of cleaning the inmates' cutlery and shoes. Following his absence at dinner time, a search was made by another inmate named John Herbert who found that the door to the room where Hollidge worked was fastened. After looking in through the skylight, Herbert fetched the porter who forced open the door with a crowbar. Hollidge was found unconscious and lying face down, wearing just his shirt, stockings and his trousers, which were about his heels. His other clothes – a coat, two waistcoats, hat, shoes, handkerchief and a scarf – were all folded up and placed on a chair. He was carried to the workhouse infirmary and attended by the medical officer, Mr Cotton, who found him cold, stiff and insensible. Despite being administered restoratives, Hollidge had died at midnight. There were no signs of injury or violence but a post-mortem revealed a wound on the scalp and a small fissure in the skull, together with a softening of the brain on one side. Death was supposed to have been caused by apoplexy, with a fall probably causing damage to the skull. However, Hollidge's state of attire remained a mystery.

1883 In the early morning, a serious fire occurred at the Cambridge Union workhouse. The men's infirmary and the nurses' quarters were completely destroyed. All the patients were rescued, including four elderly men who escaped through windows after their exit via a staircase was cut off.

9 APRIL **1910** At Chelmsford today, there was an inquest on Samuel Mortimer, aged seventy-six, who had been found in his bed in the workhouse infirmary, having cut his throat with something between a penknife and a gardener's pruning knife. Despite a doctor being immediately summoned, the man died about five minutes later. It was said that Mortimer had written a note to the workhouse master, stating that it would be his last day on earth, and making complaints about his treatment by the medical officer and the wardsman. He had been moved to a different ward with orders that he should not be allowed a knife, but another inmate had put the implement in his bag. The medical officer denied the deceased's allegations against him, but the wardsman admitted he had called Mortimer a hypocrite because of the amount of noise he had made at night. The jury returned a verdict of suicide during temporary insanity and the coroner also reprimanded the wardsman.

10 APRIL **1927** Today's *Observer* revealed that a baronet, Sir James Herbert Renals, the son of a former Lord Mayor of London, had died at the age of fifty-six in the Brighton workhouse. Sir James, who did not use his title, had been living in one of the poorest streets in the town, trying to support his wife and a family of six small children by

The Brighton workhouse, where a baronet breathed his last.

canvassing for advertisements, a trade which had become very slack. Being on the verge of starvation, he had applied for poor relief. The heir to the baronetcy was said to be a seven-year-old boy named Herbert, at present receiving treatment in the Brighton Sanatorium.

11 APRIL, 1833 At the Sheffield workhouse during the night, an old man was burnt to death. He had apparently been in the habit of getting out of bed and going to warm himself by the fire. By some accident, his clothes caught fire and he was burned to such a degree that there was no hope of recovery.

12 APRIL, 1894 A Local Government Board inquiry began today into complaints about the management of the Newton Abbot workhouse. The main evidence came from Alice Hinton, who had taken up the post of workhouse nurse in the previous December.

Nurse Hinton said that women entering the workhouse went unbathed and kept their own clothes for a week, resulting in the whole place being infested with lice, which were even found on the bread in the dining hall. She had also had to burn her own underclothes because of them. None of the inmates were ever bathed. One, Rose Hellier, had never had a bath during her twenty-eight years in the workhouse. At night, by order of the matron, many elderly inmates were stripped naked and placed into a 'jumper' – a kind of sack used as a straitjacket – and tied to their bedsteads. An elderly inmate named Sarah Bovey, who was paralysed, had been placed naked by a wardswoman in a 'jumper' every night for a week. One morning, because the old woman had made a mess, the wardswoman took a handful of faeces and put it in her mouth. Bovey had died that same night. Despite Hinton's complaints, the matron had said the 'jumpers' were used to save the washing and had not reprimanded or punished the wardswoman. Hinton testified that she had found an inmate named Mrs Nickells apparently dying. The woman was very dirty and covered with vermin. Her hair had been cut off, and her toenails were like claws, being 2½in long. Another woman, who was paralysed, had her fingernails so long that they made wounds in her flesh. Nurse Hinton had also seen an idiot woman, with bruises on her face, crouched in a corner of the workhouse yard where the guardians had built a shed for her. The workhouse boys threw stones and snowballs at the woman to make her swear and when the master's son was at home he was the ringleader. Hinton claimed that Miss Ann Mance, workhouse matron for almost thirty years, neglected her duties, and had only visited the sick ward five times over a three-month period.

Another workhouse nurse, Miss Pike, said that the beds in the nursery were unfit for pigs, and the children were under the care of two partially blind women. One day, a child was tied up to the bed with a piece of string to prevent it from running about, as it had no shoes and stockings. Eleven children had only four nightgowns between them. Neither brushes nor combs were provided for the inmates, and their food was kept in the lavatories. A temporary nurse named Elizabeth Wills said she one night found two men tied down in the bed. One was an imbecile and the other was so ill that he died the same day.

Miss Mance emphatically denied all the charges, swearing that she had never bullied an inmate in her life. She had never ordered inmates to be put into the 'jumpers', which had been introduced by a former nurse. They were under the control of the nurse and she had never received a complaint about their use. Following the inquiry, Miss Mance was dismissed. She died from a heart condition a few weeks later.

13 APRIL, 1850 A physician attending the Castlebar workhouse, County Mayo, revealed that despite the diminishing of the famine, conditions for inmates were still appalling. On the evening of this day, he recorded that:

> Number of inmates in male and female bath rooms, 122 persons — no beds, not even straw for the night — no bed clothes, all wearing their own tattered rags — some of them stretched on the earthen floor or the ward, and many of them in the sitting posture, holding their children in their arms and laps, and begging for as much straw as they might rest their children on — there were 40 of them in the female bath room, and 82 of them in the male bath room, without a seat on which to sit or rest during the day, or a bed of straw on which to lie at night. Within 6ft of the window of this ward is the privy, without a drop lid — night soil flowing over level of drop, and the floor of the privy covered with the same. To the noxious and offensive exhalation issuing from this surcharged cesspool of human ordure, 52 broken panes in the window afford so many unobstructed passes, and which, diffusing itself through the ward, renders the air, vitiated by its overcrowded, filthy, rugged inmates — foul, fetid, and pestilential.

14 APRIL, 1837 A Select Committee today began an inquiry into the conduct of staff at the Fareham workhouse where three boys, aged from four to six years, from the neighbouring Droxford Union had temporarily been housed. William Warren had left the Droxford workhouse at Bishop's Waltham in good health on 8 October 1836, later followed by Robert Withers and Jonathan Cooke. On their return to Droxford, they were found to be weak and sick, infected with scabies, had marks on their bodies, and had apparently made the seven-mile journey on an open cart without any outdoor

clothes. At the inquiry, the master of the Fareham workhouse, Thomas Bourne, said that all three children regularly wet or fouled their beds. His usual method for dealing with 'dirty children' was to punish them by reducing their food. He also birched small children without recourse to approval from the guardians. The schoolmistress at Fareham, Harriet Crouch, admitted that she might have whipped the children with a birch twig. It was also her custom to punish children by making them wear a dunce's cap bearing the word 'dirty' or by placing them in a set of stocks that she had brought from her previous employment at a private school. At the end of their time at Fareham, the boys had been housed for ten days in an outhouse which had a cold stone floor and no fireplace. The boys were only allowed out when their clothes were clean and dry, but were frequently confined to bed while their clothes were being washed. At the end of the inquiry, Thomas Bourne and John Blatherwick were both criticised for neglect. Although neither was dismissed, Blatherwick subsequently resigned his position.

15 APRIL 1913 The *Western Times* today gave details of the inquest into the death of William Nicholls, a sixty-two-year-old inmate of the Bideford workhouse, who was found drowned on the steps of Bideford Quay. Nicholls, who was partially paralysed, had been in the workhouse for eighteen years. He had spent the day before his death out with friends who had accompanied him part of the way back to the workhouse. At the Quay, which was quite out of his way, his overcoat had been taken off and was found folded on the steps with his stick beside it. He had apparently taken a small tin box containing private papers out of the workhouse and left them with a cousin, though he had not made any particular comment about it. The inquest jury returned an open verdict.

16 APRIL 1849 Today saw the conclusion, at the Central Criminal Court, of the trial of Bartholomew Peter Drouet, proprietor of a residential school at Tooting for almost 1,400 pauper children from a number of London poor law authorities including the Strand, Holborn, St Pancras and Richmond. The charge against Drouet was manslaughter and came in the wake of a cholera outbreak at the school when, it was alleged, his neglect had led to the death of 180 children.

In January, after the first cholera cases were discovered, the school was visited by Dr R.D. Grainger, an inspector for the Board of Health. His report was highly critical of conditions at Tooting and ascribed overcrowding as a major factor in the spread of the disease. In a room 16ft by 12ft, he had found four beds occupied by thirteen cholera patients, four of whom were in one bed, and three in each of the others. The boys' schoolroom, which housed up to 500 pupils, measured 94ft by 21ft and was poorly ventilated. Grainger also noted that the school had only one resident medical officer and that the totally inadequate nursing staff was being supplemented by the school's older children, some of whom were themselves still recovering from cholera. He had found bedclothes left soaked with the evacuations of the suffering children, and the few nurses who were in the wards were constantly running from one bed to another, and that the patients were most inefficiently attended. The children's diet was criticised as being defective in quality and including too much pea soup. His firm conclusion was that the school should be evacuated as soon as possible. This advice was quickly taken up by most of the school's patrons, with 1,000 children being removed. The Poor Law Board, however, argued against evacuation and persuaded the Chelsea Union to leave their children in residence, with extra nursing and medical assistance being offered to the school.

Further revelations came in an inquest held by Thomas Wakley, the Middlesex County Coroner, on several children from the Holborn Union. One of the Holborn guardians, Mr W. Winch, recalled a visit to the school during the previous year:

> The children were at dinner. They were all standing. I believe they never sit at meals. I cut up 100 potatoes, not one of which was fit to eat. These were served out to the boys. They were positively black and diseased... We asked the boys if they had any complaint of their food, and if they had, to hold up their hands. About thirty or forty held up their hands... Drouet became very violent, and... called the boys liars and scoundrels.

Several of the school's children also gave evidence. Patrick Sheen said that he shared a bed with two other boys. He never had enough to eat but was frightened of being beaten if he said so. Boys from St Pancras who had run away had been birched and then dressed in girls' clothes for several days as punishment. Henry Hartshorn, one of the boys who had raised his hand during the visit from the Holborn Guardians, earned a small amount of money shoemaking – a penny for each five pairs of slippers. Because he received so little food he spent the money on sweets, apples and pears sold to the children by the school's nurses and also paid ½d for water because not enough was provided.

Drouet was said to have been dilatory in reporting the problem to the authorities and in obtaining medical assistance which could have saved many of the children's lives. It was noted that not a single case of the disease had occurred at Tooting outside the confines of the school. In contrast, of the 155 Holborn children who had been removed to the Royal Free Hospital, not a single one had died, whilst many who had remained had since succumbed to the disease.

A view of Tooting School, scene of the outbreak.

The inquest's verdict was that Drouet was guilty of manslaughter and he was brought to trial on a specimen charge relating to the death of James Andrews and three other children from the Holborn Union. Despite the apparent weight of evidence showing Drouet's negligent treatment, the defence successfully argued that there was no absolute proof that the child would have recovered if it had not been for Drouet's actions. Following instruction from the judge that there was no case to answer, the jury returned a not guilty verdict. Less than three months later, following a period of illness, Drouet died in Margate.

17 APRIL 1831 At about 7.30 a.m., a fire was discovered in the workhouse at Fordingbridge, Hampshire. It began in the fuel-house where a quantity of furze faggots was stored. The flames rapidly spread, setting light to some thatched cottages on the opposite side of the street. The part of the workhouse occupied by the infirm and bedridden was soon on fire and the aged inmates were removed just in time before the flames engulfed the beds in which they had been lying. The town's three fire engines were vigorously worked for a long time before the blaze was brought under control. The exertions of the inhabitants of the town contributed greatly to the successful outcome of the proceedings. The conduct of the women in removing aged and sick inmates from the workhouse and in supplying the engines with water was especially

praised. Happily, no lives were lost – the wind was still and, it being a Sunday, everyone was at leisure to lend a hand.

1861 On this day Mr Noah Fox, one of the medical officers of the Nottingham Union workhouse, committed suicide by swallowing 2 ounces of opium, after which he survived only a few hours. He had for some time past been much addicted to drinking.

18 **APRIL 1901** Today saw the completion of a Local Government Board inquiry into the conduct of Arthur Battersea, long-standing master of the workhouse at Martley, Worcestershire, where his wife Caroline jointly served as matron. The master had already been suspended from duty, and the matron had submitted her resignation, citing ill-health. The matron's action meant that the master would automatically lose his own tenure.

Numerous charges were levelled against Battersea: not recording his times of leaving and entering the workhouse; selling eggs produced at the workhouse to a milk contractor who then sold them back at a profit to the workhouse; including insufficient meat in the soup given to sick inmates; providing tea of insufficient quality and quantity, and failing to issue extra tea at Christmas; improperly giving away workhouse vegetables and meat; giving workhouse children fried bacon instead of the regulation boiled beef; accepting substandard boots and shoes from a contractor; allowing a deficiency in the workhouse clothing stock to the value of almost £10; ordering sixteen syphons of soda water, rather than the four requested for a patient by the medical officer; permitting drunkenness amongst the male inmates; and the destruction, out of pique, of fifty-one currant bushes in the workhouse garden. The master denied all the charges, claiming either that they were completely untrue, or were the result of some small error or confusion. His solicitor suggested that the charges were grossly exaggerated and founded on the complaints of four of the master's fellow officers, including the porter and nurse who were hoping to obtain the 'snug little offices' of master and matron.

Following an investigation by auditors, a further inquiry was held to investigate unaccounted shortfalls in stocks of items such as butter, sugar, tea, meat, tobacco, coal and clothing. Battersea was found to have been careless and neglectful in his duties. However, given his long and previously unblemished tenure of the post, and his imminent forced departure, his suspension was lifted.

19 **APRIL 1892** Details appeared today of a remarkable elopement which had taken place at the workhouse in Nantwich, Cheshire. Among the inmates was a man known to the master as Dr Greame, who claimed he had practised in Toronto and

received his credentials at Owens College, Manchester. For some time past, he had been under the care of one of the nurses. One day recently, after the man had gone out, the master refused him readmission as he had returned in a new suit of clothes and looked altogether too prosperous for the inside of a workhouse. A few nights later, the master discovered that the workhouse nurse had disappeared. On making inquiries, he found that she had joined Dr Greame, and together they had eloped from the town. Both were approaching their fifties, the nurse being a widow.

20 APRIL, 1842 In the early evening, a large number of individuals went in procession to the Christchurch workhouse in Marlborough Street, Southwark, demanding out-relief. When this was refused, they began cursing and swearing in a most awful manner and threatened not only to break every square of glass in the building but also to set the workhouse on fire. A strong body of the L Division of police arrived who closed in on the rabble and apprehended thirty-four of the principal rioters who were marched off to the station-house in Tower Street.

1885 A fire broke out between nine and ten o'clock in the morning at Kettering workhouse in a room used to store picked oakum. The burning material was quickly thrown into the yard and doused with water. The authorities initially suspected that the fire had been deliberately ignited, some of the workhouse boys having earlier been seen in the vicinity. Further enquiries pointed the blame towards a spark from a lighted pipe which one of the adult inmates had incautiously carried into the place.

21 APRIL, 1877 At around half-past seven in the evening, a fire occurred at the Liverpool workhouse. The alarm was raised by a passing policeman who, after organising the immediate connection of the workhouse fire reel, sent a messenger to summon the fire brigade. A manual engine and the steamer *Hamilton* speedily arrived and two fire escapes also attended, with the blaze being put out after half an hour. The fire was located in the workhouse nursery which, providentially, was unoccupied at the time while undergoing disinfection and fumigation.

1883 At about six this morning, James Clarke, aged seventeen, set fire to the St Giles's workhouse in Covent Garden. He put a lighted match to bedclothes in the men's dormitory where he had been sleeping, then went down to breakfast leaving the bedclothes burning. The fire was not discovered for another hour, by which time the bedclothes had been destroyed and a hole burned in the floor. Some of the ceiling in the room below had fallen in, endangering the lives of eight sick women who were confined there. At his subsequent trial at the Old Bailey, Clarke said that his actions had been in response to being punished for some acts of insubordination. After the judge sentenced him to five years' penal servitude, Clarke, in an impudent tone, exclaimed, 'Thank you, sir.'

22 APRIL 1882 A coroner's jury at Holbeach, Lincolnshire, today returned a verdict of manslaughter against the master of the Holbeach workhouse, Walter Bridges Waterer, for causing the death of an inmate, a young man named Bingham. The man had been suffering from a skin disease and was placed in a sulphur fumigation box used to disinfect persons suffering from infectious conditions but was apparently forgotten. His cries finally attracted attention and he was released, but not until he had been so terribly burned that skin and flesh fell from different parts of his body. He died a few hours afterwards. At a subsequent trial at Lincolnshire Assizes, Waterer was found not guilty of manslaughter.

Six months afterwards, Waterer was offered the post of master at the Westbury-on-Severn workhouse in Gloucestershire. He had not, however, informed the Westbury guardians of the manslaughter charge, and when this came to light the appointment was rescinded.

23 APRIL 1836 At about four o'clock in the morning, a fire was discovered at the Loddon and Clavering Union workhouse at Heckingham, Norfolk. The numerous inmates were aroused from their beds and although many of them consisted of aged and infirm persons, all were removed without the loss of a single life. Difficulties in obtaining an adequate supply of water made it impossible to arrest the progress of the flames and two-thirds of the building was destroyed with the damage estimated to cost £3,000. A £200 reward was offered by the Norwich Union insurance company for the conviction of those responsible. A former inmate of the establishment, James Barrett, was arrested but never tried, sufficient evidence being lacking to bring about a conviction.

24 APRIL 1837 A riot occurred today at the Braintree workhouse, Essex. About thirty men went to work in the morning at the mill, and continued quietly until breakfast time, after which they refused to return to work unless each had half a pound more bread a day, with some also demanding beer. Seven of their number were taken before a magistrate who sentenced four of them to fourteen days' hard labour at Springfield Gaol. The other three were sent back, in the hope that the example of those jailed would be communicated by them to their companions, and that order would be restored. This expectation was not fulfilled, however, and a number of turbulent inmates were placed on bread and water until they went to work, an order which resulted in a riot developing.

At a specially convened magistrates' session, twenty-four men and boys were charged with refusing to work. In their defence, the men's spokesman, James Reed, stated that they did not have enough food for working men and were treated as slaves. The Bench said they were perfectly satisfied that the allowance of food was sufficient, and if the men disagreed, they should complain to the guardians and not to refuse to work. If, however, the accused had acted under a wrong impression and would return to their duty, no further proceedings would be taken against them. After this proposal was rejected, three boys were sentenced to fourteen days' hard labour in Halstead Gaol, and others to different periods of imprisonment and hard labour.

25 APRIL 1899 It was revealed that following the death of a woman inmate of the Wandsworth and Clapham workhouse infirmary, the news was given to her brother and husband, who went together to the workhouse. They were shown into the dead-house where about seven bodies were lying wound in sheets and placed on shelves with their names written in rotation on the top shelf. Two of the names were wrongly placed, however. When the nurse showed the visitors the body of their relative, she unwound part of the sheet from the face of the woman on the top shelf, but it was the wrong one. The one underneath was then shown to the visitors, and found to be the right body. Unfortunately, the names were not corrected at the time. The next morning, the undertaker visited the mortuary and measured the wrong body, which

The entrance to the Wandsworth and Clapham Union infirmary, St John's Hill.

was then removed to the deceased's previous home. Here the mistake was discovered, and the relatives and neighbours were considerably distressed. Correspondence with the workhouse authorities followed, but the relatives got no satisfaction beyond a letter of regret.

1900 Also on this day, the *Hampshire Advertiser* reported that Mr Kelly, the Master of the New Forest Deerhounds, had sent a deer – presumably a dead one – for the enjoyment of the inmates at the New Forest Union workhouse at Ashurst.

26 APRIL, 1889 This afternoon, Thomas Jaggard, a seventy-five-year-old inmate of the Thingoe Union workhouse in Suffolk, died after being shot in the chest with a five-chambered revolver. The gun, which was found near to his hand, belonged to Frederick Mathews, the workhouse labour master, who also discovered the body. Mathews told an inquest that the gun was normally locked up in a drawer but it had been inadvertently left out on a table in his room, hidden under a newspaper. He had asked Jaggard to come to the room to help clean an old gun barrel and had then left the man alone for a short time. After hearing a shot being fired, he ran back and found Jaggard lying on his back with blood pouring from his chest. The inquest heard that Jaggard had been in the workhouse for four years and was invariably of a cheerful disposition and had never spoken of suicide. The workhouse medical officer stated that the bullet had passed right through the body of the deceased and was fired from close range. The jury returned an open verdict – that the deceased had died from a self-inflicted bullet wound, but whether wilfully or accidentally they were unable to say. They also criticised the labour master's gross carelessness.

27 APRIL, 1871 The accidental poisoning of three girls at the Crumpsall workhouse formed a large part of the business at today's meeting of the Manchester board of guardians. The three, Sarah Ann Royles, aged eighteen, Margaret Akroyd, thirteen, and Mary Ann Monaghan, ten, all inmates of the workhouse school, had been suffering from severe colds, and on the previous Saturday evening, directions had been given to supply them with some medicine. The instructions were carried out by Miss Lees, an assistant at the school, who kept bottles of medicines in a locked cupboard, along with one containing carbolic acid, used for disinfecting purposes. The carbolic acid was normally stored at the rear of the cupboard but on this occasion was out of its usual position. Instead of administering cough mixture to the girls, Miss Lees picked up the wrong bottle and gave each of them two teaspoonfuls of the carbolic. They rapidly became ill and, despite a doctor's efforts, all three girls had died before midnight. An inquest returned a verdict of death by misadventure.

An aerial view of Manchester's workhouse at Crumpsall.

28 APRIL, 1871 An inmate of the Plymouth workhouse committed suicide by throwing himself from a window.

1899 An elderly pauper in the workhouse at Driffield, Yorkshire, was suffocated by fumes from a cinder fire in the potting shed adjoining the greenhouse. Robert Cook, aged eighty-seven, had been an inmate of the institution for twenty-four years.

29 APRIL, 1882 Reports appeared in the press today concerning the interment of a child who had died at the Leeds workhouse infirmary. A day or two after the child's demise, the coffin was taken to the cemetery at Burmantofts, where the burial service was conducted. The next morning the body of the deceased child was found on a slab in the dead-house at the workhouse, never having been placed in the coffin. The body was then taken by a pauper and placed in the grave, where it was afterwards discovered. The mix-up was reported to the chaplain, who was naturally indignant and grieved to find that he had been allowed solemnly to consign to dust and ashes an empty coffin. The Leeds guardians subsequently appointed a paid official to manage all future burial arrangements.

30 APRIL, 1768 Today's *Westminster Journal* gave details of a shocking incident at Bow. In the early morning, a man named Sayer went into his garden and discovered a

The Burmantofts cemetery at Leeds, with the workhouse standing behind.

stranger in the 'necessary-house'. As the man could not give a satisfactory account of himself, Sayer and his servants carried him before a magistrate who, concluding that he was a lunatic, committed him into the temporary custody of the parish workhouse. Throughout the day, the man behaved reasonably and, at about ten o'clock, the beadle and another person who were sitting up with him were persuaded to take off his handcuffs, which were hurting his wrists and making them swell. He then asked what the time was and on being told it was nearly eleven, replied, 'Tis very well; at that time I shall begin my work.' At the stroke of eleven, he attacked his two guards with a chair. The beadle escaped from the room, with the madman immediately bolting the door. He then picked up a cleaver, which had unfortunately been left in the room, struck the other man down and severed the head from the body. He next went upstairs where he cut and mangled several paupers who were in their beds. The master and mistress of the workhouse almost suffered the same fate but they barricaded themselves in their room by placing furniture against the door, which he had almost hacked to pieces when assistance came. The man was secured only by the use of firearms, resulting in one of his arms being shot through, a hand being partly shot off, and contusions on his head. He was not expected to live.

MAY

Agnes Jones, who oversaw the pioneering experiment at Liverpool workhouse to replace pauper nurses by properly trained paid staff. With up to 1,500 patients under her care – several hundred more than the number of beds – she only had four hours' sleep a night. After less than three years, the work led to her death from typhus. (*See* 18 May)

1 **MAY** **1900** On the arrival at Slough of a train from Swindon, a well-dressed baby girl was found crying underneath the seat of a second-class carriage. The child was taken to the nearby Eton Union workhouse and there placed into the care of the matron while the guardians tried, in vain, to find her mother. Within a week, following the publicity attending the incident, five ladies, including a clergyman's wife, had applied to the master of the workhouse for permission to adopt the girl. She was eventually placed with 'a family of considerable means at a fashionable health resort'. Amongst those contacting the workhouse was a woman from Plymouth who wrote asking if any lady would like her baby, which was about to be born.

2 **MAY** **1833** William Worsley, of Stanley Street, Liverpool, who died earlier this year at the age of fifty-five, was reported to have left a fortune of about £15,000 to his only surviving sister. It was discovered that for many years past the woman had been an inmate of the Manchester workhouse.

3 **MAY** **1880** James Lomax, a pauper at Huddersfield's Crosland Moor workhouse, was today charged with the attempted murder of fellow inmate Rose Ann Harrison. On the day in question, when nearly all the inmates were assembled for dinner, Lomax had entered the dining hall, walked down the centre, taken hold of Harrison's face with one hand, and run a knife into her throat. It was one he used for peeling potatoes. He was heard to say, 'I have had my revenge.' His attack severed one of Harrison's large blood vessels and she would have died had surgical aid not been promptly administered. Even so, she was in a very critical condition for almost a fortnight. The previous year, Lomax had been jailed for three months for an offence in which Harrison had testified against him. In court, he recounted that:

> When I came to the place where I should turn in to get my dinner, it wasn't the dinner I wanted at that time – it was her life I intended taking, so I went slowly up to her, and I put my left hand gently on her head. I put my hand in my pocket, and I thought of giving her a kiss before putting the knife into her. As soon as I'd done that I thought of doing my own as well at the same time, but before I could get my hand up to my neck with the knife the rolling, rattling noise that there was in my head at that time – all the pain went away from my heart. My eyes went quite bright, and all the pain left me like a flash of lightning. It was the Lord that did that. He took the guilt that she had placed in my heart, and I hope has put it into hers.

Lomax received fifteen years' penal servitude for the attack.

A typical workhouse dining hall – one of the few communal areas of a workhouse and often the scene of incidents between inmates.

4 MAY 1889 It was reported that Stuart Drought, an inmate of the workhouse at Macroom, County Cork, had been committed to trial for attempting to destroy the building. Drought, on being refused a suit of clothes by the guardians, set fire to the outbuildings and 8 tons of straw were burned. He also refused to draw water to quench the fire when the inmates were asked to assist.

5 MAY 1879 In the House of Commons, the President of the Local Government Board was asked about press reports that a Catholic inmate of Walsall workhouse named James Hawkins had recently been allowed to die in the house without a priest being summoned by the master. It was also alleged that a Catholic priest had been prevented from visiting a sick inmate named Blake because of an argument between the man's wife and workhouse officers. The President, Mr Sclater-Booth, replied that, according to regulations, the master was not bound to send for a priest, unless the pauper required it. A few days before Hawkins died, he was told that a priest was in the workhouse, but declined to see him. As regards Blake, his wife had wanted to visit him outside the allowed hours, and when this was refused she had sent the priest in her place, but he too had refused admission by the matron – something she had not been justified in doing. The President added that he had been assured by the workhouse master that there was no desire to interfere with the Roman Catholic clergy, and that every facility consistent with the rules of the house was afforded them.

6   MAY   **1848**   The *Leeds Times* today published extracts from a shocking report by the Huddersfield Overseers of the Poor about the treatment of the sick poor at the workhouse in the town. Their investigation, instigated following a series of complaints by Thomas Tatham, one of the Huddersfield Union's medical officers, revealed a damning catalogue of defects and concluded that the sick poor had been shamefully neglected. It was reported:

> [that the inmates] have been and still are devoid of the necessary articles of clothing and bedding; that they have been suffered to remain for weeks at a time in the most filthy and disgusting state; that patients have been allowed to remain for nine weeks together without a change of linen or of bed clothing: that beds in which patients suffering in typhus have died, one after another, have been again and again and repeatedly used for fresh patients, without any change or attempt at purification; that the said beds were only bags of straw and shavings, for the most part laid on the floor, and that the whole swarmed with lice; that two patients suffering in infectious fever, were almost constantly put together in one bed, that it not infrequently happened that one would be ragingly delirious, when the other was dying; and that it is a fact that a living patient has occupied the same bed with a corpse for a considerable period after death; that the patients have been for months together without properly appointed nurses to attend to them; that there has been for a considerable time none but male paupers to attend on female patients; that when the poor sick creatures were laid in the most abject and helpless state – so debilitated as to pass their dejections as they lay, they have been suffered to remain in the most befouled state possible, besmeared in their own excrement, for days together and not even washed; the food was unfit to be eaten, even by parties in health – particularly the 'soup', which was so surcharged with vegetable matter, such as cabbage, as to be nauseous, even to the smell; that gallons upon gallons of this description of 'food' has had to be thrown away; ...that the house is, and has been for a considerable period, crowded out with inmates; that there are forty children occupying one room eight yards by five; that these children sleep four, five, six, seven, and even ten in one bed; that thirty females live in another room of similar size; and that fifty adult males have to cram into a room seven and a half yards long by six yards wide; that there are at present but 65 blankets fit for use in the establishment, to fit up 79 beds; that there are but 108 sheets for these 79 beds, being 50 short of a pair each; that there is in consequence no change of bed linen whatever; that when cleansed the beds have to be stripped, and the linen hurried through the wash-tub, dried, and on to the beds again for

the same night; and that there are throughout the entire establishment the most unmistakable signs of bad arrangement, short-sightedness, real extravagance, waste of the ratepayers' money, and want of comfort, cleanliness, health and satisfaction amongst the poor.

7 MAY 1838 Three boys, named Moss, Murdock and Styles, inmates of the Tonbridge Union workhouse, were revealed to have been brought before the magistrates at Tunbridge Wells, and each sentenced to three weeks' imprisonment and hard labour. Their offence, it was said, was to have got up early in the morning and, putting their bolsters in their places in bed, let themselves out of the window and scampered for some hours over the countryside, returning at breakfast-time.

8 MAY 1837 It was reported today that the governor of the Burnley Union's workhouse at Padiham had been committed by Burnley magistrates to the House of Correction at Preston, on a charge of manslaughter. It was said that an old man, an inmate of the workhouse, who was very dirty in his habits, had been taken to the pump in the yard, and then laid upon some shavings in a corner of the house, where he had died.

9 MAY 1837 Matthew Noble, aged sixty-eight, a pauper in the Hull workhouse, this afternoon launched an unprovoked and violent attack on several fellow inmates. Noble, a resident of the workhouse for more than seven years, was formerly an Independent minister. He was said to be insane with regard to religious matters and was always preaching, but otherwise never troublesome. Holding a sharp pointed knife, he first approached a woman named Hannah Jenny and hit her on the arm. After she had run out of the room, Noble then cornered and stabbed Richard Lowson, who also managed to escape from the room. Noble next turned his attention to William Coates, who was sleeping by the fire-side. He stabbed Coates several times, with Coates's hands being terribly cut in warding off the blows. The knife once entered Coates's breast, close by the collarbone. He then attacked Thomas Hart who received a stab in his breast which caused blood to fly out every time he tried to cough. The workhouse constable, Charles Hart, was downstairs in the office when Hannah Jenny entered and screamed, 'He's murdered them all!' Lowson then entered, bleeding profusely and went with the constable back up to the room where a blood-covered Thomas Hart was crying, 'He's killed me.' The constable struck Noble with a poker and three other men hit him with a crutch, finally disarming him. It transpired that the knife with which the injuries were inflicted belonged to Thomas Hart and had been taken by Noble from a basket under

Hart's bed. Hart, aged eighty, died a few days later. Noble was charged with his murder but found not guilty on the grounds of insanity.

10 MAY **1891** Some weeks prior to this day, a private in the Shropshire Militia, named William Hancox, went missing from his regiment, and his clothes were found on the bank of the Severn near Shrewsbury, with a piece of paper attached to them requesting that the finder return them to the military depot in the town. At first it was thought that Hancox had drowned himself, but police enquiries showed that he had obtained an old suit of ordinary clothes and most probably had simply deserted. Nothing, however, was heard of him till late last night, when he presented himself at Atcham workhouse, near Shrewsbury. Giving the name of Bennett, he said he wanted to see his sister, Mrs Hancox, who was an inmate. The woman being taken to him explained that the man was not her brother but her missing husband, whereupon Hancox drew from his pocket a razor, and cut his throat in so serious a manner that he was today lying in the workhouse hospital in a critical condition. Happily, he later recovered from his injuries, though subsequently faced a criminal charge for attempted suicide.

11 MAY **1907** The Cardiff board of guardians decided today to prohibit a wedding between Joseph Da Venezia, aged twenty-six, an Italian sailor living in Cardiff, and Ellen ('Rosie') Bulley, sixteen, an inmate of the Cardiff workhouse with whom he had fallen in love. Although the girl had been born in the workhouse, and records proved she was still only sixteen, her lover claimed that the girl was eighteen and had sent the guardians statements to that effect from several people who knew her. The guardians had also been contacted by the girl's grandmother proposing that she should be sent to her in Devon, where a good home awaited her. It was said that the grandmother was a respectable woman, and that the young man was an honest and honourable lover. At any rate, he was a persistent lover, for he wrote to the girl nearly every day. The board finally agreed, however, that for the present she should remain in the workhouse. In February 1909, the story had a happy ending when, on the day after her eighteenth birthday, Rosie took her discharge from the workhouse where her suitor was awaiting her at the gate. She was expected to stay with her grandmother prior to finalising her wedding plans.

12 MAY **1907** During the early morning, fire gutted one wing of the Alresford Union workhouse at Tichborne Down, Hampshire. No lives were lost although the rescue of the final inmates was only effected by the great pluck of the workhouse master, Mr L.W. Williams, just in time and at great personal risk. The floor of their dormitory fell through immediately after they had left the building.

The Alresford Union workhouse with its fire damage clearly visible.

13   MAY 1886   Two nurses at the Limerick workhouse were in police custody today, charged with cruel ill-treatment that had accelerated the death of an elderly blind inmate of the workhouse infirmary named Margaret Bourke. The two, Jane Garvey, a paid night nurse, and Mary Fitzgerald, a pauper nurse, were on duty when the old woman had fallen out of bed. It was said she had been allowed to lie uncovered for twenty minutes, crawling about the floor, and that Fitzgerald refused to help Garvey get her back into bed until she had finished drinking her tea, which was getting cold. After they had put her to bed, Garvey had tied the woman's hands with a handkerchief. The light had then been turned out and Bourke was not visited again until the next morning when she was found dead with her hands still tied.

14   MAY 1886   At Hammersmith magistrates' court today, Mrs Sarah White of Notting Hill appeared with her son Ernest to complain about the vaccination of the boy at the Kensington workhouse while he was residing there on remand prior to a court hearing. Ernest had been made to have his hair cut, to which she had no objection, but she wished to know whether his being vaccinated without her permission was within the law. The boy's arm was in a bad state and very inflamed. The clerk to the Kensington guardians, Mr Vassie, said that the vaccination had been carried out in accordance with Local Government Board regulations which directed the medical officer to vaccinate all children admitted into the workhouse. He offered to admit the boy into the workhouse infirmary for treatment, to which the mother replied that she shuddered at the idea and left the court with her child.

15   MAY 1882   The Shardlow board of guardians today received a report from a committee appointed to investigate claims that workhouse officials had strapped in their beds patients suffering from diarrhoea, and who had died shortly after the occurrence. The committee found that inmates Samuel Eaton and Edward Bradshaw were on several occasions tied down in bed all night with towelling. Eaton had died on 2 February, and Bradshaw on 23 February, although neither had been tied down the night before his decease. Eaton had been suffering from diarrhoea. The men appeared to have been tied down because they had given the officials trouble by getting up in the night. It appeared that the men were tied down with roller towels, one round each ankle and each elbow, and tied to the bottom and top of the bed, so that the poor creatures, once laid on their backs, could not possibly turn over, and all the relief they could obtain was pushing backwards and forwards a little. All the officials, including the master and matron, had denied the accusations at first, but later admitted them.

   1894   In the early hours of the morning, a fire broke out in the laundry of the Camberwell workhouse. The occupants of an adjacent ward for elderly female inmates were removed to a place of safety. The laundry and women's ward were burnt out, but other buildings escaped damage. The fire was thought to have started in the drying house.

16   MAY 1901   A devastating fire today ravaged the old infirmary at Stafford workhouse which was occupied by eleven persons, including Ann Middleton, the workhouse cook. The borough fire brigade turned out promptly and soon subdued the flames. Four of the occupants escaped, but the remaining seven, including Mrs Middleton, perished. The alarm was raised at around 1.40 a.m. by the nurse in charge of the imbecile wards, Nurse Langatreen. She went down the passage and heard the cook calling 'Fire!' On opening the door of the corridor leading to the cook's room, she was forced back by the smoke and heat. She told the other occupants of the ward to leave the building and also removed three women and their babies from another ward. Then she got the fire-hose working and began to direct water on the burning part of the building and continued her efforts until she was relieved by the master and matron. Her brave conduct undoubtedly prevented the flames from spreading to the main block where 260 inmates were in residence. On the first floor, beyond the imbecile wards, was the cook's bedroom and then two wards occupied by the others who lost their lives. In the end room, in which four bodies were found on beds, the floor and the walls for about 3ft were untouched by the flames, which rushed through the door. Some clothes lying in a corner were not even scorched. It was thought that if the old people had thought to lie flat on the floor, they might have been saved.

17 MAY 1905 It was revealed today that a romantic marriage was to take place at Hull between a veteran member of the Hull board of guardians and an inmate of the Hull workhouse. The groom was Mr John Jickells, aged seventy-four, and his bride, Miss Margaret Bean, some forty years his junior. She had been in the workhouse for about a year, but Mr Jickells had made her acquaintance before that, he being a friend of her parents, both of whom were now dead. They were very respectable people and, dying penniless, the daughter found shelter in the workhouse. Her troubles, which came before him officially, touched his heart. He proposed and was accepted. Mr Jickells, a widower with children, had taken his prospective bride out of the workhouse, and she was staying with friends until the marriage. Mr Jickells was said to be a gentleman of means, and an extensive property owner.

18 MAY 1865 A pioneering experiment began today at Liverpool workhouse. In a scheme financed by local philanthropist William Rathbone, twelve nurses trained at the Nightingale School at St Thomas's Hospital were deployed in the workhouse infirmary. These were assisted by eighteen probationers and fifty-four able-bodied female inmates who received a small salary. Although the experiment had mixed results – the pauper assistants needed constant supervision and obtained intoxicants at the slightest oppor-tunity – it was generally perceived overall to have been a success. This was largely due to the tireless labours of the nursing superintendent, Agnes Jones, who, in 1868, died from

Liverpool's pioneering workhouse infirmary.

Liverpool philanthropist William Rathbone.

typhus contracted at the infirmary. Her efforts were a major contribution to a skilled nursing system eventually spreading to all union infirmaries in the country.

1894 It was reported that the Newton Abbot board of guardians had received a letter from Mr W.S. Gilbert, of opera fame, concerning an old street ballad singer now in residence at the Newton Abbot workhouse. It appeared that the old man, named Martin, had eighteen months previously been charged at one of the London police courts with obstructing the highway, and his case had aroused public sympathy. Mr Gilbert appealed through the press for subscriptions, and received £117, all of which, with the exception of £35, had now been spent. Martin had come to Newton Abbot to live with friends, but eventually he had to go to the workhouse. The guardians had now taken the £35, and relieved Mr Gilbert of further responsibility.

19 MAY 1900 The *Bucks Herald* today gave details of the deaths of two young children belonging to a couple named Richard and Catherine Tasker, who had been tramping in search of work. The family had stayed the night in the Winslow workhouse casual ward and in the morning the eldest child, a boy aged six, who had a history of convulsions, was found to be ill. They asked to see the master but were told by the porter that they could not see him until 11.30 a.m. and that they were to go out at once. The family continued their journey towards Leighton Buzzard, carrying the sick child in an old pram. They had just passed through Soulbury when they realised that the boy was dead. An inquest jury later recorded that he had died from convulsions but censured the porter for his conduct.

While staying at the Leighton workhouse, another of the Tasker's children, a boy aged three, became ill, retching and attacked by diarrhoea. He was given medicine by the workhouse nurse and medical officer but got worse and died two days later. The child had never suffered from fits and everything he had eaten had been shared by the parents. They had bought some milk on the road from Winslow which had smelled sour so most of it had been thrown away. A post-mortem indicated that the boy had died from 'germ poisoning' caused by eating unsound food.

The *Herald* also revealed that the family would no longer need to tramp the country as Mr Tasker had been offered work by a local employer.

20 MAY 1889 An inquest was held today at the Atcham Union workhouse, Shrewsbury, on the body of inmate Sarah Daley, aged thirty-two. Mrs Coleman, matron of the workhouse, said Daley had been in the hospital for some time. She was deaf, and paralysed on one side. Elizabeth Reynolds, another pauper, had nursed her for a while but was taken away after reports that she had been unkind to the deceased. Reynolds was on the imbecile list, and had herself been a patient in the hospital. It was the rule for convalescent patients to assist in the ward, but they were entirely under the control of the nurses. The workhouse medical officer, Mr Cureton, said that he had found numerous bruises and wounds on the body of the deceased, mostly on the legs, and the left arm (the one paralysed) was broken. The shock arising from such injuries would be sufficient to account for her death. After he had heard complaints about Reynolds's cruelty, she had been discharged from hospital duties. One patient had stated that if Reynolds were not removed she would cut her own throat. Other inmates said that Daley had an antipathy to the bath, and that Reynolds had slapped her in the face, struck her on the head, and used 'great force and cruelty' to get her into one. The jury decided that there was insufficient evidence to show how Daley's injuries had been inflicted but recommended that wardswomen should not be allowed to bathe old people without express orders.

21 MAY 1882 At about six o'clock in the evening, William Philip, who had for some time been resident in the Montrose poorhouse, cut his throat with a razor. Philip, aged fifty-five and a widower, was formerly a salmon fisherman. Death was almost instantaneous.

1882 A fire was discovered at York workhouse at about nine o'clock in the morning. When the steam fire engine arrived, its crew found that the workhouse officials, by means of a hydrant, had managed to keep the flames in check. The brigade extinguished the fire before serious damage was done to the building.

22 MAY 1885 It was reported today that the Dispensary Committee of the Ballinrobe Union, County Mayo, had asked the Local Government Board to investigate charges that had been brought against the workhouse porter by the local parish priest. It was alleged that, in the absence of the doctor, the porter attended the dispensary and dispensed medicine, extracted teeth and even vaccinated children. The porter, named Keane, was stated to have admitted the truth of the charges. The most remarkable part of the affair was that Keane was quite an illiterate man and unable, it was said, to read a label.

23 MAY 1835 An operation began today to transfer paupers from the old parish workhouse at Chesham to the new union workhouse at Amersham, a distance of some three miles. The proceedings, supervised by local magistrate, Mr Fuller, provoked unexpectedly stiff resistance. On his arrival at Chesham, about a hundred people had already collected outside the workhouse, and he was greeted with hissing, hooting and yelling. The workhouse gates were opened to bring out a wagon carrying the inmates,

The workhouse at Chesham where violent scenes took place in 1835.

but the crowd rushed up, shouting, 'Don't let them come out', and closed the gates. Fuller then read the Riot Act, after which the mob gave way and allowed the wagon out. Its progress was followed by a crowd, mostly of women and lads. The wagon was halted at Amy Mill with the crowd calling to its passengers, 'Get out. Why don't you get out?' The paupers refused to alight and one who was sitting at the tail of the wagon drew out a knife and threatened to cut off the hand of anyone who approached. Eventually the wagon was halted and damaged, with the crowd bringing the paupers back to Chesham in carts. Fuller was showered with stones and then approached by some of the crowd asking him for beer, saying they would let him go if they gave him some. He managed to escape but was hit on the back of the head by a stone which cut through his hat and penetrated through the flesh to the bone. At a subsequent court hearing, eight individuals were found guilty of riotous assemblage and given prison sentences of between fourteen days and four months.

24 MAY 1849 At Macroom in County Cork, the assistant master of the workhouse, Michael Williams, and a ward-master, Thomas Scannell, were today in custody on charges of manslaughter. Their victim was an inmate named Patrick Kelcher, whom Scannell had hit on the head with a drain shovel. As he was trying to get up, the man had again been hit on the head with a stone hammer wielded by Williams. Another inmate named Casey, who was also involved in the incident, subsequently died from his injuries.

25 MAY **1849** Details appeared today of a shocking incident at the Youghal workhouse in County Cork. A destitute and starving man named Patrick Connolly was admitted to the workhouse, and two days afterwards, on Sunday morning, took a small piece of bread beyond his allowed ration from a basket in the dining hall. He was seen by Michael Crotty, the ward-master in charge, who took both the bread and breakfast from Connolly, and reported him to the master, Matthias McRoy. McRoy ordered Connolly to be confined in the refractory cell – a windowless 'black hole' measuring 8ft by 6ft, also used as a mortuary. Later that morning, Connolly was taken out to attend Mass, and afterwards placed by Crotty back in the refractory cell. At about 3.30 p.m. the porter discovered that Connolly was ill and informed the master who, deciding that the man was just scheming to be let out, declined to go and visit him. After Connolly suffered a fit in his cell, the master and medical officer attended him but the remedies applied proved ineffectual, and after some hours' suffering, Connolly died. An official inquiry concluded that Connolly's death was accelerated, if not caused, by his having been confined in the cell and not having had any food when he was in a weak condition from previous privation. The master and ward-master were both barred from ever again being employed in the administration of relief and any further use of the black hole was banned.

26 MAY **1927** One hundred and seventy-four male inmates of Govan's Merryflats poorhouse in Glasgow today walked out of the institution and proceeded five miles to the parish council chambers in a protest against the conditions in the poorhouse. The men carried placards, one of which bore the words, 'Inmates of Govan Poorhouse get porridge seven hundred and thirty times a year.' One speaker told the council that he had been inside Barlinnie Prison, not for a criminal offence, and found that the food there was far superior to that in the poorhouse. The inmates had to be in bed by eight in summer, while prisoners had till nine. Conditions in the poorhouse were worse than those meted out to murderers and other criminals in prison. The council agreed to form a special committee to examine the inmates' allegations.

27 MAY **1838** Reports appeared today that Mr W.L. Caswell, formerly employed as a surgeon by the Bridgwater Union, had taken his own life. It was said that after twelve months' unremitting attention to his work, the board of guardians had refused to pay him the sum of £90, the charge for his services, but instead offered him £50, which he refused. Mr Caswell took legal proceedings against the board but, being of very limited means, he ultimately settled for £40. The matter preyed on his mind, Caswell fearing that his professional standing might be lowered if it became known that he had accepted a sum so far below his original and moderate demand. This had brought about a state

of temporary insanity, in which he had made his way beneath the town's sea walls and there nearly cut his head off with a razor.

1893 On this day, Charles Shaw of Church Broughton, an inmate of the Burton-on-Trent workhouse, took his own life by cutting his throat with a pocket knife he used to chop tobacco.

28 MAY **1888** At eleven o'clock this evening, John Turner, foundry labourer, an inmate of the Barnsley workhouse, took his own life. He had been in the workhouse infirmary for the past week suffering from bronchitis and pleurisy. He fell out of bed and died, having cut his own throat with a two-bladed pocket knife.

1927 An alarming outbreak of smallpox at Oldham workhouse continued today when three new cases were confirmed, all male inmates of the institution and contacts of the three cases notified a fortnight earlier. The outbreak was believed to have originated with a tramp who had spent six days at the workhouse before going on to Blackburn. All those infected were removed to the isolation hospital, and all visiting and leave was suspended.

29 MAY **1900** Charles Roberts, a pauper at the Wrexham workhouse, today committed suicide by hanging himself. The seventy-six-year-old former gardener's labourer had been in the workhouse off and on for about ten years and suffered from chronic bronchitis and asthma. It was said that he had been a quiet man who seemed generally cheerful. He was found after dinner, hanging by his scarf, which had been tied to a towel and secured to a down-spout at the back of the workhouse chapel. His knees were almost touching the ground.

30 MAY **1896** On this day, at the age of seven, future Hollywood star Charles ('Charlie') Chaplin entered the Newington workhouse in south London, together with his mother, Hannah, and his older half-brother Sydney. Three weeks later the boys were transferred to the Central London District School at Hanwell – a large residential school for pauper children from several London workhouses. They made the journey in a horse-drawn bakery van and after a period in the 'approbation' ward, Charlie moved to the infants' section while Sydney entered the main school. Chaplin later recalled that on Saturday afternoons the bath-house was reserved for the infants who were bathed by older girls – he suffered the ignominy of receiving an all-over wash with a face-cloth from a fourteen year old.

Charlie soon graduated to the rigours of the older boys' department. On one occasion, a boy of fourteen tried to escape from the school by climbing onto the roof

The huge dining hall at the Hanwell District School.

and defying staff by throwing missiles and horse-chestnuts at them as they climbed after him. For such offences there were regular Friday morning punishment sessions in the gymnasium where all the boys lined up on three sides of a square. For minor offences, a boy was laid face down across a long desk, feet strapped, while his shirt was pulled out over his head. Captain Hindrum, a retired Navy man, then gave him from three to six hefty strokes with a 4ft cane. Recipients would cry appallingly or even faint and afterwards have to be carried away to recover. For more serious offences a birch was used – after three strokes a boy needed to be taken to the surgery for treatment.

Chaplin remained at the school until January 1898, during which time he caught ringworm – an infectious disease of the scalp common amongst pauper children. Its treatment required the head to be shaved and treated with iodine, their resulting appearance making sufferers the subject of ridicule by other boys.

31 MAY 1894 At Brentwood magistrates, Ella Gillespie, fifty-four, a former nurse at the Hackney Union's schools at Brentwood, was charged with the wilful ill-treatment of children in her care. As the case unfolded, the nation was scandalised by the details of Gillespie's activities at the schools, home to around 500 pauper children, which went back over a period of eight years.

Clara Good, thirteen, testified that Gillespie had on a number of occasions knocked her head against the wall. Once, after being punished in this way for talking to another girl,

Hackney's workhouse schools at Brentford – the scene of Ella Gillespie's reign of terror.

she had required treatment in the infirmary. Another time, when she and two other girls were scrubbing the nursery floor, Gillespie had entered and knocked over two scuttles of coal. She then turned over four pails of water, and rubbed Good's head into the wet coal on the floor for having helped another girl who had been set to scrub the corridor as a punishment. Gillespie regularly gave the children 'basket drill'. They were forced to walk around the dormitory in their nightclothes, barefoot, and with a basket on their heads containing their day clothes. The children were kept at basket drill for two hours or more after being dragged out of bed.

Elizabeth Fawcett, thirteen, stated that Gillespie had slapped her face, pulled her hair, and struck her with a frying pan. Once, when she had been an infant, she had been given twelve strokes on each hand with a cane. Gillespie used to send a helper out for stinging nettles. She used then to lay the children on the bed and thrash them with the stinging nettles on their bare backs. Fawcett had seen the children forced to kneel on the wire netting that covered the hot-water pipes. She had also witnessed Gillespie throw a boy named Charles Williams out of bed, cutting his eye against the bedstead and requiring medical treatment.

Maud Garrett, also thirteen, said the children were not allowed water with their lunch. They were so thirsty that they resorted to drinking water from the toilets or from puddles in the playground.

Other witnesses reported that Gillespie was regularly drunk and that during 1893 a local brewery had supplied her with nineteen 4.5-gallon casks of beer. Supposedly 'surprise' inspection visits by guardians were invariably preceded by requests from them to be met by a carriage at the local station and to have a good lunch laid on at the school.

Gillespie was subsequently sentenced to five years' penal servitude.

JUNE

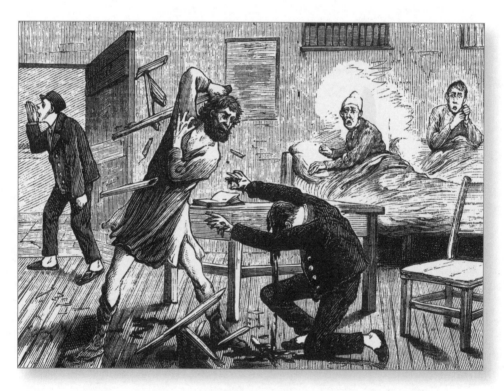

David Saleneskem's violent attack on his fellow patients. (*See* 30 June)

1   JUNE 1894   An inquest was held today at the Belfast Union workhouse following the death of Robert Spence, aged sixty-seven. Spence had been admitted into the workhouse infirmary with pleurisy. He was also afflicted with heart disease, which was the cause of his death. The inquest heard that Spence had been suffering from delusions and was transferred to the lunatic department of the workhouse, though no consultation had taken place amongst the medical staff as to the suitability of such a move. While in the lunatic ward, Spence had attempted to pull his own ear off and tried to eat himself. On two occasions he had been restrained by having his hands tied together with sheets which were then tied to the side of the bed. The coroner reminded the jury that use of such restraint was illegal in workhouses – any dangerous inmate should be transferred to a lunatic asylum for proper care. Placing a man with a heart condition amongst violent and excitable lunatics might also be considered a questionable decision. The jury recorded their strong protest against the illegal system of restraint used in the workhouse lunatic department. They also condemned the transferring of patients to the lunatic department without proper medical consultation into their mental state.

    1882   Also on this day a disastrous fire occurred in the poorhouse in the small Swedish town of Oesthammar. The building was set on fire by lightning and burnt to the ground. Out of fifty-two inmates, twenty perished in the flames.

2   JUNE 1898   An inquest was held today on James Nichol, aged seventy-nine, a blind, bedridden inmate of the infirmary ward at the Longtown workhouse, Northumberland. Nichol was alleged to have been beaten to death by a fellow inmate, Michael Carr, aged sixty, the youngest in the ward, which housed five other men, one of whom was 106 years old. Just after midnight, the workhouse master, Mr Dawes, heard shouting in the hospital. When he got to the ward, Michael Carr was sitting, clad only in his shirt, in a chair beside Nichol's bed, beating the man's face and head with two iron-tipped walking-sticks, one in each hand. The scene was awful, blood being spattered all around, even onto the 10ft-high ceiling. When Carr saw the master he lifted up the sticks and gave him a blow on the forehead which drew blood and nearly stunned him. All the other old people in the ward were paralysed with terror. Even the blind and deaf centenarian sat up in bed and asked what the matter was. An invalid in an adjacent bed managed to strike Carr a blow and cut his head. This dazed him, and allowed the master to tumble him onto the floor and secure him. He was afterwards handed over to the police. Nichol was quite dead on the arrival of the master. The other inmates stated that Carr had accused Nichol of being in the wrong bed, though he was not. Carr tried to pull him out of bed by the shoulders but, not succeeding, he began wielding his sticks. The inquest jury returned a verdict of

wilful murder against Carr, who had previously been an inmate of Garland's Lunatic Asylum.

3   JUNE   1896   It was reported that the Revd George Tripp, a somewhat eccentric clergyman, had died in the workhouse at Market Bosworth. He had been an inmate of the workhouse for two years, and although he left the premises occasionally, he only ever did so for a short time. He was kindly treated by the workhouse officials, the only thing that seemed to trouble his mind being the conversation of the other inmates. He caught a chill through walking barefoot on the plaster floors of the workhouse, which eventually led to his death from pneumonia. Tripp was at one time the possessor of £20,000, the whole of which he gave away to charitable causes. With his cheque book in his pocket no appeal was made to him in vain, with foreign missions and other institutions greatly benefiting from his generosity.

     1904   Details were given today of a legacy, worth about £150, that was to be left to the Birmingham board of guardians by an inmate of the workhouse infirmary. The testator was formerly a prosperous merchant, and had executed large orders for helmets for the army, on one occasion fashioning a Life Guard's helmet for the King. He had spent a good deal of time in travelling on the Continent, and was an ardent student of French literature. He was, however, something of a misanthrope, and lost touch with all his relatives and friends. In his latter years, he had earned a living as a metal worker, but failing health had seen him living neglected in squalid lodgings, and the thought had come to him that he would be much better off in the workhouse infirmary. A messenger was sent to the relieving officer who immediately decided that he was a suitable case for admission, and, incoherently muttering his feelings of gratitude, the old man was removed to the institution. The following day he called for the relieving officer, and handed to him his will, legally drawn up, leaving to the guardians the deserted metal shop, with plant and fittings, his books, and a sum of money, the whole of which would render the sum of about £150. The old man told the relieving officer that he was very comfortable where he was, and that he wanted to pay for the comforts he was receiving during the remaining few weeks of his life.

4   JUNE   1866   A Poor Law Board inquiry opened today at the Strand Union workhouse into charges against the management of the workhouse infirmary by Matilda Beeton, former head nurse at the institution. Miss Beeton stated that on her arrival in the previous August, she had twenty-two wards in her charge, and that all the nurses apart from herself were paupers. The nursing of the sick and the crowding of the wards had been a positive disgrace. Most of the nurses could not read and often

A 1920s view of the Strand Union's Cleveland Street workhouse in London's Fitzrovia district.

made mistakes in administering the medicines. They seemed to have complete control over the diets of the sick and, according to the patients, the rations of meat were often short in quantity. Stimulants, such as wine and spirits, were either given to the pauper nurses by the patients in order to obtain attention, or sold to them, or else were simply stolen by them. The nurses were often drunk. Able-bodied paupers wandered over the sick wards, not just husbands or wives visiting one another, but others who came to beg or buy the uneaten meals of the patients. The patients sold their food to pay for their washing, which was done by pauper laundresses. If it was not paid for, it was so badly done that the things were unwearable. The laundry women were often drunk, and they got the drink from the nurses, who obtained it from the patients. The pauper nurses were quite unfit for their office. On one occasion two of these nurses, both of whom were sick themselves, in trying to lift a sick man, had pulled him along the bed in such a way that a portion of his skin which had adhered to the sheet was torn off and a large place in his back was left bleeding. The man died the day after this happened. The sick slept all over the house, even in the receiving ward, and when this was full some clean patients were sent into the ward for 'dirty' cases. Some of the poor sick people, after being in the sick ward all day, had, in going to another part of the house to sleep, to cross an open yard in all weathers. As a result, one poor man, who had been getting well, had developed erysipelas. The man was then sent to the foul ward, and placed between an itch case and a man covered with sores. The nurses of the children in the house used to sell the children's milk to the patients for a halfpenny a pint.

1829 The *Leeds Intelligencer* noted that at the workhouse in Leeds, there were sixteen male and nine female paupers in residence whose combined ages amounted to 1,918 years, an average of almost seventy-seven years each. The oldest of the men was eighty-three and the oldest woman was aged eighty-four. The paper suggested that the figures proved 'the excellence and utility of the English system of poor laws; as, in all human probability, had not this refuge been provided for them, many of these aged and helpless persons, weighed down by misfortunes, must long ago have sunk "unpitied and unblest", under the iron grasp of poverty and want.'

5 JUNE

1894 Early this morning, John Dawson, an inmate of the Leicester workhouse infirmary, jumped from a lavatory window on an upper floor of the building down to the lawn outside. He was found by Charles Merrick, a local hairdresser, who was on business at the workhouse. Dawson did not appear to be injured by the fall and no bones were broken. Despite this, he went on to develop pneumonia which brought about his death a few days afterwards. At a subsequent inquest, Merrick said that he had asked Dawson whether he had fallen accidentally or had jumped. Dawson replied that he had jumped and was tired of life. He later said that he had meant to jump onto some railings, and also asked Merrick to cut his throat. Dawson, aged forty-eight, had been admitted from Leicester Prison and came from Whitechapel but nothing else was known of his background.

1849 Also on this day in 1849, a remarkable inmate of the Bath workhouse, John Plass, died at the age of eighty-two. Just a few years earlier, the former stonemason

The Bath workhouse chapel, built by inmate John Plass.

had taken on the extraordinary challenge of laying all the stone during the construction of the workhouse's fine new chapel. According to a plaque on the building's wall, he accomplished this task with 'much zeal and industry'. He was laid to rest in the adjoining burial ground.

6 JUNE 1835 A young labourer named Povey, working on the construction of the new union workhouse at Abingdon, Berkshire, had his skull fractured when a hammer was dropped on it.

7 JUNE 1900 At eight o'clock on this evening, a disastrous fire broke out at the Newry workhouse in County Down. The conflagration caused an immense amount of damage, with the main building being largely destroyed. Fortunately, no lives were lost. In reviewing the event, the board of guardians agreed that when rebuilding work was undertaken, the opportunity should be taken to review the needs of the establishment. In particular, support was voiced for a greater provision of infirmary facilities.

1832 At 7.30 a.m. twenty-four long-standing female inmates of the St Marylebone workhouse set out for Van Diemen's Land (Tasmania) under a voluntary emigration scheme. It was reported that they were all robust healthy-looking young women, cleanly and suitably apparelled, between sixteen and twenty-five years of age, and, except at the trying moment of departure, seeming in full and buoyant spirit. All had been given a substantial breakfast after being allowed to sleep the previous night in the same ward. Friends and relatives gathered at the workhouse door to make their often tearful farewells, with force sometimes being required to separate mothers from their offspring. The party were conveyed in two omnibuses to St Catharine's Docks, from where they travelled by steamer to board the *Renown* at Gravesend, accompanied thus far by the workhouse governor, two matrons and other officers. The cost to the parish of the whole proceedings was said to be more than £300.

8 JUNE 1791 At Clerkenwell court, William Seymour, master of Staines workhouse, was charged with assaulting a pauper and accelerating his death. The man, of unknown name, had been very ill when admitted to the workhouse in March. He had been left in the care of Mrs Seymour who put him in an old outhouse 'scarcely fit for a dog-kennel' where, despite the frosty weather, he remained for two days. Then, scarcely able to stand or walk, he was violently dragged out of the workhouse by Seymour who told him he must leave the parish. Seymour pulled the man across the parish boundary, leaving him on a common, exposed to the elements, and unable to move. He then sat drinking in a public house for two hours despite being told that the man was dying. In fact, Seymour had left the man 2 yards inside his own parish boundary and was ordered by the High Constable to take him back to the workhouse. Fearing he would have to bury the man, Seymour at first refused but was forced to comply, the removal being effected by four bearers carrying him in a chair. However, the man died before travelling 200 yards. The court sentenced Seymour to a year's imprisonment.

1899 A sixty-year-old inmate of the Stockton-on-Tees workhouse named Henry Ramsay committed suicide. Ramsay had been in the workhouse since the previous August and suffered very much from pains in the leg. At around 11.30 p.m. one of his fellow inmates in the workhouse infirmary heard something dropping to the floor from Ramsay's bed but thought he was sick and took no notice. When the night watchman came up later, however, he found Ramsay dead, with a large gash in his throat which he had inflicted with his penknife.

1903 John White, an inmate of the Isle of Wight Union workhouse at Newport, today attained his hundredth birthday. Sadly, he died just two hours later.

9 JUNE **1861** The death occurred early this morning of Rachel Brady, an inmate of the Walsall workhouse. The previous night she had gone to bed as usual, but just before eleven o'clock she complained about pains in her head – a recurring affliction – and said she felt as if she was going mad. She was discovered in bed at about 6 a.m., her body still warm. In conducting a post-mortem, the union medical officer opened the head of the deceased and in the tuber ancillare, where the brain and the spinal marrow join, found four hydatid sacs or *cysticerci cellulosae*. He had ascertained that it was not uncommon for Brady to eat sausages; and the hydatid sacs, he had no doubt, housed the eggs of a tapeworm which had probably been taken into the body through eating sausages not properly cooked, and composed of measled pork. The worm had then forced its way into the various organs, the liver, the head, eyes and brain, and deposited its eggs, which had begun to grow. The resulting pressure upon the brain from the hydatid sacs was judged to have been the cause of death.

1880 An inmate of the Sheffield workhouse infirmary, named Fox, suddenly jumped out of bed, obtained possession of a razor and inflicted a wound on his own throat. Fortunately, the injury was not of a very serious character.

10 JUNE **1842** Two boys, inmates of the St Alban's Union workhouse, having had some trifling dispute, engaged in a scuffling fight. The younger, a fine boy of eleven years of age, was felled by a blow received on his body from his antagonist, under the effects of which he lingered for a few hours and, not withstanding great efforts from the medical officer, gradually sank to his death.

1880   On the evening of this day, Frederick Jupp, an inmate of the Sheffield workhouse, committed suicide under very shocking circumstances. The deceased, aged sixty-seven and a former gardener, was admitted with his wife on 2 January but the woman died two weeks afterwards. This preyed upon Jupp's mind to such a degree that he was placed in 'the retreat' where he seemed to recover although his manner and conversation continued to be eccentric. In the afternoon of his death, he told some fellow inmates that he had taken his last meal. He also gave a man his hat which he said he would not require again. At a quarter past seven, he climbed through the top garret window, three storeys high, suspended himself by the hands for a few seconds, then let himself fall to the ground, a distance of 30ft or more. During his descent, his feet caught on a projection causing him to turn a complete somersault and to land on his head.

1908   On this day a massive boiler explosion at the Toxteth Park workhouse, Liverpool, killed three inmates. Richard Lloyd, aged sixty, Edward Rigby, fifty-four, and Henry Smith, sixty-six, who were respectively doing service in the boiler house as fireman, labourer and fitter, died instantly, while flying debris struck and seriously injured two inmates of the causal ward. Smith was blown right through the boiler-house roof and fell amongst some bushes 100 yards away.

11   JUNE   **1862**   An inquest was held at Birmingham into the death of Thomas Bullock, a gun-barrel rifler, who had committed suicide in front of the Birmingham workhouse. Several months earlier, Bullock had thrown his wife out, sold their furniture, and gone to live with another woman named Richmond. When Mrs Bullock had applied for poor relief, she had been directed to go to her husband. On doing this, Richmond had beaten her and Bullock thrown her out of the house. She was then given entry to the workhouse where, on the day of his death, Bullock had arrived, saying he had come to make arrangements to take his wife home. When she came out to speak to him, they had both started crying. She said to him, 'Don't mind; there is nothing done but we can undo again.' Bullock asked her, 'Where's George?' (meaning his little son). Mrs Bullock replied, 'He is in the house; do you want to see him?' Bullock made no reply but pulled his hat off his head and trampled it on the floor. He then walked out of the gate into the driveway, pulled a pistol from his pocket and shot himself in the head.

1914   A new scheme for grading the inmates of the Hampstead workhouse was adopted today by the Hampstead guardians. There were to be four classes, and the scheme aimed to convert the workhouse into a pleasant retreat for aged and infirm inmates of good character – these would form Class A. They would be free to receive their friends daily from 2 p.m. till 4 p.m. in the dayroom, where the floors would be covered with linoleum, comfortable armchairs provided, curtains hung at the windows, and a clock and more pictures provided. They would take their meals in their dayroom, and receive a special dietary with a weekly allowance of 1 ounce of tobacco, or 2 ounces of tea and 8 ounces of sugar. In their dormitories, curtained cubicles were to be provided to ensure privacy, and a special smoke-room allocated for the men. Class B would be for those aged and infirm over sixty who could not be placed under Class A, and for inmates of any age of good character. They would continue with their existing treatment, but with tobacco supplied to the men, and an extra cup of tea which would be made in bulk. Class C would consist of those who were neither of definitely good nor of known bad character, and would not receive any extras. Class D would include all inmates whose characters were decidedly bad. Their diet was to be inferior to that of Class C.

12 JUNE 1874 A nineteen-year-old servant named Mary Jane Taylor was charged with the murder of her illegitimate child which had been born in the Dudley workhouse in May. Taylor had left the workhouse on 1 June and the following day the body of the child was found in the canal. The child was identified by a workhouse nurse, Eliza Jones. Taylor was subsequently found guilty of manslaughter.

1929 On this day, after parading the principal streets of Whitehaven, 500 single young miners, who claimed they were destitute, entered the town's workhouse, completely filling the establishment.

13 JUNE 1906 Details appeared today of a serious outbreak of food poisoning at the Sculcoates Union workhouse at Hull. A number of old and feeble inmates had been attacked with diarrhoea after eating frozen meat from the Argentine. There had been four deaths, and the medical officer had ordered that the master should serve no more of the frozen meat, which was said to be responsible for the outbreak. Twenty stones of the meat had been destroyed owing to it being in a state of decomposition.

1896 Also on this day, it was reported that an inmate of Guildford workhouse had committed suicide by jumping down a well 150ft deep.

14 JUNE 1828 According to today's *Times*, a fourteen-year-old boy, a pauper in St Saviour's workhouse, was claimed to be responsible for the child being expected by an inmate of the same workhouse who was twice his age. The workhouse keeper told a magistrate that every means was adopted to prevent communication between the sexes. He was completely at a loss to know how the two had come into contact as the woman slept in a storeroom and the boy in a different part of the building.

The mother-to-be stated that there was a door separating her room from that of the boy, the key of which was left in her room. She admitted having used the key to admit him at night. There was also a bolt on his side, but she had never found it closed. The boy denied the allegation, repeatedly exclaiming, 'I'm not the father, indeed I'm not.' The workhouse keeper said that the woman had previously had a bastard child by another man. The magistrate committed the boy to Kingston, to which he was taken away crying. The parish officers were recommended to prosecute the mother as a lewd woman, once she had recovered from the birth.

15 JUNE 1880 At Chesterfield workhouse, an inquiry was held by the Local Government Board into the treatment of a pauper named Gregory. The man, who was suffering from 'an affection of the bladder', was ordered into the workhouse with instructions that he would require to be relieved every three or four hours. He was placed in the receiving ward and left there for fifty hours without medical aid. After this time, his friends visited him, and finding him left in a dirty condition and not even undressed, took him back to his home where he died shortly afterwards. The inspector pointed out that it was the duty of the workhouse master to send for a medical officer whenever a patient was received. He nonetheless found that neither the medical officer, who had immediately attended when he had heard about the case indirectly, nor the guardians were to blame.

The dining hall block at the Sculcoates workhouse.

16 JUNE 1837 Details were reported today of a cold-blooded murder that had taken place at Great Yarmouth four years previously, when a boy of six, the son of a Mr Wolfe, was discovered drowned in the cistern in the backyard, into which it was supposed he had fallen. An inquest at the time had returned a verdict of accidental death. Recently, however, the Revd Armstrong was called upon to attend a woman in the Yarmouth workhouse who was near to death and in a state of great torment. She revealed that she had lived in as a maidservant to Mr Wolfe at the time the child was drowned. When the boy had strewn the house with litter after she had cleaned it, she had put him into the cistern, put a pail over his head, and held him down till he was dead, and afterwards assisted his parents in searching for him. To add to her ordeal, Mrs Wolfe had always treated her with great kindness, even more so since her illness in the workhouse. It appeared that the woman's state of health made it unlikely that she would live to face trial for the crime of which she had declared herself guilty.

17 JUNE 1887 Details appeared today of events following the death of a female pauper, aged twenty, in the Macclesfield workhouse. A man she had lived with, named Earle, had previously insured her life in a burial society, and he applied for the corpse for the purposes of burial. His request was granted, and he employed an undertaker to make a coffin. When Earle applied to the burial society for the money, however, payment

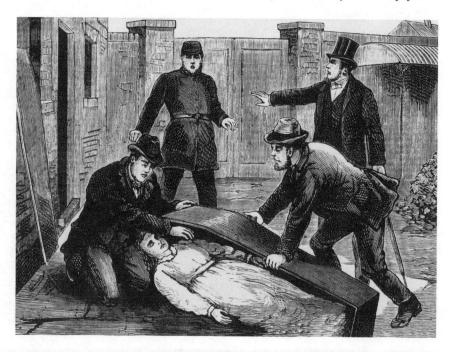

Tussles over a corpse at Macclesfield workhouse.

was refused. The undertaker, seeing he had little chance of being paid, hired two men to carry the coffin and corpse back to the workhouse. The body was turned out in the workhouse yard, the undertaker refusing to leave the coffin, saying 'he had another chap for it'. Another coffin was eventually found, and the corpse was buried after the woman had been dead for six days.

1896 In the evening, Percy Flutter, aged sixteen, the son of the master of the Pembroke workhouse, was drowned while bathing in a millpond near to the workhouse.

1915 It was revealed today that, in view of the wartime scarcity of meat, inmates of the Bury workhouse would have a change of dinner menu on two days a week. On Mondays, instead of meat stew, they would receive cheese and coffee, while on Tuesdays bacon would be substituted for beef.

18 JUNE 1885 A woman named Sarah Collinson, aged thirty-four years and a pauper inmate of Chorlton Union workhouse at Withington, was found lying dead on the floor of the establishment's washhouse. About half past twelve, another inmate had entered the washhouse and found Collinson lying with her face over a hole in the flags, which was full of water. She at once called for help, and Collinson was lifted out of the water, which was only 2in or 3in deep, but was by then quite dead. A small bruise on her forehead was supposed to have been caused by her falling on the flags, but death was thought to be due to suffocation, the water preventing her breathing.

19 JUNE 1843 The workhouse at Carmarthen was today ransacked by a mob of 'Rebecca Rioters' as part of a campaign of protests across South Wales against the high charges at the toll-gates on the public roads. A large crowd arrived at the workhouse and the master was forced to hand over his keys. The rabble then rushed into the courtyard and then entered the buildings where they smashed furniture and broke windows. The riot continued until the arrival of the 4th Light Dragoons, who brought proceedings under control and took sixty prisoners. The rioters took their name from the Book of Genesis (Chapter 24, Verse 60): 'And they blessed Rebekah and said unto her, Thou art our sister, be thou the mother of thousands of millions, and let thy seed possess the gate of those which hate them.' The raiders often included one or more 'Rebecca' figures dressed in women's clothes and wearing a wig of ringlets.

1922 In the early hours of this day in 1922, fire laid waste to a large portion of the St Faith's Union workhouse, near Norwich. The blaze began in a sitting room on the ground floor and was discovered by the night attendant who rushed upstairs to warn the master and matron, Mr and Mrs Bowman, and then began to evacuate the bedridden old people. Mr Bowman, still in his night attire, dashed

Costumed Rebecca Rioters in the midst of the fray in 1843.

downstairs and attempted to quell the flames with a fire extinguisher. However, the fire had such a hold that all he received for his efforts was the partial loss of his eyebrows, moustache and hair. Wearing only his trousers, he mounted his bicycle and rode to the Post Office and asked them to telephone the Norwich Fire Brigade. He then assembled the villagers. In the course of his rushing about, his bare feet were badly cut by glass and splinters of stone. Very quickly, officials and men of the village got to work to extricate the old people from the burning building. The flames by this time had spread at an alarming rate. Ladders were secured and the elderly were lowered from the upper room windows in slings made of blankets. Within fifteen minutes of being telephoned, the Norwich Fire Brigade arrived and hoses took water from the river 1,500ft away. Within an hour, the brigade had the blaze under control, confining it to the centre block, which was almost completely burnt away and its roof consumed. The workhouse never reopened.

20 JUNE 1810 According to *The Globe*, a 'scene most shocking to humanity' occurred this evening 'near Fitzroy Square' – presumably at the parish workhouse of St Paul, Covent Garden, on Cleveland Street:

Staff and inmates of the St Faith's workhouse holding a fire drill – a major contribution to the lack of casualties when the building was gutted in 1922.

A poor woman, actually in labour, and attended by her midwife, was delivered of a child at the door of a Poor-house, to which she in vain requested admittance. A crowd collected, and the utmost indignation was expressed at the brutal indifference shewn by the officers of the Poor-house, for while the poor creature was labouring in agony, they remained inexorable. The infant perished during this inhuman scene – at length the people broke open the door of the house and carried the unhappy mother into one of the wards.

21 JUNE **1927** The wide variety of individuals to be found in the Barnhill poorhouse, Glasgow, was illustrated in a report published today by the institution's governor. During the previous year, the admissions had included: two fully qualified doctors, one being on the verge of *delirium tremens* and the other addicted to drugs; a lawyer; a B.Sc.;

an artist, who had dissipated a fortune in about two years; the mother-in-law of one of the Deputies of the French Chamber; a man who used to own a large tailoring and clothing establishment in one of the main city thoroughfares; and another, who died at the age of eighty-four, who is said to have been one of the original founders of a large Clyde engineering firm, and who attributed his downfall to having lost £11,000 in the City of Glasgow Bank failure.

22 JUNE 1866 *The Times* today published a report by Mr Ernest Hart, a physician attached to *The Lancet*, who had visited the Whitechapel workhouse infirmary with Poor Law Board Inspector Henry Farnall. The first ward they entered contained ten beds. In one corner, a bedridden patient of middle age was lying on a very wet, hard, straw mattress. On lifting him up they found extensive bedsores which were only covered with a piece of wet rag. He was never cleaned or changed at night. Two beds beyond him lay a man with a sinus cavity on the thigh, and inflamed glands of the throat. He believed the doctor had ordered him something the day before, but nothing had yet been given to him and he was using a piece of rag he had brought in with him. Ward 5, a miserable little passage room, quite unfit for any sick person, contained three patients, one being a raving lunatic of filthy habits. He disturbed the other wards at

The frontage of the Whitechapel workhouse infirmary on Charles Street (later Baker's Row, now Vallance Road).

night and, again, was never cleaned or changed. He was lying in a state of neglect and dirt, raving incoherently, and with a form placed against his bed to prevent him falling out. Next to him was another poor man, half paralysed, inarticulate, and half imbecile, of dirty habits, who was sitting on the edge of his bed with a coloured handkerchief tied over a sore place on his foot. The third inmate was a decent old man, with all his faculties. He had an extensive ulcer of the leg, dressed with a previously wet but now dry rag, which adhered firmly to it and was tied on with a piece of string. There was no oil, silk or waterproof tissue to keep the rags moist. Many other similar scenes were discovered. Most of the patients said they were hungry, and one or two that they were half-starved. If patients got money from their friends, the nurses expected to share it. Many were on a diet which allowed meat for dinner just three times a week, with soup on three days, and bread and cheese the other day. The medicines were irregularly administered, and often not given at all. A nurse revealed the contents of her medicine cupboard – three large bottles labelled 'House Medicine', 'Saline Mixture' and 'Cough Mixture'. They had no corks. Apparently, the general custom was for the nurse at night to say, 'Anybody want medicine?' Those who did want medicine usually avoided the drastic 'House Medicine', and preferring instead the 'Cough' or 'Saline' mixture, or a combination of the two, which was said to be the favourite. Mr Hart concluded that it was a mockery to call 'this place of torture' a sick ward and hoped that Parliament would soon put an end to 'such needless and irrational cruelty and neglect.'

23 JUNE 1872 After morning service at the Chester workhouse today, the schoolmaster, Mr Howell, took the boys for a walk on the riverside Roodee racecourse. One of them, George Dobson, proposed to the others that they should gather wild celery, as he knew where it grew. The boys went to the side of the river where they gathered a quantity of roots of wild hemlock, and ate some of it. On returning to the workhouse, Dobson and Albert Kinsey were seized with convulsions, but they were regarded as fits at first, as the boys were subject to them. Another, George Clark, began to vomit, and Miss Aldis, the master's daughter, learned that they had eaten something. The house surgeon, Mr Brittain, was sent for, but tetanus had now set in. Kinsey died at three in the afternoon and Dobson at five. The others recovered after being treated with emetics.

24 JUNE 1893 The *Illustrated Police News* reported that a diminutive, wizened old woman of seventy-two, named Mary Williams, had been charged at Westminster police court with refractory conduct whilst a casual inmate of Chelsea workhouse. The assistant matron said that Williams had refused to undergo the usual bath and had used objectionable and abusive language. She had been offered the option of leaving the

house if she did not like the bath. She had delayed at dressing herself and appeared to be under the influence of drink. Williams replied that she was in bad health and suffered with rheumatism. She had not objected to the bath but would not have her head washed. She added that she had been perfectly sober, had dressed as quickly as she could, and had not used a word of bad language. The magistrate discharged Williams on assurances of her future good behaviour.

25 JUNE 1842 The death occurred at the St Marylebone workhouse of Elizabeth Pearce, aged sixty-eight. She had formerly been in affluent circumstances but, after falling on hard times, was obliged to enter the workhouse. She had frequently been heard to declare that going into the workhouse would break her heart – a prediction which was all too fatally verified.

26 JUNE 1886 Details appeared today of the practices employed in the dispensing of medicines at the Strand workhouse in Edmonton. In a report to the Strand guardians, it appeared that all the nurses between them could not recall more than twelve bottles of medicine being specially ordered for individual patients, the rest being 'stock' bottles dispensed following verbal instructions from the medical officer or, sometimes, at their own discretion. Although many of these 'stock' bottles contained unobjectionable domestic medicines, some contained drugs that should never be given except after written instructions from the medical officer. In one cupboard under the charge of a nurse had been found 'stock' bottles containing julep, cough mixture, iron tonic, peppermint mixed with julep, diarrhoea mixture, effervescing mixture, gall acid mixture, potash mixture, quinine mixture, ether mixture, black draught, white draught, eye lotion, liniment, chloral mixture, aperient pills, opium pills, two pots of white ointment – one said to be mercurial and the other zinc, but not labelled. Some of the bottles had been found with their labels washed off, and some which were marked 'poison' half washed off. The doctor in charge admitted that he had gradually lapsed into the practice owing to the pressure of work and to save time in specially dispensing for individuals.

27 JUNE 1923 At Liverpool today, the West Derby guardians discussed the case of John Nield, the Communist member of the city council, who had recently become an inmate of the union's Belmont Road workhouse. Since his entry, Nield had received a number of visitors – rather more than would normally be permitted. He had also made a variety of complaints about his treatment, including the quality of the food, and his being refused permission to leave the workhouse to attend a council meeting. One of the guardians, the Revd H. Longbottom, said he had sampled the workhouse lunch and found that the bread was better than he received at home. The board agreed that Nield should receive no special privileges whilst resident in the workhouse. A body of the unemployed who had gathered outside the workhouse to escort their leader to a meeting would therefore wait in vain.

28 JUNE 1923 At about eight o'clock this morning, James Hotchin, a former butler at Cowick Hall, near Snaith, was found dead in one of the lavatories at Goole workhouse. He had apparently tied a handkerchief around his neck and attached it to a hook. He was found in a sitting position. Hotchin, aged sixty-six, had been an inmate of the workhouse more than three years. Some years earlier he had been a patient in an asylum and had an overwhelming dread of being sent back there. In recent months, he had been heard threatening to take his life and placed under continual observation, but this had been relaxed a few weeks earlier because it was considered that he was improving.

29 JUNE 1903 At the Pickering Union workhouse today, a violent incident occurred in the vagrant ward, where a number of casuals were carrying out their tasks. John Moore, aged twenty-seven, who had been behaving oddly since his admittance two days earlier, suddenly lifted a stone hammer and dealt a murderous blow on another vagrant who was working nearby. Moore continued to rain heavy blows on the man's body and head until an official, attracted by cries of murder, dragged him away and summoned the police. While the injured man was being attended to, Moore was lost sight of, but, after a search, he was discovered suspended by a rope tied to some bars across a window in the workhouse yard. A police officer cut the man down, in an unconscious state, and both he and the other casual, named as William Reed, aged sixty-eight, were taken to the infirmary in a critical condition.

30 JUNE 1880 On this day, it was reported that a shocking murder had been committed in the City of London workhouse infirmary on Mile End Road. The episode began when a police constable found a man lying insensible in Aldergate Street. The officer conveyed him to the workhouse where he was placed in a separate room in the infirmary. His pockets were examined, and in them were a passport and other papers identifying him as David Saleneskam, a native of the village of Paruts, in the province of Kalviarany, Russia. A few hours later, Saleneskam recovered consciousness but proved unable to speak more than a few words of English. The next day, a man named Harris, a Polish Jew, who had been an inmate of the infirmary for several months, was sent for to talk with him. Saleneskam seemed very pleased that Harris could speak his own tongue, and readily entered into conversation with him. They conversed together during the day, Saleneskam seeming very quiet and calm though somewhat strange in manner. At about seven in the evening, Harris was sitting at a table reading, with another patient named Hollingworth also in the room. Suddenly, Saleneskam jumped out of bed, caught hold of a chair, and rushing at Hollingworth aimed a terrific blow at him, which he managed to avoid. Saleneskam then darted at Harris, and dealt blow after blow upon his head, smashing the chair into pieces and literally knocking out the man's brains, which were scattered about the room. After Hollingsworth shouted for help, Saleneskam was overpowered and strapped to the bed. When the police arrived, they found the murderer in a state of raving madness. He was later committed to the criminal lunatic asylum at Broadmoor.

1896 Also on this day, a murderous attack was made on Thomas Arter, master of the Basingstoke workhouse, by an inmate named John Castle, aged seventy-one. The assailant, a tall and comparatively powerful man, struck the master on the head with a spade, rendering him unconscious for a long time.

JULY

Inmates leap to safety as flames engulf Manchester's
Tame Street workhouse. (*See* 27 July)

1 JULY 1913 The Chapel-en-le-Frith board of guardians were reported to have changed the diet in the union's casual ward following the death of a journeyman painter named John Lightfoot. During wintry weather, Lightfoot, who had no money, had walked from the Aston workhouse at Birmingham in search of work. After a night in the Chapel-en-le-Frith workhouse he had breakfasted on bread and water, then walked fifteen miles through snow to Bakewell, where he received bread and water gruel for supper and for breakfast the following day. He continued twelve miles further through the snow where he died from heart failure, accelerated by insufficient food and exposure to cold. In light of the incident, it was proposed to alter the diet in the Chapel casual ward from bread and water to bread and gruel.

1840 On this day, at a session of Yorkshire's West Riding magistrates, there were only two applications for orders of maintenance in Bastardy. The first was against the master of a workhouse in the union from where the application came, and the second was against a poor law guardian in another union.

2 JULY 1890 With its implied slight on the efficacy of workhouse medical care, the manufacturers of 'Clarke's Blood Mixture' got good mileage out of an endorsement purportedly from an inmate of Hull workhouse. Over a four-year period, it appeared virtually daily in papers across the country. Interestingly, the wording of the text varied considerably over the years, but the misspelling of the workhouse address (on Anlaby Road) was never corrected:

> I feel duty bound to inform you of the wonderful effects of Clarke's Blood Mixture on me. I have had suffering over two years of a severe nature. I first consulted the best medical aid I could possibly procure, till my means were run out, and with a sad heart I was compelled to come into the workhouse hospital, where I now am. I had been in here 18 months, and my legs gradually got worse. I began to think they would never get better, till I read of 'Clarke's Blood Mixture', and then I determined that when I could raise the means I would try it; so I commenced to deprive myself of little necessaries till at length I raised eleven shillings. I commenced to use the Blood Mixture on Monday, May 6th. I then had five wounds on my left leg, one very large on the ankle bone, one on the shin about the size of half-a-crown, and three on the calf almost as large. The right leg was somewhat similar, but there were three sores which I thought would break into one. All are perfectly healed up now but one small place on the left ankle about the size of a shilling. There are fifteen patients in the ward that I am in, and they were surprised to see my legs when I had taken the Mixture a

week, and there are three of them now using it. I am very sorry, indeed, that I cannot purchase another bottle. You may judge for yourself how I am fixed after being in here eighteen months. My sister, Mrs Bullmer, lives at No. 26, Grimsby-lane, Market-place, Hull, and if you would kindly send me a small quantity I should be able to get it, and I shall never forget it as long as I live.

Yours faithfully,

EDWARD STATHERS

No. 8 Ward, Analby-road Workhouse Hospital, Hull.

3   JULY   1909   An inquest today heard that a number of the inmates at the Kingston Union workhouse had been affected by poisoning, believed to be due to ptomaine in minced mutton which had been served out to them for dinner a few days earlier. The matter came to the attention of the authorities following the death of an old man of seventy, named John Henry Loader, who had eaten the mutton and died two days later. Thirteen other adults and eleven children who ate the meat also showed signs of poisoning and had to receive medical treatment.

4   JULY   1929   The Belfast board of guardians was reported today to have succeeded in its 'back to butter' campaign. Margarine had been introduced into the institution as an economy measure during the First World War, at a time when butter was so severely rationed that it was rarely seen, and even margarine was difficult to obtain. Proposals by the guardians to revert to butter, at an additional cost of £1,000 a year, had been repeatedly vetoed by the Ministry of Home Affairs on the grounds of extravagance, with the Ministry declaring that for adults margarine was quite as good as butter. Now, after considering fresh reports on the subject by visiting medical officers, the Ministry had sanctioned the requested change. Healthy inmates, as well as the sick and infirm, would now receive butter on their bread, and there was rejoicing in the workhouse.

5   JULY   1907   At Plymouth workhouse, an early morning fire caused serious damage to a three-storey block occupied by 300 men and women. All of the inmates, many of whom were old and feeble, were safely evacuated. Some, however, had to escape in their night attire and suffered severely from exposure as the weather was very cold and the ground wet from recent rain. The fire, which originated in a store on the top floor, destroyed the roof of the building and burnt out the upper dormitories. The guardians were left facing the difficulty of obtaining temporary accommodation for the inmates.

6   JULY 1925   It was reported today that on searching the belongings of an old lady who had been admitted to the Saddleworth workhouse in Yorkshire's West Riding, the relieving officer had found £90 in gold and treasury notes hidden in an old skirt. It was also discovered that another inmate had £1,000 deposited in a bank in a neighbouring county.

7   JULY 1862   An inquest took place today at the West London Union workhouse, Smithfield, following the suicide of inmate William Bailey, aged sixty-three. The deceased was a member of a respectable family but through misfortune had entered the workhouse, where he was made wardsman on account of his excellent character. His body was discovered by a woman who ran about crying and wringing her hands and saying, 'Bailey has hanged himself in the bath room.' He was discovered hanging from a beam by two leather straps tied around his neck. He was instantly cut down, and the doctor sent for, who pronounced life extinct. Mr James Hall, master of the workhouse, said it was known in the house that Bailey had formed a deep attachment, though one of a purely honourable nature, for a nurse in the infirmary – the wife of a soldier who had been on foreign service for some years. Their main opportunities of meeting were in the storeroom where each had to go for supplies, and it appeared that three days before his suicide the two had had some slight disagreement and she refused to speak to him. This greatly depressed Bailey and three days later, on his birthday, he procured some drink and made himself slightly intoxicated. Bailey had been much respected, and the straps with which he hanged himself were used by him to enforce order among the refractory boys. The nurse involved, weeping bitterly, admitted that she and deceased had been very partial to each other. The jury returned a verdict of 'suicide, while in a state of temporary insanity.'

8   JULY 1898   News emerged today of an unusual scandal at the West Ham workhouse after one of the guardians, Mr Rayner, and his friend, Mr Pontin, visited the establishment. It was said that after taking an interest in a centenarian inmate, Rachael Perry, they had kissed her. When this was reported, a special meeting of the guardians was held to discuss the matter. Mr Rayner said he was happy to apologise, but had only 'osculated' the 103-year-old after obtaining permission and did not consider an apology was really required. The board expressed its strong condemnation of his conduct.

9   JULY 1926   An unusual story was told at Southend County Court today concerning Edwin Gell, a former mental attendant at the Rochford workhouse. After hearing rumours that the institution was haunted, Gell had been reading a ghost story

in a London paper. As it was time for the night nurse to come on duty, he had thrown a sheet over his shoulders and waited for her at the doorway. He soon heard footsteps, but instead of the nurse appearing, it had been the medical officer. He reported the incident to the guardians and Gell was dismissed. A nurse later told the board that she had seen an apparition parading the wards and grounds, his hands above his head, and suggested that Gell was responsible for this too, something he strenuously denied. He now charged the guardians with trying to rob him of his pension contributions and claimed the sum of £25, money he had paid towards his superannuation benefit.

10 JULY 1899 Today's *Western Mail* reported that Patrick Traynor, a seaman, aged twenty-five had died at the Cardiff workhouse while having an operation under chloroform. Traynor had been admitted to the workhouse in March with a sinus wound an inch deep on the outside of his right thigh. Two previous operations had taken place without incident, the first under chloroform and the second under ether. At the third, Dr Campbell Jenkins, Assistant Medical Officer at the workhouse, had again administered chloroform. Traynor at first appeared to take it all right, but suddenly his face became livid. He then gave a gasp and died almost immediately. Traynor's heart had appeared to be sound and no obvious explanation could be offered for his reaction.

11 JULY 1876 An inquest was held at the Leeds workhouse today on the body of Henry Nowillray, aged twenty-six, who had died there two days earlier. A policeman had found the man a month previously, lying insensible in Bridge Road, Kirkstall.

A view of Cardiff workhouse (left) in around 1910.

He was unable to speak further than to tell the surgeon at the workhouse his name and age. He could take no food, as his teeth remained firmly clenched, and what was given to him had to be injected through his nose, something which continued from the time of his admittance to the workhouse until his death. There were no marks of violence on his body, and a post-mortem examination indicated that death was caused by congestion of the brain. Every effort had been made by the workhouse officials to get information about the deceased, but without success.

12 JULY 1838 The *Morning Post* today recounted that a waggoner named Bailey had come to magistrates at London's Mansion House accompanied by seven small country boys, all in the garb of workhouse inmates. On his way into the city, he had overtaken the boys who appeared exhausted with fatigue. They had said that they belonged to the workhouse at High Wycombe, some thirty-two miles distant, and that the master there had instructed them to run away, with the threat of severe punishment if they dared to return. They had accordingly departed and walked towards London until they were overcome with fatigue and hunger, having been given neither bread nor money to buy it. Two of them carried a letter of recommendation to a Mr Brown, a fishmonger of Lower Thames Street, who had previously employed a boy from the same workhouse. Each of the other boys had a slip of paper directing them to another master. Sir Peter

The Wycombe Union workhouse at Marlow, from where the boys met by Bailey would have started their trek to London.

Laurie declared that it was scarcely credible that such a course could be pursued in a union workhouse. Mr Hobler, a barrister, suggested that the boys had heard about a runaway workhouse boy having been successful in obtaining a situation in London and were trying the experiment themselves. Alderman Pirie, without saying anything, put his hand in his pocket, and gave each boy as much money as would support him until the authorities at High Wycombe had been heard from. The boys, who appeared mostly to be orphans, bowed most respectfully to the magistrates then proceeded to the Giltspur Street Compter to be lodged.

13   JULY **1888** An inquest at Middlesbrough workhouse this evening heard that pauper inmate George Squire, seventy-one, had committed suicide by cutting his throat with a razor. Squire had at one time been in good circumstances but, after taking to drink, became destitute, and had to take refuge in the workhouse. In recent years he had suffered from chronic bronchitis and lately had occasionally seemed in low spirits. On the night of his death, he had risen from his bed, walked to another inmate's box, and taken out a razor. Before anyone could get up he had cut his throat from ear to ear and died before the medical officer's arrival.

An aerial view of the Liverpool workhouse, now the site of the city's Roman Catholic cathedral.

1893 On this day the master at Liverpool's Brownlow Hill workhouse, the largest in England, informed the committee that 3,053 inmates were now in residence, with 920 cases under medical treatment in the workhouse hospital. In the past week, twenty deaths had taken place in the institution.

14 JULY **1888** At Norwich Assizes today, John Revel Burrows, sixty-one, faced trial for the manslaughter of John Mickelburgh at the Kenninghall workhouse. Mickelburgh, aged eighty-two, had been suffering from bronchitis and was placed in the old men's ward where Burrows, also an inmate, was employed as a nurse. As Mickelburgh required frequent attention and was very irritable, the two men frequently quarrelled. During the night, Mickelburgh called to Burrows for help in getting in and out of bed. They finally began to argue and a struggle began. After Mickelburgh received a blow on the chest, he cried out, 'Lord have mercy on me. You have hurt me.' He also increasingly complained of pains in his chest and difficulty in breathing and died ten days later. The evidence presented against Burrows proved unconvincing, however, and he was acquitted.

15 JULY **1865** The medical journal *The Lancet* today began publication of a series of reports on the state of London's workhouse infirmaries. The articles were compiled by Mr Ernest Hart, a physician attached to the staff of *The Lancet*; Dr Francis Anstie, from Westminster Hospital; and Dr William Carr, a poor law medical officer. Their accounts, which were based on a site visit to each institution, painted a relentless picture of insanitary conditions, inadequate ventilation, poor nursing, defective equipment and overcrowding. *The Lancet* investigations played a significant part in a growing campaign for reform which eventually resulted in the 1867 Metropolitan Poor Act. Workhouse infirmaries in the capital now had to be on separate sites from their parent workhouse, and with a separate management.

The subject of the first *Lancet* report was the workhouse of St George-the-Martyr on Mint Street in Southwark. Conditions there often left much to be desired:

Each ward had an open fireplace; a lavatory and water closet in a recess or lobby; in some instances the latter served for two or three wards. In several cases the grossest possible carelessness and neglect were discovered in some of these wards. Take the following in illustration:—Thirty men had used one closet, in which there had been no water for more than a week, and which was in close proximity to their ward; and in an adjoining ward so strong was the ammoniacal smell that we had no doubt respecting the position of the cabinet, which we found dry. In No. 4 ward (female), with 17 beds, the drain-smell from a lavatory in a recess of the room was so offensive that we suspected a sewer-communication, and soon discovered that there was no trap; indeed it had been lost for some considerable time. Apart from this source of contamination of the ward, there were several cases with offensive discharges: one particularly, a case of cancer, which, no disinfectant being used, rendered the room almost unbearable to the other inmates.

Nursing care at the workhouse was largely in the hands of female inmates:

On interrogating some of the pauper female nurses on the subject of their duties, and especially on their mode of washing those who were incapable of doing it for themselves, they admitted that the 'chamber' was the favourite utensil, and even defended its use. Intemperance is common amongst them; indeed, so great is the evil that the medical officer considered it prevailed to the extent of 90 per cent.

16 JULY 1857 It was reported today that Richard Empson, a lunatic attendant at the St Martin-in-the-Fields workhouse, had been murdered by an inmate named John Payne, aged twenty. Two days earlier, Payne had accosted a policeman in the Strand, saying he wished to get into prison. The constable said he would only arrest him if he did something to warrant it, whereupon Payne went to the door of a nearby tailor's shop and walked off with a dummy wearing a coat. The officer immediately detained him and took him to the police station. The next morning, a magistrate, after concluding from Payne's manner that he was deranged, sent him to the workhouse. There, after refusing to do some light work, he became so violent that he was put in a straitjacket. The next day, he was put under the supervision of George Dixon and Richard Empson. At about midday he asked for his Bible and his cross. While Dixon went to get these, Payne tried to escape but was again secured with a straitjacket. At bedtime, Empson loosened the fastenings and went to bed in the same ward. Payne later asked for some water and while Empson was getting it, loosened the other fastenings. Dixon then went out to wash himself, but a few minutes later he heard the cry of murder. He ran out into the yard and found Payne, who rushed at him with a shovel and struck him several times. He managed to escape inside and bolt the door of the ward. He then found Empson lying on the floor in a pool of blood. He was still alive but died shortly after. He had two wounds on the left temple, and a poker was lying nearby, which Payne had attacked him with. At his trial for murder, Payne was acquitted on the grounds of insanity and ordered to be detained indefinitely.

17 JULY 1830 It was reported today that investigations were taking place into the sudden and mysterious death of Mr J.S. Gardner, master of the St Andrew's workhouse, Islington. He was suspected of being poisoned by a young female pauper named Hartwell with whom he had formed an intimacy, which he broke off. The woman had been heard to threaten him.

18 JULY 1838 The death was reported of a remarkable inmate of the Uckfield Union workhouse at Maresfield. George Watson, aged fifty-one, became widely known as the 'Sussex Calculator' and though considered dim-witted in his everyday conduct, possessed astonishing powers of memory. He could recall accurately where he had been on any day during the past thirty years, whom he had seen, and on what business. He could give the date of Easter Sunday for a century past, and knew the birthdays and ages of all his acquaintances, often raising a laugh against single ladies of a certain age by stating the day of their birth in company. One of his favourite amusements was to recount the acreage, population, size of the church, and weight of the tenor bell of every parish in the county. In recent years his wandering habits had led to his deterioration, acquiring such dirty ways that the workhouse became the only place where he could be taken in.

19 JULY 1865 An inquest was held following the death of Thomas Clutterbuck, an inmate of the St Giles's workhouse. A wardsman, Simon Scanlon, said that he had been called to the deceased whom he found having a fit, and with his head jammed in the folds of a turn-up bedstead. He had pulled at the head and tried to lift it up, but the man had firmly fixed his head in the bedstead during the fit. Another pauper had come up and quietly suggested that the bed should be turned down. After this was done, the man was released but died soon afterwards. The inquest heard that several other inmates had failed to assist Clutterbuck. Richard Taylor, who received 2s a week to look after the deadhouse, admitted that he had seen the deceased having a fit but said it had been no more his place to help than anyone else's and he had put his head under the bedclothes again.

1767 At Leeds, on this day, the worst thunderstorm in living memory took place. It struck one of the chimneys of the workhouse and shivered the slates from the ridge to the eaves. It then entered the garret, and struck a poor woman dead. It likewise struck an old man sitting at a window down below, whetting his knife, setting fire to his clothes, and burning him so badly that it was thought he would not recover.

20 JULY 1888 The report of a meeting of the Swansea board of guardians gave details of an extraordinary incident at the workhouse the previous evening. A nine-week-old baby, in the custody of its parents, had been brought to the workhouse and, being found to be ill, was placed in the hospital ward along with its mother. The infant, unfortunately, died during the night and the following morning the parents departed, leaving the body in the custody of the master and apparently not caring what became of it. The mother had been about eighteen years old and clearly well educated while the father, a young Irishman aged about twenty, was 'of the low, vagrant type' who evidently had great influence over her.

21 JULY 1876 Details appeared today of an awkward situation that had arisen at Leeds workhouse where two women named Sarah and Martha Emsley were inmates. Three weeks earlier, it had been reported that Sarah had died. Her relatives took the body away, drew out £8 from her burial club, bought mourning wear, and committed her remains to the grave. Although one of them remarked on a change in her appearance, they agreed that the features often alter after death. It later emerged, however, that a mistake had been made in the Christian name of the deceased, and that it was Martha, and not Sarah, who had been interred. The relatives of Sarah Emsley were now complaining to the guardians that they had been put to the trouble and expense of burying an entire stranger, and purchasing mourning clothes, to say nothing of the three weeks' grief, and were wishing to know what compensation they might expect for the blunder.

1906 On this day the *Weekly Irish Times* gave details of a report on the insanitary state of the Carlow workhouse compiled by the union's medical officer, Dr Rawson. He recommended the closing of the dairy, the meat store and the master's office, the latter being unfit for habitation. The porter's room, communicating with the master's office, received the emanations from the sewer, and was highly dangerous. In the school playground was an open pond of filthy sewage. He also recommended that no visitors be admitted during the next fortnight owing to the cases of scarlatina in the institution.

1916 It was revealed today that the Islington workhouse was being used for the wartime internment of male German aliens. All of those being held were married to English women who were allowed a half-hour visit each week. The men were employed in occupations such as tailoring, boot-making and mail bag manufacture, with the income generated being passed to their families. A separate section of the site was also being used to detain naturalised German prisoners.

22 JULY 1863 The medical officer of the Fermoy Union workhouse in County Cork recorded the beneficial effects that had been obtained by the installation of a Turkish bath in the establishment. It had been successfully used in the treatment of

rheumatism, scrofula and various cutaneous conditions, all of which formed a large proportion of the diseases most commonly met in workhouses. In every instance, the treatment had produced relief, and in many it had effected a rapid cure resulting in both medical and economic benefits for the establishment and its residents. All the inmates, with the exception of the very old and infirm, were now making weekly use of the facility.

23 JULY 1856 Two girls, inmates of the St Marylebone workhouse, were today brought before a magistrate and charged with riotous conduct. The girls claimed that they and others had been severely beaten with canes and a horsewhip, and that they had been singled out to appear in court because they had no marks of violence on their bodies. The magistrate sent for three other girls who, on being examined, were found to have weals and bruises on their backs, shoulders and elsewhere. The master of the workhouse, Richard Ryan, admitted the use of the cane but claimed that the girls were of the worst class and so violent that the canes had needed to be used in self-defence. Two porters at the workhouse, Charles Brown and Matthew Green, had also meted out similar treatment on the young women.

Publicity about the floggings provoked a major scandal. Green and Brown soon resigned from their posts, but the Marylebone guardians decided that Ryan should only be reprimanded, with the threat of instant dismissal if such conduct was repeated.

At an inquiry by the Poor Law Board, a number of inmates described how they had been treated. Nineteen-year-old Mary Ann Sullivan related that after an argument with Ryan about her work, she had been locked in a cell for several hours. She was then dragged out and whipped by Ryan. Green and Brown had also taken turns to beat her, with one or other of them holding her down by the hair. The inquiry's report regretted the level of disorder that existed in the Marylebone workhouse and the failings in its management. As well as demanding the master's immediate dismissal, stricter rules and regulations were imposed on the running of the establishment to prevent any recurrence of the recent incidents.

Ryan's departure became a cause of public celebration and was marked by the publication of *The Women Flogger's Lament of Marylebone Workhouse!* – a street-ballad sung to the tune of 'Oh Dear, What Can the Matter Be?'

Oh dear, here's a shocking disaster,
My name it is Ryan, a poor workhouse master,
I have now got discharged and my sentence is passed, sirs,
Because I went flogging the girls.

The two flogging porters and me are crushed down, sirs,

One porter is green and the other is brown, sirs,

We would not have it happened for five hundred pounds, sirs,

Flogging the dear little girls.

Chorus

Oh where shall we wander, or where shall we roam, sirs,

As we walk through the streets folks won't let us alone, sirs,

Kicked out of the workhouse in Marylebone, sirs,

For flogging the sweet little girls.

1927 Also on this day, a porter at the Newmarket workhouse was married. After the ceremony, twenty-eight tramps formed a guard of honour, holding up their 'drums' – the tin cans in which they used to obtain hot tea.

24 JULY **1857** Shortly after eight this evening a fire broke out at the Lambeth workhouse on Princes (now Black Prince) Road. It began above the infirmary at the top of the west wing and was discovered when a sick inmate noticed flames flickering through the roof. A general cry of 'Fire!' ran through the ward, with the master and other officials soon arriving. The scene which ensued amongst those lying prostrate and suffering from disease was said to be of the most horrifying and agonising character. The workhouse staff and a number of able-bodied inmates carried sick persons out using armchairs. Other patients, gaining strength from the danger, sprang from their beds in acute distress. Before long, firemen from Waterloo Road were at the scene, with upwards of 100 police constables also in attendance. In the course of halting the fire, some 1,000 tons of water were poured into the building. Shortly after the final patients had been removed to safety, the roof of the ward collapsed. The origin of the blaze was thought to have been connected with plumbers who had been at work in the ward that day.

1896 The inmates of Camberwell's Gordon Road and Constance Road workhouses today had their annual summer excursion to the seaside at Bognor Regis. A special 650-seat train was chartered and at around 9 a.m. the party set off. The group consisted mostly of elderly inmates aged sixty to ninety, together with a number of young children from the workhouse. They were also accompanied by a boys' band from the South Metropolitan District School. Dinner and tea were provided at the Bognor Town Hall after which the men were given tobacco, and the women and children sweets. However, many of the group had apparently obtained money from their friends and after being liberated from the workhouse had headed straight for the nearest public

Camberwell's elderly inmates enjoying their dinner at Bognor Regis. The bottles of beer that contributed to their high jinks are clearly visible on the tables.

house before boarding the train. On arrival at Bognor, they had continued drinking and then gone for their dinner at which beer was also served. After dinner, there were more visits to the local public houses. It was later reported that a number of cases had occurred of disorderly conduct and indecent behaviour on secluded parts of the beach.

25 JULY 1838 The small town of Llandovery, Carmarthenshire, was thrown into a state of great excitement by a serious fire at the new workhouse. When the alarm was raised, at about two in the morning, crowds rushed to the scene and assisted in trying to extinguish the flames, which rose to a great height. Despite their efforts, the workhouse, whose construction was virtually finished, was almost entirely destroyed apart from one wing and some outer buildings. A large quantity of workmen's tools and other materials were also lost in the blaze. The cause of the fire was a mystery, but the hand of an arsonist was suspected.

26 JULY 1927 The *Nottingham Evening Post* today recounted the tale of a solicitor, Mr Harry Wilson, and a lady who sought his advice as to her legal position, her husband having vanished some five years earlier. The man, who had lived at Streatham, had come home one evening, gone out to post a letter, and then vanished.

While arrangements were being made to presume the man's death in court, Mr Wilson, who was closely associated with the West Ham board of guardians, was told of a strange case that had baffled them for some time. There was a man in the workhouse infirmary who could remember nothing. He had been found wandering in the countryside, and for a time had been in Maidstone Union infirmary. But one day he had a transitory memory of West Ham, and he was quickly transferred there – guardians always being eager, for the ratepayers' sake, to send a man to his 'native' place. Mr Wilson went to see him, and when his photograph was given to the wife, she came to the conclusion it was her long-lost husband. She saw him and grew more convinced. Gradually, as he heard her voice and was brought back to his children, his memory returned. But he had no recollection of how he came to be there.

27 JULY 1899 In the late evening, great excitement arose in the Ancoats district of Manchester when a serious fire occurred at the workhouse on Tame Street. The seven-storey building, a former cotton mill, provided labour for able-bodied paupers during the daytime and housed tramps and vagrants overnight. When the fire broke out, seven men in bed on the third and fourth floors soon found themselves imprisoned. On rushing to the stone staircase, they found that smoke had made it impassable. Pursued by the fire from floor to floor, the apparently doomed captives revealed themselves one after another at windows to a horror-stricken crowd outside. A fire escape brought by the brigade was hindered in its access by a shed in the old mill yard. The best that could be done for those on the point of leaping for their lives from the upper storeys of the building was for the firemen to climb onto the shed and hold life-sheets on its roof. This was done, and six of the desperate men jumped down one by one. Great shrieks arose from the onlookers as the men, all elderly and all unpractised in such a proceeding, dropped or fell. They did so with more or less success, one breaking his leg which caught on a sill. More than one injured his head, and one rebounded from the life-sheet onto the shed roof. Some were burnt as well as maimed, but all survived. The seventh inmate, who had climbed onto the roof of the burning building, had a narrow escape. He was reached by the fire escape and lowered by a lifeline.

28 JULY 1906 Chairman of the Poplar board of guardians, Will Crooks, himself a former child inmate of the workhouse, today gave evidence to an inquiry into the administration of the union:

> The staple diet when I joined the Board was skilly. I have seen the old people, when this stuff was put before them, picking out black specks from the oatmeal.

These were caused by rats, which had the undisturbed run of the oatmeal bin. No attempt was made to cleanse the oatmeal before it was prepared for the old people.. The inmates were badly clothed as well as badly fed. Not one of them had a change of clothing. Their under-clothes were worn to rags. If they washed them they had to borrow from each other in the interval. The inmates' clothes were not only scanty, they were filthy. On one occasion the whole of the workhouse linen was returned by the laundry people because it was so over-run with vermin that they would not wash it.

Will Crooks who, as the title of his biography proclaimed, went 'from workhouse to Westminster'.

1910 A man named Basil Leon Monsdale was taken to Knutsford workhouse today on a magistrate's order, as it was alleged he was suffering from delusions. He had not been in the workhouse more than twenty minutes when he managed to escape and was hotly pursued through the town and down on to a marsh. He eluded his pursuers there and they eventually found him drowned. It was presumed he had scrambled through a ditch and could not climb up the other side.

1934 It was reported today that, during a recent week, as many as twelve casuals who had arrived on motorcycles had been admitted to the Belford Institution, Northumberland. The master was of the opinion that the introduction of hot dinners was responsible for the influx of new arrivals, many of whom he had never seen before.

29 JULY **1904** Today's *Western Times* reported that every Sunday, eighty-four-year-old Robert Bennett, an inmate of the City of London workhouse at Homerton, walked to the asylum at Colney Hatch to visit his wife, a round trip of some eighteen miles. Since his admission to the workhouse, he had never missed a Sunday, and had never been late on his return.

30 JULY **1848** A report appeared today relating to the adventures of a lunatic woman, now an inmate of the Bolton workhouse. She had left home two weeks earlier to visit Lady Ellesmere, to whom she wished to make some complaint. At Clifton Junction railway station, the carriage of Mr Jacob Fletcher of Peel Hall was awaiting a French gentleman who was coming to visit him. The gentleman in question arrived on the same train as the woman who, being rather peculiarly dressed, was assumed by Mr Fletcher's servants to be a companion of the foreign visitor. She marched forward to Mr Fletcher's carriage, the Frenchman bowing to her with Parisian politeness, thinking she was one of Mr Fletcher's household sent to escort him. When the carriage arrived at Mr Fletcher's residence, she was taken to be a friend of the Frenchman, but a feeling of delicacy prevented either from asking for an explanation. At length they sat down to an elegant repast, when the conduct of the woman became so extraordinary that Mr Fletcher and his friend looked at each other in astonishment. An explanation ensued. The French gentleman declared that he knew nothing of Mr Fletcher's visitor, having found her in the carriage when he entered. The woman was then requested to withdraw, but she was by now too fond of her new quarters and obstinately refused to move. A policeman was sent for, who took the unfortunate woman away.

31 JULY **1862** The *Birmingham Post* published details of an inquest into the death of sixty-year-old Alfred Miller, an inmate of the Birmingham workhouse. A fellow inmate

named Ambrose Boon said that Miller had had a reputation as a great glutton. The regular dinner allowance for each man in the workhouse was a pint and a half of soup and 4 ounces of bread. On the day of his death, five men had given Miller their allowance of soup, and he had drunk the lot, as well as his own. In the ward after dinner, many of the inmates had been teasing Miller about his shirt. Shortly afterwards, the clean linen was brought in and Miller had changed his shirt, the old one being tied up and put under the form on which they were seated. Later on there was some horseplay involving Miller's dirty shirt, and a man named William Grice tried to grab it. Grice then took Miller's arms from behind and, putting his knee to his back, pulled Miller over, when his head struck the pavement. Miller ended up on his back upon the ground, with Grice on top of him. After a wardsman told Grice to get off him, Miller staggered to a seat, sat down and, closing his eyes, appeared to go off into a fit. Some water was fetched and sprinkled on his face, while someone went for the house surgeon – who soon arrived, but quickly pronounced Miller dead. A post-mortem revealed a serous effusion on the brain, congested lungs, a fat and flabby heart, and a stomach very full of soup. The jury, not being convinced that Grice had initiated the struggle or that the blow to his head had brought about Miller's demise, returned a verdict of accidental death.

AUGUST

A depiction of the grim scene discovered in Charles and Eliza Hatton's bedroom. (*See* 8 August)

1   AUGUST 1845 In Parliament today, MP Thomas Wakley asked a question about the inmates of Andover workhouse who, whilst employed in the task of crushing bones, 'were in the habit of quarrelling with each other about the bones, of extracting the marrow from them, and of gnawing the meat which they sometimes found at their extremities.' The Home Secretary, Sir James Graham, expressed disbelief that such things could be happening but promised an immediate inquiry. So began a train of events that was to shake the workhouse system.

An initial investigation by Henry Parker, the Assistant Poor Law Commissioner responsible for Andover, soon discovered that the allegations were largely true. However, under pressure from his superiors and huge press interest in the matter, he mishandled matters and was asked to resign by the Poor Law Commissioners who wanted a scapegoat for the affair. On 8 November 1845, the Commissioners acknowledged the validity of the outcry against bone-crushing by forbidding its further use. The disquiet rumbled on until March 1846, when a Select Committee began its inquiry into the matter.

It soon emerged that, due to some administrative error, inmates at Andover had been given short rations, even though the union had in 1836 adopted the least generous of the Commissioners' six standard dietary plans. A succession of witnesses revealed the grim and gory details of bone-crushing. It was heavy work, with a 28lb solid iron 'rammer' being used to pummel the bones in a tub. Apart from the appalling smell, it was a back-breaking and hand-blistering task, yet boys of eight upwards were set to it, working in pairs to lift the rammer. Men also suffered scarred faces from the flying shards of bone.

Witnesses at the inquiry included former workhouse inmates such as sixty-one-year-old Samuel Green:

> I was employed in the workhouse at bone-breaking the best part of my time...
> We looked out for the fresh bones; we used to tell the fresh bones by the look of
> them, and then we used to be like a parcel of dogs after them; some were not so
> particular about the bones being fresh as others; I like the fresh bones; I never
> touched one that was a little high; the marrow was as good as the meat, it was
> all covered over by bone, and no filth could get to it... I have picked a sheep's
> head, a mutton bone, and a beef bone; that was when they were fresh and good;
> sometimes I have had one that was stale and stunk, and I eat it even then; I eat
> it when it was stale and stinking because I was hungered, I suppose. You see
> we only had bread and gruel for breakfast, and as there was no bread allowed
> on meat days for dinner, we saved our bread from breakfast, and then, having

had only gruel for breakfast, we were hungry before dinner-time. To satisfy our hunger a little, because a pint and a half of gruel is not much for a man's breakfast, we eat the stale and stinking meat.... I have seen a man named Reeves eat horse-flesh off the bones.

The workhouse master, Colin McDougal, a former sergeant-major, was revealed to be a brutal tyrant and often drunk. The matron, Mary Ann McDougal, was little better and said to be 'a violent lady'. The McDougals ran the workhouse like a penal colony, keeping expenditure and food rations to a minimum, much to the approval of the majority of the guardians. Inmates had to eat their food with their fingers, and were denied the usual extra rations at Christmas. Any man who tried to exchange a word with his wife at mealtimes was given a spell in the refractory cell. McDougal had also attempted to seduce some of the young female inmates, as had his seventeen-year-old son who had been taken on as a workhouse schoolmaster. McDougal's treatment of the dead was no better. On one occasion, a dead baby was buried with an old man to save on the cost of a coffin. Babies born in the workhouse were rarely baptised as this cost a shilling a time. Another revelation concerned Hannah Joyce, an unmarried mother who, after her

Andover – the scene of one of the worst workhouse scandals.

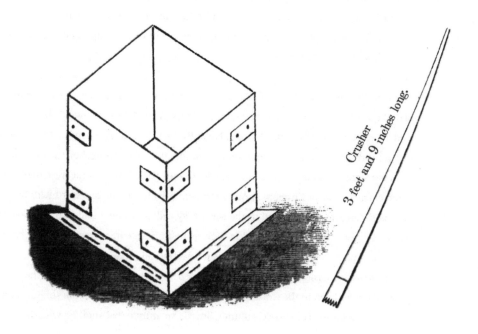

Crusher

3 feet and 9 inches long.

A rammer and tub used in bone-pounding at Andover.

five-month-old child died suddenly, was forced to carry its coffin a mile on her own to the churchyard for an unceremonious burial.

The Select Committee's report criticized virtually everyone involved in the scandal. The McDougals were found to be totally unfit to hold such posts; the guardians had failed to visit the workhouse and had allowed the inmates to be underfed; Assistant Commissioner Parker had placed too much confidence in the Andover guardians; and the Poor Law Commissioners had mishandled the whole affair. In the wake of the scandal, the Commissioners were replaced in 1847 by a new Poor Law Board, which was far more accountable to Parliament.

The Andover guardians appear to have come out of the affair little the wiser. The master appointed as successor to McDougal was a former prison officer from Parkhurst Gaol. After only three years in the post, he was dismissed for taking liberties with female paupers.

2   AUGUST 1929 The remarkable quantity and quality of the eggs supplied to the Belfast workhouse was highlighted in the *Irish Times* today, after Thomas

Morrow was fined £10 for selling eggs to the Belfast Union that were stained. A Ministry of Agriculture inspector had examined a consignment of eight cases of eggs sent by Morrow to the workhouse. In one half-case of 180 eggs, 145 had been stained, 29 were fresh, and 6 were bad. A second case was in much the same condition. Morrow was said to have supplied 9,180 dozen eggs to the institution over a sixteen-week period. The presiding magistrate at the hearing professed his astonishment, first as regards the number of eggs supplied to the workhouse, and then as to the fact that about five-sixths of the eggs in two cases, taken at random, were not up to standard.

3   AUGUST   1817   On this day, London's St Saviour's workhouse, situated on the Kent Road, was burned to the ground. The premises were set on fire by the flue of an adjoining gingerbread baker's. The inmates were rescued with difficulty but fortunately none perished in the inferno.

4   AUGUST   1897   The inmates of the Edmonton workhouse were reported to be greatly annoyed by a plague of flies. At the weekly meeting of the guardians, the workhouse master produced some verses on the subject which had been written by an inmate. The opening stanza ran:

> Oh, the flies, the horrid flies!
> Ev'ry moment, though one dies
> Tragically, and a hive
> Of them hourly caught alive
> They still come. Oh! they still come.
> Driving almost everyone
> Nearly mad, or, rather, quite,
> By their sting and by their bite.

5   AUGUST   1897   Today's issue of the journal *London* condemned the enormous wastage of food that was taking place in the nation's workhouses. The problem existed, it suggested, because inmates were served with prescribed quantities of bread and other items, whether or not they were able to eat that amount. The elderly, in particular, often had reduced appetites or had difficulty consuming the regulation portions of some foods, such as meat or bread. Any food left untouched at the end of a meal was thrown away or used to feed pigs. In the Poplar workhouse alone, it was calculated that as much as 16 tons of bread per year was wasted in this way.

The solution proposed to the Local Government Board was of more flexibility in the serving of items such as bread and meat, with inmates initially being given half their allocated ration, and able to help themselves to the remainder. Providing bread in the form of slices rather than the traditional hunk could also prove beneficial. It was noted that experiments along these lines had been carried out at the Hampstead and Chorlton workhouses and had resulted in savings of about 40 per cent. At Chorlton, the bread saved in this way had been turned into bread pudding, so adding a 'delicacy' to the inmates' fare.

6 AUGUST 1841 Details appeared today of an inquiry by the Poor Law Commissioners relating to the Revd Edward John Howman, a guardian of the Downham Union, Norfolk, following complaints about his presence at surgical operations performed on female paupers at the workhouse. Howman had admitted being present when inmate Mary Ann Leedale had undergone an operation for a venereal condition, which required the exposure of her person. He claimed, however, that he had always taken a considerable interest in medical and surgical cases among the poor and had been present at several operations, in some cases even giving personal assistance to patients. The Commissioners were persuaded that his motives for attending the operation on Leedale were honourable, and that he would have equally been present at it if the patient had been a male, or if the disease had been totally different in its character. The Commissioners considered, however, his conduct was imprudent and likely to impair his reputation as a guardian. They recommended that, in future, only bona fide medical staff should be allowed to attend surgical operations performed in a workhouse, unless otherwise specifically requested by the patient. In addition, the matron, nurse, or some other female belonging to the establishment should be present at all operations on female inmates.

1879 At Sheffield, Thomas Bishop, aged seventy-nine years and too aged to work, had for several weeks been living on bread and water. On at least one occasion, he had fallen to the ground in sheer exhaustion, from lack of food. On this day, he left home, and was soon afterwards found in a back street with his hands covered with blood. 'I have nowhere to go, and nothing to eat,' he said, 'and have been trying to cut my throat.' He died a few days later. At the subsequent inquest, the coroner said that the man was starving, and having a horror of the workhouse, committed suicide.

7 AUGUST 1894 At seven o'clock this morning Edward Gill, aged fifty, a long-time inmate of the Hackney workhouse at Homerton, threw himself from a third-storey

The lofty ward blocks at Hackney workhouse.

window into the courtyard of the workhouse, a distance of about 50ft. A letter was found in his pocket addressed to the workhouse master:

> 6th August, 1894. Mr Mason, — I write this to let you know that I am in my right mind while I do it. I have been here 27 years this or next month, I can't say which. May God forgive me for what I have done. He has given me good health for 50 years the 13th of last month, July. I know what I have done. I have fled in the face of the Almighty. I cannot help doing it. Farewell all my friends and well-wishers. EDWARD CHARLES GILL, born 13th July 1844 at No. 2 Upper Rathbone Place. May God forgive me for it.

1908   At the end of a lengthy trial, ten members and ex-members of the Mile End Old Town board of guardians were convicted of conspiracy to commit fraud and of corruptly receiving gifts. In return for bribes, the men had awarded numerous contracts to a local builder named James Calcutt and then approved the payment of excessive bills that he had submitted. All were found guilty and all but one given prison sentences. The ringleader, Rowland Hirst, a former mayor of Stepney, and in whose public house much of the bribery took place, received the severest sentence of a £250 fine and two years' imprisonment with hard labour.

A rare photograph of proceedings inside a courtroom showing some of the Mile End guardians facing trial.

8 AUGUST 1894 London's East End police were called this afternoon to 295 Old Ford Road, Bow, the residence of unemployed packer Charles Hatton, aged forty-four, and his wife Eliza. The alarm was raised by their landlord, who had not seen them about the house and so had sent a lad to climb up to their bedroom window where the couple were seen in bed, apparently dead. The room was broken into and the bodies of Mr and Mrs Hatton were found side by side, the woman's hand resting on the husband's shoulder. Both were quite dead. On a table near the bed was a glass which had contained poison, later identified as oxalic acid. On the dressing-table was a letter written in pencil:

> We have been forced to this rash act, as we can stand it no longer, and we dread going to the workhouse. We hope God will forgive us. We have nothing further to pledge, and we cannot continue as we have been doing. I have been out of work for over seven months, and cannot get anything to do. CHAS HATTON. P.S. My sister lives at 243, Bethnal Green Road. She will identify our bodies.

On searching the two rooms occupied by Hatton and his wife, police could not find a crumb of food. In a drawer of the dressing table they found a large number of pawn tickets, including one for Eliza's wedding ring.

9 AUGUST 1886 It was reported today that William Garman, thirty-three years of age, an inmate of the Gateshead Union workhouse, took his own life by jumping from an upper window of the building, a fall of some 60ft.

10 AUGUST 1839 At York workhouse this afternoon, a number of the younger inmates began complaining of pains in the head and stomach. Some brought up the contents of their stomachs which proved largely to consist of the soup of which they had partaken at dinner. Mr Walker, the workhouse surgeon, ordered emetics to be administered to those affected and these, together, with other remedies, led to their recovery within a few hours. The incident received wide publicity, with reports circulating in some quarters that poison had been deliberately put in the soup. On further investigation, Mr Walker concluded that the soup in question had been excessively fatty, and also lacking in the usual quantity of potatoes. As a result, he declared, the soup had been altogether too rich to be readily digested by persons of a tender age.

Not everyone was quite so convinced, however. A portion of the soup was also sent for analysis by a local chemist, Mr W. White of Monk Bar. His report confidently declared that the sample had been 'free from any extraneous matter usually classed under the term poison'. However, accompanied by one of the guardians, Mr Bell, he had visited the workhouse to inspect the culinary utensils where:

> In a room... ill adapted for the purpose of preserving meat, we found a beast's head at that time offensive to the smell [which] the Master informed us would not be cooked until the following Wednesday. This room adjoins and opens into a short and very narrow yard considerably tainted with all the effluvia rising from some privies at one end, at that time under progress of being razed. The head not having been previously cleaned, a quantity of unwholesome mucus was attached to it.

It further transpired that the water used in the workhouse came both from a pump and from the river, although it was said pump water was generally used to make soup.

11 AUGUST 1894 Criticisms of understaffing at the Oldham workhouse infirmary were reported today following an inquest on a patient named Cole who had committed suicide. Cole had been admitted to the infirmary a week earlier, and the doctor had indicated that he had suicidal tendencies. Nurse Wallace, who was in charge at night of the whole infirmary, said there were 230 beds, in three blocks of buildings, and her only assistants were six inmates – four men and two women. She had put the patient in charge of one of the inmates, but he at the same time had eighteen other patients to look after. When both the nurse and the assistant were temporarily absent, Cole had got out of bed and thrown himself from a window on the third storey of the building. He had died shortly afterwards. The coroner remarked that it was absurd to expect one woman to efficiently overlook three blocks that had over 200 patients in them, with nobody but irresponsible assistants under her.

12 AUGUST 1861 Reports appeared today of the unhappy state of affairs at the workhouse of St Margaret and St John Westminster whose soap-opera-like intrigues had been the subject of an inquiry by the Poor Law Board. One of the most serious charges was made by the schoolmaster's wife, Mrs Bernell, who claimed that the matron, Eliza Burridge, had tried to poison her. One dinner-time, during the previous November, she had been handed a plate of meat by the matron, which had some white powder at the edge. Becoming suspicious, Mrs Bernell had commented upon the powder – at which point, she claimed, the matron had gone pale and become confused. The powder was transferred to an envelope and later analysed by a chemist who pronounced it to be pure arsenic. A Poor Law Board inquiry was told that Bernell's husband kept a stock of various chemicals but not, he said, arsenic. It also emerged that complaints had been laid against Mrs Bernell over supposedly immoral books such as *The Woman of Pleasure* and *Aristotle* which she had loaned to the workhouse's young schoolmistress. Following the inquiry, the matron was peremptorily dismissed from her post.

13 AUGUST 1854 In the morning of this day, the central part of the workhouse at King's Lynn, Norfolk, suddenly collapsed. The building, dating from around the twelfth century, had originally been a church. Large cracks had appeared in the 80ft clock tower, and with cracking sounds coming from the walls and floors, the workhouse master, Mr Thurlow Nelson, had ordered the inmates to evacuate the building. At 10.45 a.m. the workhouse clock stopped and Mr Andrews, a local clockmaker, climbed up into the tower to repair it. At 11.20 a.m., with a tremendous crash, the workhouse tower collapsed killing the clockmaker whose body was found entangled in the clock wires. The second fatality was an inmate named Cana who had refused to leave the building. He was found doubled up with his head crushed. The master, initially thought also to have perished, was extricated from the rubble and suffered only a dislocated shoulder and bruising.

1900 On this day an inquest was held on Charles Bridgland, aged eighty-eight, an inmate of the Hastings workhouse. Two months prior to his death he had fractured his hip during an epileptic seizure and had become virtually immobile. The jury found that Bridgland had died from blood poisoning caused by bedsores.

The old King's Lynn workhouse before its sudden collapse.

14 **AUGUST** **1834** The Poor Law Amendment Act today received royal assent, bringing into effect the biggest shake-up of the poor relief system in over two centuries. Poor relief, funded as before by local poor rates, was henceforth to be administered by groups of parishes known as poor law unions, each of which was run by a locally elected board of guardians, and which was to provide a central union workhouse. For the able-bodied pauper, it was intended that there should be an end to out-relief – it was now to be the workhouse or nothing. The workhouse was intended to be a deterrent, with conditions inside deliberately less attractive than could be obtained by even the lowest-paid independent labourer.

15 **AUGUST** **1871** At the Neath Union workhouse, an inquest was held following the death of the infant child of one of the inmates, Elizabeth Ann Thomas. Thomas said that she had come into the workhouse in April but, for some reason, had not been bathed or medically examined. She claimed that she had not been suffering from any disease or complaint at that time. The child was born nine days later and, at her confinement, certain symptoms had given rise to suspicions by the staff that Thomas was diseased. The child had been weak and delicate, and at times had sores on the head and a discharge from its nose and ears. Its eyes later become affected,

and the nurse said she would tell the medical officer, Dr Russell, as soon as she saw him. However, Dr Russell did not examine the child until a week later, by which time its eyes were closed up. He separated the eyelids and a quantity of matter flowed out but the sight was gone. The child died three days later. A verdict was returned of 'Death from syphilis.'

16 **AUGUST 1831** Elizabeth Cooper, seventy-five, died this afternoon at the workhouse of St Giles, Cripplegate. At the subsequent inquest, the treatment she received in her final hours was described as abominable. The previous evening, Cooper, who had suffered from a bowel complaint for several days, had called out to the nurse, 'Sarah Hunt, come to me, for God's sake, I am very sick and dying.' The nurse told her to 'puke away' and paid no attention. Another inmate later called the nurse to Cooper, who had become insensible, but no doctor was sent for and the nurse went to bed. At eight the next morning Mrs Cross, mistress of the workhouse, visited Cooper, but still no doctor was called in. The woman continued in a stupor until four in the afternoon, when Hunt came and pinched her nose violently. She then tied up her jaws, and tied her legs together, though she was still breathing, and left her for a short time. On finding she was not dead, Hunt thrust the sheet violently against her face. An inmate who tried to remonstrate with her was told to go to the devil and mind her own affairs. Another nurse untied Cooper's jaws and legs, and gave her some wine, but she died half an hour later.

The inquest heard that Cooper and Hunt had been on bad terms. The previous Sunday, Hunt had said she should have the pleasure of tying Cooper's jaw up. She was intoxicated when she committed these acts, and indeed was seldom sober. Another inmate said Hunt had knocked Cooper's head from side to side of the bed, and tore her cap off in her last agonies. Medical evidence was inconclusive, with Cooper being supposed to have died from excessive vomiting. The inquest jury returned a verdict of 'Died by the Visitation of God'. Hunt was later put on trial for her actions, however, and received a twelve-month prison sentence.

17 **AUGUST 1833** The death occurred of Ann Parker, an inmate of St Margaret's workhouse, Westminster, at the advanced age of 101 years. It was said that a portrait also existed of an old woman in the same workhouse, who had died on 26 June 1739, at the age of 136 years.

1898 On this day in it was reported that the workhouse at the Russian town of Rukovishnikoff had been totally destroyed by fire with at least thirteen inmates having been burnt to death.

18 AUGUST 1877 At the Nuneaton Union workhouse, an unmarried inmate named Hannah Coleman, aged forty-five, was at supper with the other inmates. They had some conversation as to the probable duration of their stay in the institution, and Coleman jocularly remarked she would rather have a watery grave than die in a workhouse. No sooner had she uttered these words than she fell on her left side, was caught by one of the other inmates, and expired a few minutes later. The workhouse medical officer, Dr Hammond, attributed her death to heart disease.

19 AUGUST 1916 An inquest was held today into the death of Frederick Bryan, forty-seven, master of the Lewes Union workhouse, and Winnie Rushworth, sixteen, book-keeper at the institution, who were found dead in the master's sitting room on the previous Thursday. A servant told how, at about 12.20 p.m., Bryan asked for a jug of hot water as the two were going to try a sample of café au lait which had been brought to the workhouse. Two days earlier, the master had told her not to touch a jug at the back of the cupboard in the room as it contained poison he was mixing to kill rats in the garden. At 1 p.m., another servant went to the room and saw the master and book-keeper sitting down apparently asleep. She asked the master if he was ready for dinner, but received no reply. An hour later a seamstress at the workhouse visited the room and saw the master and the young woman sitting in chairs dead. Two cups which had contained coffee were on the table, with a bottle of potassium cyanide and a bowl of bread. It was stated that Miss Rushworth was in an advanced state of pregnancy. All the master's books were in order, and his wife, who was away when the tragedy occurred, stated that she had always been on good terms with her husband and had never noticed any familiarity between him and the girl. The jury returned a verdict that Bryan had committed suicide and persuaded Miss Rushworth to do so to, which the coroner said amounted to a verdict of murder against him.

20 AUGUST 1891 In Lincoln, the dead body of an inmate from the city's workhouse was dragged from the Fossdyke, a navigable canal connecting the Rivers Witham and Trent. The coat and hat of the deceased were found lying on the bank, and in the coat pocket was the following letter:

> This statement I wish to make, that Bob Simpson is cruel man to the sick men. He does his best to kill them. A prison warder would treat you no worse. I have never been a lover of Unions, but the way in which I have seen him treat other poor, helpless inmates has made my blood run cold. I would rather die in the streets. Yours, T. Eason, a native of Lincoln.

Whoever reads this statement, I should like it to be brought before someone.

Mrs Maddison, No. 129, Portland Street, is my sister.

Good-bye, God bless you all. —T. Eason.

21 AUGUST 1895 A shocking quarrel, with fatal consequences, occurred today at the Bedale Union workhouse in Yorkshire. A middle-aged woman, named Margaret Appleton, who was employed as help at the workhouse, sent a man named Richard Dixon, aged fifty, to dig some potatoes in an adjoining garden for the inmates' dinner. As he had not returned with the potatoes after an hour she went into the garden to inquire the reason. Following an altercation between the two, Mrs Appleton snatched the gripe (a potato-harvesting fork) from him and struck him across the head with it, inflicting a wound about 3in long. He seized the gripe from her and struck her several times, including several blows at the back of the neck which fractured her spine and caused instant death. Dixon walked into the vagrants' ward, and said to the porter, 'Boynton, I have killed Margaret.' Blood was then streaming down his face, which he said was the result of the blows that the deceased had inflicted.

The workhouse at Bedale, North Yorkshire.

Initially charged with murder, Dixon subsequently pleaded guilty to manslaughter, with medical evidence showing that Appleton had struck the first blow. He was sentenced to five years' penal servitude.

22 AUGUST 1883 On this morning, a contractor's coach carrying the bodies of dead paupers from the Clerkenwell workhouse mortuary to the Great Northern Cemetery at Finchley broke down on Exmouth Street, Clerkenwell. According to some reports, five coffins – three of adults and two of children – then rolled into the road. An excited crowd gathered and remonstrated with the driver. He told them that the payments from the guardians were so low that he could not afford to take them to the cemetery one at a time, but had to wait until four or five were ready for burial. Further allegations emerged that the coffins were identified only by a name chalked on each of them and that during the journey the writing rubbed off. Although an investigation by a committee of guardians refuted the allegations, it was agreed that the union should acquire its own hearse, coach and horses for use at pauper funerals.

23 AUGUST 1931 The vagrants' ward at Leicester workhouse today had more than eighty casuals in residence, including a tramp named Thomas Fullerton. At dinner time, the labour superintendent instructed the assembled throng to remove their hats. All complied except Fullerton, who refused to do so. On being further ordered to uncover his head, he threw the plate containing his dinner at the officer, hitting him and damaging his uniform. Fullerton followed this up by kicking him. The next day, in court, the magistrate asked the man, 'Have you a religious objection to taking your hat off at meals?' Fullerton replied, 'It was just an idea of my own.' He was sentenced to fourteen days' imprisonment.

24 AUGUST 1856 Mary Lawson, a widow aged seventy years of age, an inmate of the Bradford Union workhouse, took her own life this morning by cutting her throat with a pair of scissors. The gash, about 4in long, had been inflicted in a most determined manner on the right side of the neck below the ear, resulting in almost instantaneous death. Another inmate, Mary Withers, observed blood flowing from beneath the privy door in the old women's yard. She pushed open the door and was horrified at finding Lawson sitting with her head thrown back and life extinct. The scissors, with string attached to them, were on her knee covered with blood. The deceased had been admitted into the workhouse two weeks previously, and was very low and dejected in her spirits.

25 AUGUST 1892 A meeting of the Southampton board of guardians today learned that the examiner's reports on boys' and girls' schools had considered them unsatisfactory. One of the guardians, Mr H. Kitcher, noted that at the boys' school, inmates had to get up at half-past five and work at scrubbing up to breakfast time, and then again until nine o'clock, with some then going into the school, and some into the tailor's shop. He thought the boys were fagged out before they got to the school, and that might account for the bad examination returns.

1897 On this day in 1897, following an inquest on an elderly inmate of Bethnal Green's Well Street workhouse who had died from the effects of an over-loaded stomach, the establishment was described as a pauper's paradise. The deceased, Thomas Fyfe, aged seventy, was the third inmate of the workhouse to have died in this manner. Keen to play down suggestions that paupers were being too well fed, work-house officials said that the man had a weak heart and could have died at any time from the least exertion. The extra food he had eaten was probably given to him by a fellow inmate who was unable to finish his own prescribed portion.

1912 Also on this day it was reported that a young woman, brought up in the Sedgefield workhouse and now in service, had asked to spend her fortnight's holiday at the workhouse. It appeared that the girl, an orphan, looked upon the institution as her real home.

26 AUGUST 1901 This morning, a labourer named Robert Hughes, aged forty-one, committed suicide in the Blackburn workhouse. Hughes, who was admitted to the lunacy ward in June, was seen apparently sleeping soundly in his bed at 3 a.m. Half an hour later he was missed, and a search by the attendants revealed that he had hanged himself with his braces in an outhouse. Hughes had returned from war service some months earlier, and entered the workhouse classified as a harmless imbecile. He became engaged to marry another inmate, and spent about £40 on preparations but, at the last moment, she changed her mind and a different inmate became his bride. When the bridegroom's savings were exhausted, the pair returned to the workhouse, where the romance ended with Hughes committing suicide.

27 AUGUST 1906 An inquest was held today into the death of Fanny Jane Hayball, who, following her escape from the Chard workhouse, had drowned herself in the town reservoir. The deceased, a lace mender, aged thirty-six, had been suffering from fits of melancholia. While visiting a doctor the previous Friday afternoon, her strange conduct had prompted him to send for Police Sergeant Attwood, who had taken her to the workhouse, pending her removal to the asylum. On the way there,

she asked him to cut her throat and kill her and, because he refused, she lay down and cried. The workhouse master declined to take responsibility for looking after the girl, but permitted her to be detained in the workhouse waiting-room, with a woman assigned to watch her. Later in the evening, Hayball became restless, and asked the woman to hang her. She eventually went to the toilet where she overpowered her keeper. She then made good her escape through a window and later drowned herself in the reservoir.

28 AUGUST 1891 The Revd Michael Arthur O'Meara, chaplain of the Barton Regis workhouse, Bristol, for the past seventeen years, committed suicide on this day. The Revd O'Meara, aged sixty-six, had been in bad health for some time and the guardians had recently granted him two months' leave to visit Ireland. His wife found him lying on his bedroom floor quite dead, having inflicted a fearful gash in his throat with a razor. He had written a note stating that he could endure life no longer.

1894 An inquest took place into the death of James Cooper, twenty-four, an imbecile patient at Bradford workhouse, who had died after being kicked in the stomach by a fellow inmate. Cooper, an inmate of the workhouse for about eight years, was said never to have worked and had suffered from fits since infancy. Another inmate, who acted as wardsman, said that on the previous Thursday evening he heard some 'fratching' going on on the steps leading from the imbecile day wards to the bedrooms. He had heard Cooper say to Patrick Scanlon, 'You must not touch "Dummy" again.' Cooper was sticking up for another man named James Killerby, who was deaf and dumb, and who always looked to Cooper as his friend. At this time, Cooper was two steps lower down on the stairs than Scanlon, and they were facing each other. Cooper was just about to turn round when Scanlon 'let out' with his foot and kicked him in the stomach. Cooper appeared to be severely hurt, and died three days later. Dr William Proctor, medical officer to the union, gave his opinion that the cause of death was peritonitis, due to external violence which could have been produced by a kick. The jury returned a verdict of manslaughter against Patrick Scanlon.

29 AUGUST 1838 An inquest was held today at Kingsland Road on the body of an old man named Phillips, an inmate of the Shoreditch workhouse, who committed suicide by cutting his throat. The man had apparently deliberately sharpened the knife with which he killed himself. It was said that he had previously been in good circumstances and that illness and poverty had preyed on his mind.

30 AUGUST 1805 After a visit to the workhouse at Bury in Lancashire, the philanthropist and prison reformer James Neild was far from impressed at what he had found. He criticised the use of a private contractor to run the establishment, a practice known as 'farming the poor'. There was no daily table of diet prescribed for the inmates. He discovered that there were twenty-eight children in the workhouse, who were in a state of nearly total ignorance, although several of them had spent fourteen years of their lives there.

31 AUGUST 1888 In the early hours, at a quarter to four or thereabouts, the body of woman was discovered in Buck's Row, Whitechapel, just a little way from the Whitechapel workhouse infirmary on Baker's Row. She was found lying on her back, legs straight out, and with her skirts raised to her waist. Her throat had been slashed from ear to ear and her neck severed back to the vertebrae. Her abdomen had been slashed and ripped, with one of the wounds extending from the base of the abdomen to the breastbone. The woman was soon identified as Mary Ann Nichols – the first generally accepted victim of the killer who became known as Jack the Ripper.

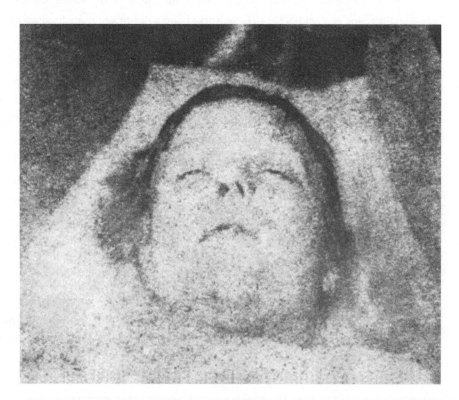

A mortuary photograph of Mary Ann Nicholls.

Nichols, aged forty-two at her death, had been a regular habituée of London's workhouses including ones at Lambeth, Mitcham and Edmonton. That list could now be said to include Whitechapel as her body was taken to the workhouse's nearby mortuary at Eagle Place, off Old Montague Street. It was also discovered that she had kept a 'souvenir' of her workhouse visits: her petticoats were stamped 'Lambeth Workhouse R.R.' – the establishment in question being located on Renfrew Road.

SEPTEMBER

Frantic attempts to evacuate children from the fire engulfing
Liverpool workhouse. (*See* 8 September)

1 SEPTEMBER 1850 It was reported today that two Penrith workhouse inmates, Felix Lough, a widower with three children, and Mary Jackson, a widowed mother of four, had recently eloped to Gretna Green. After discharging themselves from the workhouse, the couple – both of advancing years – had made the thirty-mile trip to Gretna on foot. On their arrival, they found that they lacked the means to pay the officiating priest, who demanded a fee of twenty times what cash they had. However, Felix Lough, in a most melancholy strain, explained that his wife was dead, as was Mary Jackson's husband, and that they were both paupers from Penrith workhouse. Then, becoming quite convulsed and letting flow a flood of tears over his wrinkled cheeks, in the most affecting manner exclaimed, 'For goodness sake do marry us, for Mary Jackson was the first sweetheart that I ever had, aye, long before I was married to my first poor wife, but then she would not have me; now she has consented to be my wife. Oh, do marry us!' 'Yes, yes, it is all true, do wed us,' said Mary Jackson. The priest was moved with compassion and he married them. Soon afterwards they set off on their return walk to Penrith, arriving there footsore and completely exhausted. Having no place to lay their heads, they applied to the relieving officer for assistance. The newly married couple were now spending their honeymoon back in the workhouse – apart from each other.

2 SEPTEMBER 1929 There was a lightning strike today by inmates at the Hamilton workhouse in Lanarkshire. A large number of male paupers refused to carry out their duties until several complaints and demands, one of which was for a putting green, had received attention. The governor summoned the police and about twenty inmates were expelled. The inmates complained that grievances already placed before the governor had not been put to the House Committee. They demanded that the inmates engaged as hospital warders should be provided with extra rations of tobacco, tea and sugar, and that heating apparatus should be installed in the wood factory.

3 SEPTEMBER 1863 At Beverley police court, six Irish labourers were charged with maliciously setting fire to the rugs and mattresses while spending a night in the vagrant ward of the Beverley Union workhouse. The damage was discovered by the master, Mr Hudson, when he went to let them out of their ward the next morning. He immediately locked the outer door to detain them until he had spoken to some of the guardians, but when he returned an hour later, the birds had flown. The case was at once put in the hands of Superintendent Pattinson of the borough police who, after making enquiries as to the road taken by the men, set off in hot pursuit with one of his men. Despite their having two hours start,

the officers eventually caught up and apprehended the fugitives some twenty miles away at Holme-on-Spalding-Moor. Each was sentenced to a month's imprisonment with hard labour.

4 SEPTEMBER 1837 A vicious attack was carried out today on Mr Jonathan Fielding, the elderly governor of the Prestwich workhouse, Manchester. The assailant, an inmate named Joseph Dennerley, had first entered the workhouse nine months earlier. A man of violent temper, he had frequently been disorderly and was regularly absent from the workhouse without permission. As a result the governor had taken him before the magistrates on five occasions, resulting in spells of imprisonment. Dennerley had frequently threatened revenge on the governor. At the start of his most recent three-week sentence, he was reported to have said, 'I'll make him shut his eyes before the month is up.'

Prior to the attack, Dennerley was engaged in weaving, and came into the dayroom where the governor was making some 'sough' – a paste used by weavers – in a pan on the fire. Dennerley picked up a drying iron, which was heating up in the fire, and struck the governor on the head. He then landed a second blow which knocked the old man to the floor. Looking down at the body, Dennerley exclaimed, 'I have killed him.' He then tried to make his escape but was apprehended and taken to the workhouse kitchen. There, he seized a kitchen knife which he drew across his throat, causing blood to flow. The knife was taken from him before he could inflict serious injury and he was placed in the workhouse dungeon. The master was given immediate medical attention but died five weeks later. Dennerley was tried for his murder but acquitted on the grounds of insanity and imprisoned for life.

Three months after the murder, the son of the deceased, also named Jonathan Fielding, committed suicide. A silk weaver by trade, he cut his throat with one of his own weaving tools and died five hours later. He was said to have been depressed following the death of his father. He had been married for just six months and his wife was carrying their first child.

5 SEPTEMBER 1836 At Lambeth Street magistrates, Thomas Prior, sixty-four, a cook in the workhouse of St Ann's, Limehouse, was today charged with administering arsenic to a female who was in a state of pregnancy by him, with a view to producing abortion.

Rhoda Meade, thirty-two, stated she had been an inmate of the workhouse for almost two years and assisted in the kitchen. About six months previously, an improper intimacy had taken place between Prior and herself, and she became pregnant. Prior told her she must take something to make her miscarry and gave her a bottle. On taking a spoonful of the mixture, which had a white sediment at the bottom, she became very ill and vomited a great deal, but recovered after attendance by the parish doctor. At Prior's request, she later took two further doses from the bottle, but none produced the desired effect.

Mr Warring, the parish beadle, produced a bottle matching Meade's description, which had been found in Prior's kitchen cupboard. He had also found some white powder wrapped in a paper marked 'Arsenic – poison'. Prior stated that he had bought the arsenic to kill black beetles and denied giving it to Meade. He had offered her something to drink, telling her that it might be poison and it was up to her whether she drank it or not.

At a subsequent hearing, the beadle produced a piece of root found in a further search of Prior's cupboard. Meade stated that the accused had boiled up a piece of the root then given her a spoonful of the liquid, telling her that it would cause miscarriage. He gave her the same thing on two further occasions, and each time it made her very ill, but did not produce the desired effect. Mr Burn, the parish surgeon, identified the root as hellebore, a strong vegetable poison. The substance might produce miscarriage by its violent effect on the system, but was very rarely administered internally. Prior said he had boiled down a part of the root for a lotion for a scorbutic condition with which he was troubled, and had told Meade she might try it if she liked, but that it was poison.

Prior was committed for trial at Newgate and subsequently sentenced to fourteen years' transportation.

6 SEPTEMBER 1902 This evening, Harriett Harrison Asgodby, aged thirty-four, assistant superintendent of nurses at Manchester's Crumpsall workhouse, was found in her bedroom with a handkerchief tied round her throat. Miss Girdlestone, the lady superintendent of the workhouse, found the body stretched face downwards on the floor near the bed. She noticed a silk handkerchief tied loosely round Asgodby's throat, and on removing it she found another handkerchief tied very tightly. Her face was very swollen and discoloured. The doctor was been summoned and tried artificial respiration, but without success. The handkerchief had to be cut before it could be removed. An inquest was told that the deceased was an efficient and experienced nurse and was usually of cheerful disposition, though subject to occasional fits of slight depression, which had become rather more marked during the recent months. A fortnight earlier she had made a will, but it contained nothing indicating that she intended to kill herself. The jury returned verdict of suicide whilst temporarily insane.

1904 Also on this day it was reported that, when requested to break a few stones, George Ablett, an able-bodied inmate of the West Ham workhouse, had declined, adding, 'They will have to be boiled first.' His joke cost him six weeks' hard labour.

7 SEPTEMBER **1895** Today's *Yorkshire Gazette* gave details of a letter that had recently been sent to the Auckland board of guardians by Watson Dickinson, a miner from Waterhouses. Its contents had given rise to some amusement:

> Having noticed that you have some orphan children and other class of people you want rid of from your Workhouse, I thought it a likely place to get a wife from. I am a respectable working man under forty years of age, a widower with no encumbrance, a good set-up house, a coal-hewer by trade, and want a wife, as I am completely sickened of housekeepers, having had no less than eighteen in as many months. If you can fit me up with a respectable lassy between thirty and fifty I would be glad, and would be glad to take an orphan girl into the bargain free of charge. I prefer a single woman before a widow, as widows won't do for me. I have no particular fancy to beauty; a plain girl will do for me, only she must be clean and industrious. If you have one please let me know and I will come with a trap and take her away free of charge to the Guardians. Let me know soon, please.

The letter was handed over to the workhouse master to deal with as he felt fit.

8 SEPTEMBER **1862** In the early hours of the morning, a devastating fire broke out at Liverpool's Brownlow Hill workhouse. The alarm was raised at about 2 a.m. when Miss Kennan, the schoolmistress, discovered dense smoke issuing from the windows of a children's dormitory. The workhouse governor, Mr Carr, at once ordered all the workhouse hoses to be readied and trained on the burning interior of the dormitory. Unfortunately, low water pressure limited their efficiency. The dormitory, some 50ft in length and running north and south, had staircases at its centre and southern end. The location of the fire, raging mainly at the centre of the structure, allowed inmates occupying the southern portion to be readily evacuated. Those at the northern end, however, had no means of escape despite valiant efforts to extricate them through the windows.

The following morning, the ruins presented a grim spectacle. The dormitory roof was completely destroyed, as were a large portion of the floor and central staircase. The parts of the floor which remained were covered with partially burned bedding among which lay the charred and disfigured remains of the victims of the flames. Some were horribly mutilated having been crushed by falling debris. In a row of fourteen iron bedsteads along one wall lay the fourteen bodies of lifeless children, charred and blackened and partially covered by roof fragments. Twenty-one children, all aged four to seven years, were burned to death or suffocated, together with two nurses.

9 SEPTEMBER 1846 An inquest was held at the Elephant and Castle Tavern, King's Road, into the death of Mary Anne Jones, aged nineteen, former inmate of St Pancras workhouse, whose body was found in the Regent's Canal. Fellow inmate Jane Dowling deposed that Jones had left the workhouse in June and, despite not having enough to eat, had sworn not to return there, lest she should be put into the 'shed' by Miss Stone, the matron. The shed, a dark room 26ft by 18ft, was a place of confinement where inmates were placed for misconduct and at that time had upwards of sixteen in it. Jones declared that she had been so ill-treated by Miss Stone, that rather than return to the 'house' she would drown or poison herself. Dowling said she herself had been in the workhouse five or six years, and had been kept in the shed for up to five months at a time, where inmates picked oakum and feathers. The workhouse also had a 'black hole' where she was once kept for forty-eight hours, having nothing to eat or drink but bread and water. The jury found that the deceased had drowned herself rather than return to the workhouse, being driven to distraction by the thought of the treatment to which she would be subjected in the shed.

10 SEPTEMBER 1866 The wife of Thomas Nichols, a rope-maker of Silkmill Place, Hackney Wick, today died from cholera in the Hackney workhouse infirmary. Later in the day, the second of his sons to succumb to the disease died in the German Hospital at Homerton. In the evening, his seven-year-old son Thomas was also discovered to have been attacked by cholera. The parish surgeon, Dr Vinall, was summoned and gave an order for the boy's immediate admission to the Hackney workhouse infirmary. At the workhouse gate, the matron, Mrs Driscoll, refused to admit the boy saying he should be taken to the German Hospital for treatment as his brother had been. The child, seated on a form in the gateway, kept vomiting and his skin turned a blue hue. Mr Oxley, a young assistant to the workhouse surgeon, tried to persuade the matron to relent as the night was cold and wet. The matron refused to give ground, even after the surgeon's deputy had issued an order to admit the boy to the workhouse's 'iron house' which was equipped for treating cholera cases and had empty beds. Mr Driscoll, the workhouse master, arrived on the scene and despite deterioration in the boy's condition, sent him in a cab to the German Hospital – where he died the next morning.

At a subsequent inquest, the jury decided that the boy's death had been accelerated by the delays at the workhouse gate and constituted an error of judgement by the master. The Poor Law Board also held an inquiry, but before they could deliver their conclusions, the Driscolls resigned, citing 'failing health superinduced by the late inquiries'.

11 SEPTEMBER 1927 John Henry Phipps, aged sixty-eight, an inmate of the Barrow-upon-Soar Union workhouse at Mountsorrel, was found in the grounds of the institution with a wound in his throat. He was carried to the workhouse infirmary but died the same evening. It was thought that his mind had become disturbed following the discovery, a few days earlier, of his younger brother hanging in the stables at Nanpantan Hall where he had been a groom for more than fifty years.

12 SEPTEMBER 1899 It was reported today that an aged couple, inmates in separate infirmary wards of Reading workhouse, had just celebrated their golden wedding anniversary. The husband, Edward Hague, was aged seventy-three, while his wife had seen ninety summers. They had been in the workhouse for almost a year, the old lady now being bedridden, while the husband, said to be fairly hearty, was 'as deaf as a post'. The Reading guardians had granted the couple special privileges for their celebration, with a small side ward being set aside for their use, and special food allowed them. The couple entertained their son, daughter, son-in-law and grandson during the afternoon and at tea.

1900 Also on this day, a jury at Canterbury returned a verdict of manslaughter against Walter Carter, an epileptic patient in the workhouse infirmary, who was seized with a fit and attacked James Wells, aged seventy-six, an inmate dying of senile decay. Carter pulled Wells out of bed and kicked him, leading to his death three hours later.

13 SEPTEMBER 1881 The Dudley board of guardians today began a public inquiry into allegations by the workhouse porter, Jesse Rushton, of irregularities, immorality and drunkenness among the officers and inmates of the institution. Rushton stated that he had seen the master, Joseph Rodgers, drunk in the house on many occasions. Another officer named Turner said that the master had swept ornaments off a mantelpiece in his room because he would not fetch him brandy. The master admitted that a man named Nupon entered the house as a tramp, but being found useful he had remained in residence for several years. A female inmate had become pregnant by Nupon and a child had been born. Rushton himself admitted that he and his friends had had private suppers and had drunk quarts of ale at the expense of the ratepayers.

A subsequent investigation by the Local Government Board uncovered many further irregularities: the accounts of the consumption of provisions in the house were kept in an improper and careless manner; there was improper consumption of provisions by the officers; the meals provided to the children did not follow the official dietary and were often deficient; the consumption of coal had been extravagant; inmates had been provided with beer; the master had admitted insobriety; there were no proper arrangements for the industrial training of the children; and there was no proper accommodation for the imbeciles. Much of the blame for these defects was placed on the guardians. It was also said that the overcrowding in the Dudley workhouse was worse than in any other in England and Wales.

14 SEPTEMBER 1877 A bizarre train of events began this evening when the master of Burton-on-Trent workhouse went in search of the establishment's porter. Not finding him at the lodge, he spoke to the schoolmistress who said that the man had recently spent the whole night under her window and the following morning accused her of having had the master in her rooms. The master then visited the schoolroom, at which point the porter's fist smashed through one of the window panes. The master asked him what he was doing there, to which the porter retorted by asking the master what he was doing with the schoolmistress alone in her private apartments. At a subsequent meeting of the House Committee, the porter claimed he had been paying his addresses to the schoolmistress for two years and that they were engaged to be married. After the master had taken the schoolmistress to a recent agricultural show in Burton, he had been watching their conduct. The schoolmistress said that she was astonished to hear of the alleged engagement. If she wished to get married, the porter would be the last man she would choose. Under her questioning, the porter admitted that she had never even shaken hands with him and had scarcely ever spoken to him in her life. He added, however, that they would make a very happy couple if they were married. The committee concluded that the porter had either invented his claim or was labouring under a delusion. On being told that his services were no longer required, he left the room still persisting in the truth of his statements.

15 SEPTEMBER 1887 At two this morning, a fire was discovered in the laundry of the workhouse at Killarney, County Kerry. The master and inmates at once set to work to contain the blaze, with assistance soon being rendered by the military and constabulary and a party from the nearby county asylum. Fortunately, the night was calm and the fire was confined to the laundry, which was totally destroyed. Following recent malicious damage to the workhouse garden, the fire was suspected of having

been deliberately caused, arising from a refusal by the authorities to give out-relief and recent prosecutions for the adulteration of milk.

1900 On this day it was reported that the Holbeach workhouse in Lincolnshire had been taking in paying guests. Because of the shortage of cheap lodging-house accommodation in the town, the master was providing overnight hospitality for a fee of fourpence per night. This was brought to the notice of the guardians who condemned the practice, but the master explained that he had had to accommodate a man with 12s in his possession who could not obtain a bed elsewhere. One member of the board suggested they should make a charge of 1s per night, but it was decided to instruct the master only to admit casuals, and, in the event of money being found upon them, to appropriate it towards the cost of the hospitality provided, according to the regulations of the Local Government Board.

16 SEPTEMBER **1796** At around midday, a devastating fire began in the workhouse at the small village of East Witton, in the North Riding of Yorkshire. The flames rapidly spread to adjoining buildings, most of which were covered with thatch. This, coupled with a strong wind, and occurring at a time when most of the inhabitants were in the fields reaping, meant that the fire burnt with an irresistible fury. In the course of a few hours about a dozen families were totally ruined with the destruction of sixteen dwelling-houses and outbuildings, and a large quantity of corn and farming utensils, all of which were uninsured.

17 SEPTEMBER **1853** In London's East End this morning, a young woman was walking in Victoria Park when she suddenly fell to the ground in an exhausted condition. The police on duty outside the park gates were called, and carried her to the Bethnal Green workhouse at Bonner's Fields where she partially recovered and asked permission to go into the yard. After the woman had been gone some considerable time, the suspicions of the servants were aroused and one of them went in search of her. They discovered the woman lying in front of the seat, utterly exhausted. A search was made in the soil, where the body of a newly born male child was found with bruises around its head. The body was quite warm, and there were two cuts on the face. A surgeon called to examine the body said it was fully developed, and he had no doubt it had been born alive.

1894 Jeremiah O'Mahony, an inmate of the Skibbereen workhouse, County Cork, committed suicide by hanging himself from a tree. It was thought that the man had become depressed after being diagnosed with some incurable disease.

1922 A romance at Poplar workhouse resulted today in the wedding of inmates Eliza Dobbins, aged sixty-nine, and Harry Green, seventy-one. The streets from the workhouse to Poplar Parish Church were crowded with people heartily cheering the bride and groom. The bride was dressed in a blue silk frock and black hat, and walked to the altar on the arm of the Mayor of Poplar, Mr Charles Sumner, who gave her away. She was attended by Miss Sybil Harris and Master Geoffrey Harris, the godchildren of the matron. The bridegroom was attended by Alderman David Adams who acted as best man. After the service they travelled by car to the workhouse, where they were met by pipers and drummers. A reception was held in the boardroom, followed by a wedding breakfast provided by the matron. The health of the bride and bridegroom was toasted in whisky sent by friends, and afterwards Mr and Mrs Green entertained a few friends in their new married quarters in the workhouse.

18 SEPTEMBER 1895 It was reported today that the Plymouth board of guardians had received a letter from a gentleman at Torquay, inquiring whether the guardians would assist him in finding a wife. He stated that he wanted a woman between twenty-four and thirty years of age, slim and passably good-looking, but he did not care what her religious creed was, so long as she was respectable. The letter concluded, 'Please grant me permission to go over the workhouse on any visiting day and select a wife for myself. It will be one woman less on the rates of Plymouth, my native town. I will leave the matter in your hands, as I would rather have a poor woman from the workhouse than one who required no sympathy.' The letter was referred to the chairman of the House Committee.

19 SEPTEMBER 1926 A disturbance was caused in a men's ward at the West Ham workhouse late this evening. Lights in a large dormitory were suddenly turned on and the inmates started singing. The doors were barricaded, and mugs, mats, bowls and other crockery were flung from the windows. The fire hose had also been used. The police were sent for and the three men who were the ringleaders were arrested. They later received sentences of fourteen days' hard labour.

20 SEPTEMBER 1888 Chesterfield workhouse was today the venue for the inquest on Joseph Mulline, aged sixty-two, who had become an inmate of the institution on the previous Monday. Two days later, Mulline, who was afflicted with partial paralysis, was having his dinner and began coughing and choking. Despite the efforts of those around him, he died before the arrival of medical assistance. The jury found that the deceased had died from suffocation while attempting to swallow a piece of beef or potato.

21 **SEPTEMBER** **1895** At the
Bodmin workhouse, recently connected to the mains water supply, members of the town fire brigade gave the
board of guardians a demonstration
of how any fire could now be dealt
with. A discussion followed concerning a letter from the Local Government Board, asking whether provision for inmates escaping in the case
of fire had been made in accordance
with a recent inspection report. The
Board resolved to reply that certain
internal rearrangements, coupled
with the new water supply, made
any further provision unnecessary.
A resolution to purchase a 'jumping
sheet' was lost by a large majority.

Edward Aigstrop's drunken assault on
Mary Brinsley.

1870 A shocking assault took place today at St Giles's
workhouse. An inmate named Mary Brinsley was sitting in the yard when the porter,
Edward Aigstrop, with whom she was on friendly terms, beckoned to her. She went up
a flight of steps to him and he asked her to have a drink with him. She saw that he had
already been drinking and refused. He then asked her to fetch some beer. When she
refused to do this and laughed at him, he struck her in the eye – her only eye, the other
having already been lost. Another inmate saw that the eye was bleeding, and went to tell
the governor who took Brinsley to the doctor. The eye appeared to be completely gouged
out. At a subsequent magistrate's hearing, an eye specialist who had examined the eye,
said that the lower part of the eyeball had a deep cut about an inch in length. Although
the wound had healed and she had a little sight, it was getting worse and a cataract
was forming. Aigstrop admitted having been drinking. He said that when Brinsley had
laughed at him, he had hit her with the back of the hand, not meaning to hurt her.
The magistrate committed him for trial.

22 **SEPTEMBER** **1896** The magistrates at Cromer in Norfolk committed for
trial, for attempted suicide, Frederick Cripps, hairdresser, who had been found in the
sea off Sheringham, clasped in the arms of his wife who had drowned. Both were fully
dressed at the time. Cripps, aged fifty-two, who appeared very ill and dazed, said he

was truly sorry. His wife had suggested they commit suicide together for, their means being exhausted, she could not endure the idea of the workhouse.

1880 On this day a shocking occurrence at the Louth Union workhouse, Lincolnshire, resulted in the death of one of the inmates. Amongst those in the workhouse sick ward were two men named George Robinson, aged about forty, and William Chapman, aged sixty-four. The previous night, a quarrel had taken place between the two, but at bedtime all was quiet. In the morning, however, the dispute was resumed. A fight took place, and pair struggled until completely exhausted. Chapman was knocked down and fell heavily on the floor, his head coming in contact

The fight between George Robinson and William Chapman which resulted in Robinson's death.

with a bedstead and the skin being peeled off his face. Robinson then staggered to a chair but died a few minutes afterwards. An inquest found that Robinson had suffered from heart disease and the violent exertion had resulted in his death.

1906 Also on this day, the Pontefract guardians had a lively discussion as to whether women should smoke, and decided that smoking be allowed only under medical direction.

23 SEPTEMBER **1881** Margaret Johnstone, aged thirty-five, an inmate of the South Dublin workhouse, was killed in a quarrel with another inmate, Anne Taylor, who slept in the same ward. At 7 p.m. they were locked up for the night by the ward mistress, Mrs Hoey. Half an hour later, while Mrs Hoey was away having her tea, an alarm was raised in the ward with screams and loud knocking on the door. The door was burst in and Johnstone was found dead on the floor lying in a pool of blood with a deep wound in her throat and a knife beside her. Mary Wilson, an inmate who had come in from an adjacent ward after hearing the commotion, later told a court hearing, 'I put my hand on Maggie Johnstone's neck, and my fingers went into a little hole in her neck (indicating close to the jugular vein). This knife (producing a black-hafted table-knife) was lying beside the dead woman, who was lying on the floor with her feet to the door.' Taylor was subsequently charged with Johnstone's murder.

24 SEPTEMBER **1847** Details appeared today of the experiences of a poor woman named Mary Catheray at the Hull workhouse. The woman, in an advanced state of pregnancy and accompanied by her ten-year-old daughter, had come to Hull from Leeds to meet her husband who, with the couple's four other children, had travelled there some days earlier to seek work. The mother, being taken ill on the journey, had been directed with her daughter to the Hull workhouse, known as Charity Hall. She had seen two men and told them she was poorly. According to Catheray, one accused her of being a liar, while the other told them to go to the vagrant office, elsewhere in the building. A man named Short was called and took the two upstairs, saying 'It's such b—rs as you comes to impose on folks.' He then threw her down on the floor two or three times, severely cutting her elbow. The little girl began to cry and said, 'Mother, don't let us stop here or they will kill us.' They then left Charity Hall and went into West Street when the mother went into labour at the door of Mr Foster, a rag dealer. Three passing ladies helped her inside and, shortly afterwards, she gave birth to a son just inside the door. Short was later fined 10s for assault.

25 SEPTEMBER 1928 Three casual inmates of the Boston workhouse in Lincolnshire were in court today, charged with refusing to perform their allotted labour task. The trio had instigated a revolt involving thirty-five inmates, all complaining that their gruel was not fit to eat. The medical officer had been called to examine the gruel and pronounced it perfectly wholesome, though slightly discoloured. Apart from the three charged, the inmates had then resumed their work of sawing wood for two hours. William Bennett, the ringleader of the revolt, received a month's hard labour, while his accomplices, George Bennett and John McQueen, were each given twenty-one days'.

26 SEPTEMBER 1842 At around nine o'clock in the evening, William Skipper attempted to set fire to the St Faith's Union workhouse near Norwich. Skipper, who had been an inmate of the workhouse until earlier the same day, used a lucifer match to set alight a 5-ton stack of straw standing near a few yards from the establishment but the building was undamaged.

27 SEPTEMBER 1893 Henry Cressell, an old man known as the 'Islington workhouse lawyer' because of his readiness to take workhouse officials to court, began proceedings against Robert Musto, master, and Alfred Edwin Lee, storekeeper, at the St John's Road workhouse, where he was an inmate. Cressell alleged that after complaining that the soup given him for dinner was more like bone-liquor than pea soup, he had been dragged from his place in the dining hall by the two men, rushed down the corridor, his head banged against the wall and rapped on the knuckles by the master, and had then been thrown bodily into the yard. In reply, the master said that Cressell was noisy and insolent and had to be taken out of the dining hall for the purposes of discipline. The magistrate, Mr Bros, who had earlier visited the workhouse and seen the dinners which were being served, said there might have been some cause for the complaint of the soup being improperly cooked, but the materials were good, and the food he had seen himself was certainly good. He concluded that the master was justified in putting the man out of the dining hall and dismissed the case. A few months later, it was reported that Cressell was departing on a free passage to Australia in order to avoid a pauper's grave.

28 SEPTEMBER 1867 The *Illustrated London News* recorded the opening of the new casual wards at St Marylebone workhouse, which provided a night's accommodation for tramps and vagrants. After first visiting a local police station to gain a ticket of admission, new arrivals were washed with plenty of hot water and soap, then given a supper of 6 ounces of bread and a pint of gruel. They were then

The coffin-like beds provided at St Marylebone workhouse for what were officially referred to as 'the houseless poor'.

issued with a warm woollen nightshirt and sent to bed, with their own clothes cleansed and fumigated overnight. In the dormitory, whose walls were adorned with the Ten Commandments and other scriptural texts, inmates slept in narrow 'bunks' just above the floor, and separated by partitions just high enough to prevent the intermingling of the breaths of the occupants of adjacent berths. After rising at 6 a.m., and a breakfast similar to the previous day's supper, up to four hours work was required, with the women with being set to clean the wards or pick oakum, while the men broke stones. 'A board of Good Samaritans could do no more', the paper concluded.

29 SEPTEMBER 1908 A scandal which had brought unwelcome publicity to Cumberland's Longtown workhouse was brought to a conclusion today at a meeting of the Longtown guardians. The affair had begun when the workhouse master, Thomas Murray, intercepted a parcel addressed to the workhouse nurse, Margaret Jeffrey. The parcel, which was sent by a male inmate of the workhouse named Dallas, had contained a bottle of whisky and a letter addressed to 'My darling Maggie'. The master

claimed that he had read the letter because it contained objectionable references to himself, and he had intercepted the whisky because the regulations provided 'that the master must prevent spirituous liquors being sent to inmates.' He later brought serious allegations about the conduct of Nurse Jeffrey and Dallas before the guardians. An inquiry by the Local Government Board concluded that the master's actions had been 'unwise and reprehensible' and advised him to resign, which he now did. The inquiry had also discovered that Nurse Jeffrey's appointment had never been reported to the Board and that she had never provided any testimonials as to her nursing qualifications. Accordingly, Miss Jeffrey also resigned.

30 SEPTEMBER 1927 Following the poisoning of thirty inmates at the Fulham workhouse, three of whom had died after a meal of corned beef, the Fulham guardians were today reported to be putting sausages on the workhouse menu in its place. At a meeting of the board, one member suggested that sausages were even more mysterious in their contents than corned beef. An investigation was being made to find out which was the more suitable food.

OCTOBER

A sparsely furnished dormitory at the Cootehill Union workhouse in County Cavan. The bedding – blankets and a straw-filled mattress and pillow – was rolled back against the wall during the days and the beds used as seats. The 'squalor and wretchedness' of the place led visitors from the *British Medical Journal* to call for the workhouse to be closed down. (*See* 12 October)

1 OCTOBER 1890 An inquest took place today into the death of Bristol workhouse inmate Elizabeth Clevely, who had hanged herself. Fellow pauper Rose Philips, who slept in the same room as the deceased, said that on the previous Sunday night, Clevely had been complaining of sleeplessness. When Philips woke up the next morning, she saw Clevely's bed empty. She immediately opened the door and found the woman hanging from the ceiling. Helen Jones, nurse at the workhouse, said that she heard that Clevely was hanging in the passage and hurried to the spot and cut the woman down. She was hanging by a round towel, and had some bandages round her neck. She was quite dead when cut down. Other witnesses stated that Clevely had attempted her life twice, once by hanging from a beam in the hospital kitchen, and a second time with a knife. Dr Henry Grace, workhouse medical officer, testified that he had certified Clevely as insane but the Bristol magistrates had refused to consign her to an asylum. The inquest jury found that the deceased committed suicide whilst of unsound mind, and also considered that the magistrates had committed a grave error in judgment in not sending her to the asylum.

2 OCTOBER 1894 At Lincoln City Police Court, John Seymour, a labourer from Grimsby, was charged with setting fire to woodsheds at the Lincoln Union workhouse in the early hours of 21 September. The sheds, used to store firewood chopped by male inmates, had contained about 33,000 bundles at the time of the fire, of which 17,600 had been destroyed or damaged.

A typical workhouse wood-chopping shed.

Seymour, who had entered the workhouse casual ward on several occasions, had made a statement confessing to the crime. After hearing the police evidence, he asked, 'Has it done much damage?' After being told that it had burnt most of the bundles of firewood, he replied, 'That's a good job, too. There's a good many men working there for nothing, and it prevents people getting a living outside.'

3 OCTOBER 1900 A terrible tragedy was discovered at Manchester's Crumpsall workhouse, this morning. During the night, George Pescott, twenty-six, an attendant in the imbecile ward, had become annoyed with the noisy behaviour of an inmate named Francis Southgate who suffered from 'general paralysis of the insane' – a form of dementia associated with advanced stages of syphilis. In an effort to subdue him, Pescott had knelt on Southgate's chest and held his throat, while a second attendant named Hirst held the man's legs. Another inmate, James Tattersall, said that Hirst had whispered to Pescott, 'You've done enough.' The struggle later resumed and Tattersall was instructed by Pescott to hand him a towel which he then twisted around Southgate's neck. At about 3 a.m. Pescott again applied the towel when, according to Tattersall, Southgate said, 'I've had enough, Mr Pescott, you'll hear about this.' Pescott then tightened the twist in the towel with the aid of a poker. There was a gurgling sound and Pescott removed the towel and went away. Coming back to look, he exclaimed, 'Good God! The man is dead. I'll go for the doctor.' As they lifted Southgate onto his bed, he was 'drawing his last'. An inquest on Southgate was told that he had died of asphyxiation. He also had damage to his larynx and a bone in his throat, together with a total of thirty-four scars on his legs, chin and cheek. Southgate was later convicted of manslaughter and was sentenced to seven years' penal servitude. It emerged at his trial that the workhouse housed 120 certified lunatics because the county asylum had no room for them. The workhouse had no padded room and violent lunatics were restrained by tying their wrists and ankles to their beds using ordinary bedsheets.

4 OCTOBER 1850 Some remarkable revelations were made at today's meeting of the St Marylebone guardians. First, during a recent absence of the chaplain and his deputy, one of the paupers had been ordered by the master of the workhouse to don the reverend gentleman's surplice and to conduct an entire service. It was said that there had been much giggling by other inmates during the proceedings. The chaplain, Mr Moody, appeared very indignant that any notice had been taken of the matter. The other disclosure was that carrier pigeons had been kept in the workhouse. It seems that the late master had regularly employed them to receive early news of the winning horses at Goodwood and Epsom, and to place bets accordingly.

He had been a great better, and was said to have died with a betting-book in his hand. An extensive system of gambling was said to have prevailed in the workhouse. It was also revealed that a vestryman, who had no claim whatever to the birds, had caught and sold them, keeping the entire proceeds for himself.

1870 On this day a meeting of the Neath Union guardians was told that the water supply to the workhouse was inadequate and, in consequence, some of the cooking was done using water drawn from the adjacent canal.

5 OCTOBER 1838 At about two o'clock this afternoon, some inmates at the Greenwich workhouse were removing some oakum from in front of an understairs cupboard when they became aware of a sickening smell emanating from inside. On opening the cupboard doors, they discovered the body of Thomas Robinson, a pauper who had been missing for ten days. It was in an advanced state of decomposition. The head was lying on a coil of rope with a large pool of blood underneath, and was nearly severed from the body. Nearby was a 6-inch razor with which the act had been committed. An inquest was later told that when Robinson, aged sixty-three, had gone missing, he was assumed to have absconded – a common occurrence at the workhouse. He had been a well-liked man, who never quarrelled, though had appeared dejected in recent weeks. At his last meeting with his son, at the workhouse gate, Robinson had burst into tears saying, 'I shall never see you again.'

6 OCTOBER 1894 The *Ipswich Journal* today reported a serious allegation of neglect against the master of the Ipswich workhouse, following the death in the workhouse infirmary of James McDermott, a forty-nine-year-old army pensioner. An inquest heard that McDermott, a regular heavy drinker, had occasionally been allowed to sleep overnight in the cells at the police station. However, on the evening of 29 September, his physical condition was such that one of the union medical officers, Mr Elliston, had directed him to be removed to the workhouse infirmary. After McDermott arrived at the workhouse, the master, Mr Henry Sidney, had decided that he was just suffering from the effects of drink and so detained him for a day in an unheated receiving ward without medical attention. Another inmate stated that during the night, McDermott had not slept at all and was so ill that his head had to be raised during fits of violent coughing. On 2 October, the workhouse medical officer, Mr Staddon, had discovered McDermott's situation and ordered his immediate removal to the infirmary but he died there four hours later. A post-mortem by Dr Brogden revealed the cause of death to be chronic pneumonia. The jury returned a verdict of 'death from natural causes' but that the master had been guilty of dereliction of duty in his dealing with McDermott.

7 **OCTOBER 1836** William Horseman, a long-standing inmate of the workhouse of St Paul's, Covent Garden, was charged at Bow Street magistrates of illicitly smuggling spirits into the establishment. The gatekeeper, Peter Attwell, said that on the occasion in question, suspecting Horseman had spirits concealed upon his person, he had searched him and found a flat stone bottle containing a quarter pint of rum, hidden between his shirt and waistcoat. Horseman told the magistrate that he was troubled with a very bad cold and asthma and took the rum to merely mix with hot water and sugar to ease his complaints. Attwell stated that when Horseman had left the workhouse earlier that day, he had warned him not to bring back spirits. He believed he had done so previously from having observed the inmates in an intoxicated state from the use of spirits which could only have been supplied by the accused. The workhouse master stated that Horseman acted as a messenger for the paupers and was allowed out occasionally. He was generally a very orderly, well-conducted man. Horseman was fined 10s, in default of which he would spend seven days in the House of Correction.

8 **OCTOBER 1889** Details were reported today of a daring robbery at the workhouse in Hull. A young man named William Lancaster was charged with having induced another inmate, a boy named Alfred Pearson, to steal a purse containing nine £5 notes, £14 in gold, and 10s in silver, from a cupboard at the workhouse. The money was the property of George Johnson, the institution's baker and cook. Johnson testified that he habitually left his coat in a cupboard of the bread-room when he arrived in the morning. Lancaster, being aware of this, persuaded Pearson to steal the purse if ever he found there was more than £7 in it, and gave the boy a key which fitted the cupboard. After the purse went missing, the police were called and interrogated the boy who confessed what had happened. Lancaster had first told him to bury the purse in a woodshed, then later to hide it somewhere further away. Lancaster had said he would discharge himself, and then change the notes at Leeds, but would return and share the money with Pearson. He had also told the boy they would be able to buy tools with which they would commit burglaries. After Lancaster's arrest, he said, 'This lot will about do me; I'll put a knife into his young guts if I ever have a chance; I'll be hanged for him.' He was later sentenced to fifteen months in prison.

9 **OCTOBER 1847** Today's *Northern Star* reported great excitement in Bolton at rumours that John Rothwell, aged seventy-two, an inmate of the workhouse, had been flogged to death by one of the male nurses. At an inquest into Rothwell's death, fellow inmate James Rostron testified that Rothwell had been afflicted with dysentery and was moved into the workhouse infirmary where the nurse, Henry Bicknell, was in the habit of beating the inmates with a whip. Once, when Rothwell had refused to go to bed, Bicknell had said if he did not go, he would make him. He fetched his whip and beat Rothwell's legs, then struck his ribs and back with the butt end. Rothwell, who was wearing only a shirt at the time, got into bed and cried out 'Murder!', upon which Bicknell got hold of a sheet, and tied it over his mouth to prevent him being heard. A few days later, at about two in the morning, Bicknell beat him again to get him into bed, but when Rothwell refused he struck him several times over the temples, making him fall on the floor. Mr Sharp, the surgeon, said that a post-mortem indicated that the cause of death was dysentery, but he considered the conduct of the nurse towards the deceased was most brutal. The jury recorded 'their abhorrence of the brutal and inhuman conduct of Bicknell' and recommended his immediate dismissal.

1926   Samuel Rowe, Exeter's premier glass smasher, who on nearly 150 occasions had been the central figure in police cases, was back in prison today, this time for two months. In his latest escapade, 'Sammy the Smash' had broken another pane of glass at his customary haunt, Milk Street lavatories, waited for a constable, and later told magistrates that he preferred prison to the workhouse, the former he thought having improved, while the latter 'was getting worse'.

10   OCTOBER   **1882**   At Nottingham police court today, Edward Robson Morley, formerly clerk to the Nottingham guardians, was charged with having embezzled sums of £39 and two sums of £3 5s. In 1874, an imbecile woman named Emma Reynolds had been an inmate of the workhouse, when she was found to be entitled to the interest of £130 under her father's will. She signed an authority to Morley to receive the money, to be disposed of as he thought best. Morley induced Edward Cryer, brother and trustee of Reynolds, to pay him the sum of £39 for his sister's maintenance, and later to forward £3 5s each half-year in part payment. Out of the £39, £7 had been spent in travelling expenses and in legal charges; but the remainder was unaccounted for, as were the two sums of £3 5s. Morley did not deny the receipt of the money, but said that it was taken without felonious intention. At his subsequent trial, Morley was found not guilty as no evidence was produced that the money in question had been disposed of improperly. Three years later, Morley was found guilty of a charge that while still employed by the guardians he had obtained money by forging a letter purporting to come from the then chairman of the board.

11   OCTOBER   **1909**   Reports appeared today of a mystery surrounding the deaths of three inmates of the Hemel Hempstead workhouse after they had all been bathed on the same day. The first fatality was a fifty-four-year-old man named Howells, who

expired twenty minutes after bathing. He was said to have been in the terminal stages of consumption, and had needed carrying to the bathroom. He had been an inmate of the workhouse for a fortnight and had no known relatives. Edward Almond, who died six hours after being given his bath, had been suffering from broncho-pneumonia. He was fifty-six, and had a brother living in the locality. The third of the victims was a man named Adams who had died four days after the bath, following which a haemorrhage had occurred. He was aged sixty-eight and had been suffering from bronchitis. It later emerged that the bathing had been carried out by the workhouse porter, Herbert Goodson, without the presence of a nurse as regulations required. The temperature of the bath in each case had been 89.5 degrees, which the workhouse medical officer claimed was well below the minimum of 98 degrees that he had laid down. Overall responsibility for bathing inmates was, however, in the hands of Nurse May Bellamy, whom an inquest found to be guilty of culpable negligence. Bellamy was committed to trial for manslaughter but later acquitted of the charge.

12 OCTOBER 1895 As part of its campaign to improve the nursing and administration in Irish workhouses, the *British Medical Journal* today published a report from its Commissioners following their visit to the workhouse at Cootehill, County Cavan. They were dismayed by the 'squalor and wretchedness' that greeted their eyes as they toured the buildings. The aged inmates' quarters were particularly grim:

> The rooms were dirty, the patients were unkempt and unwashed, and as the only materials that we saw for the toilet were a tin basin and a dirty round towel this was not to be wondered at... There are no indoor conveniences, and that the privies are at some distance from the wards, and therefore unavailable in bad weather or at night; to meet this difficulty the old people are provided with open pails or buckets; in the sick wards these buckets are enclosed in a wooden chair. It must also be observed that the infirm wards are locked on the outside from 7 p.m. until 6.30 a.m. The greater part of that time the ward is in darkness, and the only assistance available is such as the inmates can render to each other. The pails remain unemptied until the morning in both the sick and the infirm wards. We pictured to ourselves these wards locked up, the windows closed to husband the feeble warmth of the stove; the inmates on their narrow beds, from which they may slip to the floor in their weakness and there remain until the morning; the filthy-smelling buckets, some doubtless upset in the dark; no water to be had, no help available except in case of dire need; we turned away sick at heart that such things should be. In the sick wards the nurse is at hand, but there is no

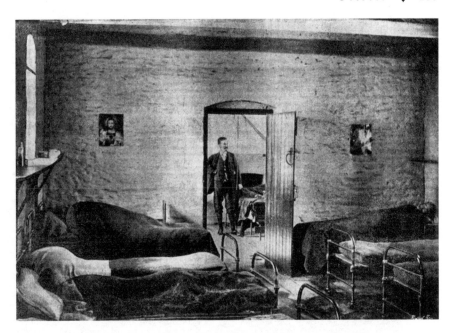

The miserable interior of an infirmary ward at the Cootehill workhouse.

night nurse, and the excreta of the sick poison the air in those crowded wards. In the lunatic wards the same unsavoury method prevails, and the well-known dirty habits of the feeble-minded add to the foulness of the surroundings.

13 OCTOBER 1886 At the Toxteth workhouse today, an inquest was held on the body of John Kenington, a painter by trade, aged forty-nine. On the previous Friday he had attended the stoneyard opened by the guardians for the relief of the distress in Toxteth. George Patterson, who had been working alongside Kenington, said he had seen him breaking a large stone on the top of his pile, and splinters were flying about. He heard Kenington cry out and, thinking something serious was the matter, went up to him. Seeing some blood, he lifted up his chin and saw a wound from which blood was gushing as if coming from a leaky pipe. One of the men in the yard brought a handkerchief to hold against the wound. Dr Smart, the workhouse medical officer, who was quickly on the scene, said the wound was a very deep one. It was dressed immediately, and the man seemed to progress favourably, but at about 4 a.m. on Monday morning, he had found him almost pulseless, and saw him die shortly afterwards. A post-mortem revealed a large clot of blood about the size of a small orange behind the windpipe, and another clot of blood at the entrance to the windpipe, almost blocking it up. Suffocation from the pressure of this clot on the windpipe was the cause of death.

Blood pours from the neck of John Kenington (centre left) after a shard of the stone he was breaking punctured a major vessel in his neck.

14 OCTOBER 1904 Three men appeared at the Sligo Petty Sessions following a violent incident at the Sligo workhouse. One of the inmates, named Rooney, had made a brutal assault on a feeble man called Mulhall, throwing him on a bed, pulling out half his beard, and nearly choking him. Mulhall had retaliated by stabbing Rooney in the head with a bread knife. Two other able-bodied inmates named Farrell and McTernan refused to interfere, and Rooney was finally overpowered by workhouse officials. In Rooney's defence, it was said that he had refused to eat his soup at dinner, as it was made from water in a tank in which a number of rats had been drowned, and Mulhall had mocked him. The magistrates sentenced Farrell and McTernan to seven days' imprisonment with hard labour. For his assault on Mulhall, Rooney also received seven days.

15 OCTOBER 1894 A man named James Mariano Williams applied this evening for admission to the Lewisham workhouse. It was not his first experience of the establishment. After a previous stay a few months earlier, Williams, a former journalist, had published an unfavourable description of the dying moments of inmates in the workhouse infirmary, leading to criticism of the establishment by the Local Government Board. His latest admission was to prove equally controversial.

Williams claimed that he received no supper and at 9 a.m. the next morning was given gruel and dry bread but was by then too ill to eat. The master had said to him, 'I think I have seen your face before. As you are so ready with your pen you shall not pick oakum or break stones, but I will give you some writing to do.' The medical officer then examined Williams and certified him as a lunatic, whereupon he was transferred to the lunatic ward where he was, he said, subjected to the ravings of a dying man. The next day, according to Williams, he was dragged from his sick bed, and forcibly removed to the Cane Hill lunatic asylum, although the medical staff there could find no trace of insanity in him. His subsequent complaints about his treatment resulted in a lengthy inquiry by the Local Government Board where it was revealed that he drank alcohol to excess, had talked about killing himself, and had been sleeping rough prior to entering the workhouse. In their report, the Board concluded that the workhouse officers had acted in good faith and with due care in dealing with Williams.

16 OCTOBER 1882 An inquest took place today at the Sunderland workhouse concerning the death two days earlier of James Reay, aged eleven, an inmate of the workhouse industrial school. On the morning before his demise, Reay had complained of feeling unwell. He was suffering from a headache and was sick. He was put to bed but did not remain there and his condition was not considered serious enough to send for the doctor. That evening, he went to bed in the usual way and a light was left burning. He was heard to cough during the night but not visited. At around 5.45 a.m. he was found dead in his bed. A post-mortem indicated that the boy had a defective development of the left lung from birth which caused a strain on his heart and he might have died suddenly at any time. The jury recommended that a medical officer should be consulted at once under similar circumstances in the future.

17 OCTOBER 1878 A meeting of the board of guardians at Listowel, County Kerry, today heard allegations by the workhouse chaplain, the Revd Mr Moynihan, that a pregnant inmate named Bessie Flavin had been offered money to conceal the identity of the child's father. Father Moynihan said he had visited Flavin in the workhouse and asked her how she came to be there. She said she was pregnant by a man named Howard. Being suspicious from the doubtful manner of her reply, he had asked her to tell him the truth. She confided that she had recently been taken by the workhouse master into the surgery where the acting medical officer, Dr Gentleman, awaited her. On being left alone with him, he had offered her £10 to conceal the name of the real father and invent some other. She had consented to this and signed an agreement. The man who had seduced her was, in

fact, a local bank clerk named Shanahan. An inquiry by the Local Government Board decided that, due to Flavin's background and the 'discrepancy in her evidence, compared with that of the respectable and well conducted officers of the workhouse' they could not place much reliance on her allegations.

1902 It was reported today that Sir William Gordon Macgregor, a baronet, had been admitted to the West Ham workhouse at Leytonstone. The old man – actually only fifty-six, but his silvery hair and beard making him look older – was said to be suffering from locomotor ataxy and was an inmate of the workhouse infirmary. Sir William had for a long time been 'something in the City' and was innocently associated with a gang of swindlers over 'bucketshop' frauds and the 'Jubilee Syndicate' swindle in 1897 when his name was used on their circular without his knowledge. In more recent times, he had depended upon a weekly allowance from a relative, who had now died. The publicity given to his presence in the workhouse led to many offers of marriage, and in March 1903 it was reported that the 'pauper baronet' had left the workhouse and had married a rich American woman. In fact he first became betrothed to a wealthy Bristol woman then, when she changed her mind about the matter, instead married her sister, a Miss Alice Gulliver, in a register office adjacent to the workhouse.

18 OCTOBER **1890** A serious explosion occurred at the Ballinasloe Union workhouse, County Galway, while the master was searching in his room for an escape of gas with a lighted match. Much damage was done to the workhouse, with the door of a chapel some 50 yards away being broken. The master and porter were severely injured, the latter receiving a fracture of the skull from which he was not expected to recover.

19 OCTOBER **1867** On this day, Poor Law Inspector Mr R.B. Cane paid his first visit to the Kirkheaton workhouse, one of the four institutions then being operated by the Huddersfield Union. The elderly premises did not impress Mr Cane, who described it as 'wholly insufficient in every respect.' The male residents comprised two men and sixteen boys who all shared eight beds in two small rooms. Six women, twenty-one girls, and two infants occupied thirteen beds in another part of the house. Two of the elder girls, affected by incontinence, slept together in the same bed, which was in a very lamentable state. Three of the boys with a similar affliction slept together in the same bed which was also in an abominable condition – the urine had not only saturated the bedding and the boards beneath the bed, but had found its way through the floor into the room below. In the kitchen, Mr Cane observed that the copper in which the foul linen was boiled was also used for cooking the food of the inmates.

20 OCTOBER 1856 An inmate of St Pancras workhouse named Arthur Stanley, aged forty-three, was confined to a padded room on account of his violent behaviour. The man was later found hanging from an iron bar near the ceiling of the room. He had unfortunately been entrusted with a handkerchief which, by an unusual effort, he had affixed to the bar and managed to tie around his neck.

21 OCTOBER 1850 Officers from the Shoreditch workhouse today attended the Worship Street court to seek advice on how to proceed against an inmate named John Sayers, aged sixteen. A few days earlier, another inmate named William White had noticed that Sayers had not touched his basin of breakfast gruel. Not wanting to let it go to waste, White, with Sayers' consent, consumed the gruel but noticed a brown-coloured sediment at the bottom of the bowl. Sayers told him that it was only the brown sugar used to sweeten the gruel. A few hours later, White was seized with such violent pains and sickness that he took to his bed, and continued in a state of excruciating suffering until the workhouse medical officer, Mr James Clarke, was called in. White successfully responded to treatment, but the liquid discharged by him had been thrown away, leaving no opportunity for analysis of its contents.

Sayers was later reported to have said that he had mixed up some stuff to give to the 'Old Prophet' – a reference to an inmate called Tom Pickard, who had predicted that Sayers would die on the gallows. According to another witness, Sayers had said that the 'stuff' was arsenic, and that he could access the workhouse surgery at any time and obtain any drugs he wanted. Sayers was sorry that White had taken the substance, which was not meant for him.

The magistrate, Mr Arnold, eventually decided that no substantive proof had been offered against Sayers, and he could only recommend that the parish authorities continue to watch the matter. Sayers was escorted back to the workhouse in the charge of the beadle.

22 OCTOBER 1828 The master of the Aldgate workhouse attended a hearing at London's Mansion House with a bandage around his head after being beaten in revenge by one of the paupers. The master stated that despite his best efforts to prevent the introduction of gin into the workhouse, the inmates managed regularly to get drunk. As might be expected, the gin inflamed more passions than one, and a female pauper had managed to make her way into the men's quarters where she was discovered in close conversation with a male inmate. When the master ordered the woman back to her proper place, her paramour had knocked him down and kicked him violently about the head and body. The assailant was then taken into custody. Soon afterwards, William Lamb, messenger to the paupers, was detected conveying seven small bottles of gin into the workhouse. The Lord Mayor remarked that it was an injustice to the distressed to keep in the workhouse persons who could afford to purchase gin. He asked the messenger, who was himself a pauper, what could have led him to take in such quantities of gin as made his companions drunk.

Messenger – Oh, your Lordship, they begged so hard of me to bring 'em a drop that I couldn't help it. They told me they were all so sick, that if they didn't get gin they would never get over it. (*A laugh.*)

The Lord Mayor – That does not justify you. They might have done dreadful mischief.

Messenger – But if I hadn't brought 'em gin now and then, your vorship, I could never live in peace with 'em. They'd d—n and b—t me so, your vorship, that I wouldn't be able to sleep a wink. (*Laughter*) You never knowed any think like their language.

The Lord Mayor – What! Both men and women?

Messenger – Lord bless you, yes; the vomen's the vorst. If I vouldn't fetch them a drop of max, they'd d—n me off my legs. I'm obligated to do it, your vorship; but, poor creeturs, they gets it but seldom.

The Lord Mayor – You must go to Bridewell for this. The mischief to which you are accessory is very great.

Messenger – What was I to do? They pays me wages, and when they are sick in the bowels, a'nt they have nothing to comfort 'em? If they gets a little tossicated, it's because their stomachs is empty.

The master refuted this attack on the workhouse, and said that if it had not been for the gin, which brought many of the unfortunate paupers to their present conditions, there would be no disturbance whatever amongst them. The assailant was committed for trial, and the messenger sent to Bridewell for a month.

23 OCTOBER 1892 Details emerged today of the mysterious disappearance of two officers at the Hampstead workhouse where a new master and matron, Mr and Mrs Graves, had recently been appointed. At a recent meeting of the guardians, Mr Graves requested five days' leave of absence from the workhouse, which was granted. At the same meeting Miss Lyon, who for several years had been assistant matron of the workhouse, tendered her resignation, which was accepted. The following Saturday, Mr Graves departed for his leave. On the same day Miss Lyon obtained permission from Mrs Graves for two hours' absence, in order, she said, to meet her sister at Waterloo Station. Mrs Graves later received a telegram from Lyon stating that she was going on to Southampton, as her father was very ill there, and that she would return the following Tuesday. She did not return, however, and had not been heard from since. It transpired that she had sent her boxes away from the workhouse before she left.

Mr Graves, too, had not been heard of. It was said that all his accounts were in order and no reason for his disappearance could be found in that direction.

1900 At Luton workhouse today, the death occurred of Nurse Binks, aged twenty. She had been reported to the Luton guardians on the previous day for drunkenness, with the workhouse medical officer recommending her dismissal. After an interview with the board of guardians, when she confessed that she could not resist the craving for drink, she was given a month's notice. Binks, who had threatened to commit suicide if she was dismissed, left the workhouse unobserved during the afternoon, and returned in an intoxicated condition. She was told to go to her room, and an hour later was found unconscious from the effects of laudanum. Despite the efforts of two doctors, she could not be saved.

24 OCTOBER **1929** The master of the Keighley workhouse, Norman Card, was today reported to have been dismissed following a Ministry of Health inquiry into allegations about his conduct. Card was said to have been guilty of improper actions towards a maid, drinking, sending inmates for drink, and of touching the bedclothes of a girl who had been sleeping in the workhouse dining hall after a dance.

1899 On this day it was revealed that at the St Pancras workhouse infirmary, Highgate, a man named Alfred Edwards had jumped from one of the building's

A ward block at the St Pancras workhouse infirmary where leper Alfred Edwards jumped to his death.

upper windows. The 70ft fall had resulted in his instantaneous death. Edwards, sixty-two, had been suffering from leprosy for twelve years or more. A spokesman for the infirmary said Edward had lived in an ordinary ward just like other chronic cases, just having his own special eating and drinking vessels. He had enjoyed being out in the gardens, smoked his pipe and had what he liked to eat. There had been no danger from him as leprosy did not flourish in northern climes, especially in the face of modern sanitation.

25 OCTOBER 1838 A meeting of the St Pancras vestry met today to discuss religious instruction at the workhouse. The chairman, Mr Horspool, reminded members that, in 1834, it had been decided that employing a chaplain was an unnecessary expense and, accordingly, they had thrown open the workhouse doors on Sundays, allowing the inmates to go where they pleased, requiring only that they be home at the proper time in the evening. In order to deal with the spiritual needs of the aged and infirm who were incapable of enjoying this privilege, a number of 'respectable Dissenters' had offered their assistance. So many, in fact, that making a choice had presented a great difficulty. However, a minister of the Established Church, the Revd H. Stebbing of St James's Chapel, had stepped forward to offer his services without payment. Two years later, he had been voted a letter of thanks with an award of £50 which he had donated towards the support of the schools. As two further years had now elapsed, he proposed a similar resolution. The motion was carried unanimously.

1913 Today at the Whitechapel workhouse in South Grove, Mile End, a lunatic evaded the attendants and, scaling a water pipe, reached the roof. For over an hour he kept the officials at bay in view of hundreds of people who collected in the street. Although paralysed in one leg, he showed remarkable agility in climbing from one part of the roof to another. He rained slates down on the attendants, and, becoming hot with his exertions, took off his coat and hung it up by the chimneys. Failing in their efforts to get him down, the officials tried directing a water hose on him, and when this failed they sent for the fire brigade. At intervals the man addressed the crowd below, telling them he had been badly treated inside, and that he would have to be brought down forcibly either dead or alive. Many in the crowd expressed sympathy with him, and cheered his efforts in keeping the attendants at bay. When the fire brigade arrived, an escape was put in place and several members of the brigade climbed up. After talking with the man for a while they persuaded him to come down voluntarily and he was taken inside the building and secured by the officials.

26 OCTOBER 1873 A pauper at the Plympton St Mary Union workhouse in Devon committed suicide by hanging himself. He appeared to have made a rope for

Some rather lethargic inmates picking oakum at Whitechapel workhouse.

that purpose using hemp taken from the room used for oakum-picking – a task given to inmates involving the teasing apart of old ropes into their constituent fibres.

27 OCTOBER 1894 Today's *Ipswich Journal* recorded the sad case of a man named Bayles, aged seventy-one, a labourer of Stradbroke in Suffolk. His situation was brought to the attention of Mr Henry Thirkettle, relieving officer to the Hoxne Union, who immediately visited the man's dilapidated cottage. Bayles, who shared the home with another old man, was found lying on the brick floor in a corner of the room, with nothing on but his shirt, trousers and stockings. He was unconscious, and throwing his arms up and moaning as if in pain. Dr Howe, the medical officer of the district, was summoned and at once ordered Bayles' removal to the workhouse infirmary at Eye, a telegram being despatched to summon a cab for the purpose. Some clothing was put on to the man, and brandy and water were given to him by Mr Thirkettle. On his arrival at Eye, Bayles was put to bed in the sick ward, and was shortly afterwards seen by the workhouse medical officer, who found him to be unconscious, pulseless and extremely cold. The officials made great efforts to give him brandy and other stimulants, but he was unable to swallow them and he died the following evening. It was said that Bayles had been lying for four days in the corner of the room where Mr Thirkettle found him.

28 OCTOBER 1836 In the American papers received today, it was reported that the roof of the workhouse at Rochester, New York, on which over 100 persons had collected to witness a balloon ascent, suddenly fell in, with a tremendous crash, causing a considerable number of men and boys to sustain serious injuries. Some were found to have broken their limbs and their backs, and one of them had an axe-handle forced completely through his leg. It later emerged that several had died from their wounds.

1896 This day marked the 106th birthday, at the Wandsworth Union infirmary, of what was said to be the country's oldest workhouse inmate, Mrs Jane Blower.

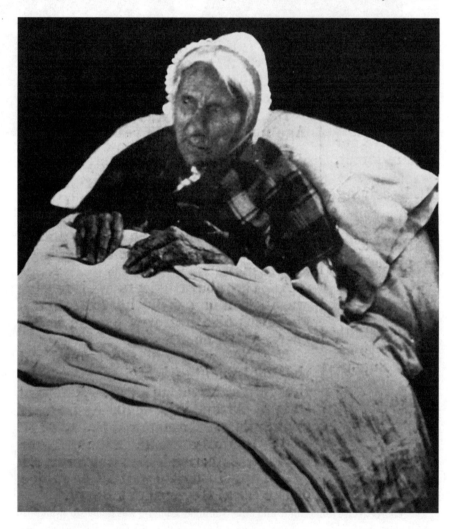

Mrs Jane Blower, at the age of 106, was still active and regularly ran the length of the workhouse ward. Her son, a mere youth in his eighties, was also an inmate of the same workhouse.

29 OCTOBER **1909** Today saw the posthumous publication of the autobiography of Henry Morton Stanley. Best known for his journalism and African expeditions, most notably his locating the missing explorer Dr David Livingstone, Stanley's formative years were spent in the St Asaph workhouse in North Wales which he entered in 1847 as a fatherless five year old, then named John Rowlands. It was, according to Stanley, a miserable experience. The scourge of the workhouse was a one-handed schoolmaster called James Francis whose cruelty seemed to know no bounds. On one occasion, Francis appeared to have been implicated in the death of a classmate of Stanley called Willie Roberts. On hearing of Willie's death, Stanley and several other boys sneaked into the workhouse mortuary and discovered his body covered in scores of weals. In 1856, Stanley had a violent showdown with Francis, in which he ended up knocking the teacher unconscious and thrashing him with his own blackthorn cane. Terrified of the consequences of his actions, he absconded over the workhouse wall and later ran away to sea.

30 OCTOBER **1838** Ralph Richardson, aged seventy, a pauper in the St Martin-in-the-Fields workhouse, was found dead just after seven this morning. A nurse discovered his body hanging by a rope attached to a nail in the wainscoting of the room in which he resided. She raised the alarm and one of the male paupers cut down the body which appeared quite lifeless. Richardson had been in a very infirm state of health which was thought to have also affected his mind.

1855 At about four this morning, a gas explosion occurred in the tramp ward of the Birmingham workhouse. The block, some 60ft square and 20ft high, was built of brick and covered in tiles. The accident appeared to have been caused by the ward's gas fire being moved about by some of the inmates trying to get a light for their tobacco and fracturing an under-floor gas pipe. Just before the explosion, a number of the men awoke and raised the alarm with cries of, 'There's an escape of gas! For God's sake let us out, or we shall be suffocated!' The night watchman, named Weare, opened the doors to let the men out and those who were able immediately rushed into the yard. Weare and a companion then entered the room carrying a lighted lantern. A most awful explosion followed which blew the building to pieces with the roof and walls showering down on those still inside. It was with the utmost difficulty that those trapped under the ruins were released. When they were taken out, many were literally naked, their clothes, rugs, and even shoes, having been burned and torn from their bodies, and many of them presented a most frightful appearance. Remarkably, there were no fatalities. Sixteen tramps were seriously injured and fourteen others suffered more minor injuries.

A plaque at St Asaph workhouse commemorates its unhappy association with H.M. Stanley.

31 OCTOBER **1900** A desperate murder took place today at the Saffron Walden workhouse, where a tramp named Thomas King, aged thirty, attacked William Woollard, superintendent of the stone-breaking department, with a hammer weighing 6lb. King first struck Woollard several times on the head, then knelt on his chest and battered him again. Woollard was removed to the workhouse infirmary but died shortly afterwards from his terrible injuries.

NOVEMBER

Islington workhouse inmate William Edwards
suffered a fractured skull after falling from a
ladder while cleaning windows. The use of
inmates classed as 'imbeciles' for such work was
criticised at his inquest. (*See* 14 November)

1 NOVEMBER **1839** In the early hours of this morning, the death occurred of Gwenllian Thomas, a seventy-four-year-old inmate of the Brecon workhouse. Mrs Thomas, and her husband of more than fifty years, William, had just been admitted to the workhouse and, as required by the regulations, placed in the separate women's and men's quarters. On being sent to bed, Mrs Thomas continually called out for her husband, expressing her anxiety for his comfort, but her cries went unheeded. At around midnight, she was found groaning at the bottom of a deep precipice near the workhouse. It appeared that she had jumped from one of the windows, some 16ft above the ground. She was carried back into the workhouse but death soon put an end to her suffering.

The workhouse at Brecon.

1951 At today's meeting of Lancashire County Council's Health Committee, Alderman Harry Lord said that 'terrible conditions' still existed in several former workhouses in the county. The Bury institution at Jericho still had only one bath for seventy-nine men, the dormitories were 50 per cent overcrowded, and men had to wash themselves in the same room where dishes were washed. When he had visited it he had been so moved that he had to go out before the inmates could notice his emotion.

2 NOVEMBER **1841** At a quarter to midnight, an alarm was raised that a fire had broken out in the laundry block of the Belper Union workhouse, Derbyshire. Many of the crowd that gathered refused to give assistance and even attempted to

intimidate those doing so, such was their wish to see the fire spread and consume the whole of the buildings. The blaze, however, was extinguished by two o'clock.

3   NOVEMBER **1899** A fire during the night totally destroyed the Westhampnett Union workhouse, near Chichester. Although parts of the building were four storeys high, all 115 inmates were safely evacuated thanks to the fire escapes installed on the premises. An old man suffering from heart disease later died from the shock, however. The damage to the building was such that it was decided to close it permanently.

4   NOVEMBER **1851** Following his visit on this day to the workhouse school at Southwell, the Education Committee's Inspector for the East and Midlands region, Mr H.G. Bowyer, observed that, 'The cause of the compulsory resignation of the late master and mistress is a remarkable instance of the low tone of morality so frequently exhibited by the present race of workhouse teachers. She was old enough to have been his mother.' The two teachers in question had been dismissed after it emerged that thirty-eight-year-old Maria Richardson had become pregnant by William Sumner, seventeen years her junior.

1901 William Copley, master of the Malton Union workhouse for the previous eight and a half years, was today charged at Malton Police Court with falsifying accounts and forging tradesmen's signatures, with the intention of defrauding the guardians of the union. Copley was alleged to have carried out a large number of such acts. In the previous April, he had paid a local grocer, William Wardell, the sum of £1 12s 6d for 5 stones of Yorkshire bacon but had then claimed reimbursement of £2 3s 9d. In May, he had submitted receipts which were purported to be payment to provision merchant Mr R.S. Wallgate, for a consignment of yellow soap, even though no soap had in fact been supplied. On another occasion, he had pretended to order 24lb of lard from Mr William Baker and forged a receipt to the amount of 16s. He was committed for trial at York Assizes.

5   NOVEMBER **1823** In East London, a serious fire broke out at the workhouse of St George-in-the-East. The blaze began in a room where inmates were employed in picking oakum and above which were several sleeping rooms. There were over 400 individuals on the premises who were rushed out into the yard and street. The parish fire engine soon arrived and set to directing water onto the conflagration. A search of the wards over the oakum room revealed four females who had been deprived of life, suffocated by smoke. One of these, it was said, had escaped in a state of nudity but had returned for her clothes and in consequence fell victim to her modesty. The body of a male inmate was subsequently recovered.

1861 In the morning, Mr Samuel Walker, fifty-three-year-old master of the Ashbourne workhouse, read prayers as usual to the male adult inmates. He was then not seen until about half-past nine when the porter found him hanging by the neck from a beam in the chapel. He summoned one of the female inmates who assisted in cutting down the body which was warm but quite dead. An inquest later that day returned the verdict that the deceased hanged himself whilst labouring under temporary derangement.

1866 Also on this day, Poor Law Board Inspector Mr R.B. Cane visited the Preston workhouse. His report described the establishment as 'old, ill-arranged, and unsuitable in every respect'. The wards were dark, low, close, gloomy, unhealthy and 'dangerously crowded', with many of the inmates, including patients with syphilis, sleeping two to a bed. In the 'itch ward', four patients, two men and two boys, had recently been sleeping together in the same bed. In the same ward, six men were occupying two beds, three in each bed. The man in the middle of the bed had his feet to the top of the bed, and his head came out at the bottom. In the midst of the ward, and in full view of the others, an adult patient was standing naked while a pauper attendant painted him over with a brush dipped in an application for his disease.

6 NOVEMBER

1901 It was reported today that the famous Nottinghamshire and England fast bowler John Jackson had died in the Liverpool workhouse infirmary in his sixty-ninth year. Known as the 'demon bowler', Jackson's first-class career, which had extended from 1855 to 1866, had come to an end after he sustained a serious injury whilst playing against Yorkshire. He visited Australia in 1863–64, at which time he was regarded as one of the best fast bowlers in the kingdom. Despite a small allowance from the Cricketers' Friendly Society, and the help of friends, Jackson had spent his declining years without a permanent address and on the brink of the workhouse, whose doors he finally entered.

7 NOVEMBER

1861 An inquest was held on the body of plumber George Newton, thirty-nine, who had met his death while working at Nottingham workhouse. Newton had gone down a well in the workhouse wash-up room to saw a suction pipe. He had pulled on the rope for a light, which was let down to him but soon went out. A rope being used to pull Newton up from the well then went slack. Another man went down the well, which was believed to be 36 yards deep, but his light also went out and he was drawn back up. A man named Sharp then descended with a lantern and, near the bottom, found the deceased with his legs fast in a ladder and his head hanging downwards. Sharp's light went out but a rope was let down to him and he tied it around the deceased's legs to pull him up. Sharp told the inquest that he had found great difficulty breathing in the well and had felt a dreadful sleepy drowsiness, almost as if he were drunk. It was said that Newton had lit a fire in the well the previous day to try and clear it.

8 NOVEMBER 1904 Following a circular from the Registrar General, proposing that any reference to the workhouse could be omitted when registering the births of those born in such institutions, it was today reported that the Honiton guardians had discussed the matter. The clerk's suggestion that the workhouse address be specified as '1, Love Lane' provoked much laughter. Eventually the name 'Marlpit House' was agreed. The *Western Times* commended the new scheme, which aimed to remove the stigma that attended workhouse children. It cautioned, however, that 'there is no need for giving to the workhouse a high-sounding appellation, [conveying] the impression that the unfortunate child was born within palatial walls. A simple title is all that is necessary.' The paper considered that the address proposed for the Okehampton workhouse, of 'No. 1, Castle Walk', was 'preferable to those aristocratic names which have been so readily adopted in some unions.'

9 NOVEMBER 1879 Details emerged today concerning the recent death of Charles Cartwright, aged sixty-four, who had been for many years an inmate of the Chorlton workhouse. Cartwright had squandered two fortunes of £40,000 and £80,000 respectively. He lived contentedly in the workhouse, and employed a portion of his time in writing poetry and also sermons for some clergymen of his acquaintance. When in possession of his wealth he had driven to his works in a

The entrance to the Chorlton workhouse, with a carriage at its gate.

carriage drawn by four horses, and he now seemed unable to restrain his extravagance when temporarily out of the workhouse. At one time his friends allowed him £1 a week which according to the clerk to the guardians he used to spend in driving about in cabs, smoking expensive cigars, or dining at the most expensive restaurants. When his last half-crown was reached, he gave that to a cabby to drive him, still in state and with a choice Havana, back to the workhouse.

10 NOVEMBER 1846 James Tuke, a Quaker, visited some workhouses in the west of Ireland that were suffering the growing strains placed on them by the famine which was now in its second year. At the workhouse in Swineford, County Mayo, he recorded that on this day:

> 120 were admitted beyond the regulated number. Hundreds were refused admission for want of room, some unhappy being pushed on the high roads and in the fields. Influenced by terror and dismay – leaving entire districts almost deserted – the better class of farmers, in numbers, sold their property, at any sacrifice, and took flight to America. And the humbler classes left the country in masses, hoping to find a happier doom in any other region. In this Union, 367 persons died in the workhouse; the Master of the workhouse also died. In the adjoining Union, Ballina, 200 were admitted to the workhouse beyond the number it was built for (1,200). Hundreds were refused admission for want of room and 1,138 died in the workhouse; the medical officer of the workhouse was also carried off. In another adjoining Union, Ballinasloe, all the officers of the workhouse were swept away, and 254 inmates of the workhouse perished.

11 NOVEMBER 1893 A touching workhouse romance was revealed today in a letter from an inmate of the Birmingham workhouse to the master, Mr Mitchell, and the guardians. Literally transcribed, the missive ran:

> Mr. Mitchell Governor Master and Esquire: Sir and gentlemen of the Committee, I Thomas Hughes have been your servant now 8 years, and desire to thank you all for your kindness to me and now gentlemen I am going to say I have Buried my wife 14 years and have been a poor wanderer since as I have not got a soul Living on Earth that I can speak to but gentlemen since I have been to the Old Women with my paper there is a female that noticed me as soon as I went and She said I believe that man is come for to be my husband. I never spoke for some time until I looked at her and said do you realy think so she said yes at least I

hope so. I said well if you will Consent to be my Wife I shall pledge myself to make you a happy Husband if the Gentlemen will allow us to be married. We shall be very happy I am sure as we are Both their servants and quite Satisfied we are able and willing to do anything that comes in our way and we desire nothing in this world but to marry and live Happy together. The female is 63 years of age and I am turned 80 years and we are both well and Hearty able and Willing to do any thing that comes and now Gentlemen we pray you to Grant us this our only Hope of our Blessed Comfort we also desire to continue in our Sittuations as we do not desire any Change. We are perfectly satisfied with our position and desire to be thankful Gentlemen I will appear before you on Friday.

We remain your Humble Servants. Thomas Hughes 80 Emma Llewllen 63.

1899 A man named Kenny, who occupied the post of gateman at the Kilrush workhouse in County Cork, committed suicide at 8.30 a.m. by hanging himself with a rope from the rafters within the lodge. The man, when discovered by another pauper helper, was quite dead.

12 NOVEMBER **1874** Details appeared today of the opening of an official inquiry at Cheltenham workhouse into a large number of charges brought against the master and matron of the establishment, namely that they had: inflicted punishment without reporting to the guardians; been absent from house after hours; not visited the men's wards at night; not reported property possessed by deceased paupers; misappropriated property of the guardians; scalded the milk and kept a number of fowls; fed visitors from the workhouse supplies; disposed of lard, and not accounted for money received from the sale of rags and bones; improperly cut up the pigs and kept the best joints preserved; given lumps of fat, cow's udder, lights and pipes to the paupers; used burnt sugar to colour the beef tea; failed to report complaints; bullied the inmates; allowed drunkenness in the house; permitted the officers to not dine together; and given out the officers' rations for the whole day. The proceedings were expected to last four days.

13 NOVEMBER **1839** Today's *Times* reported a court hearing at Wigan where a charge of violent assault had been brought against the workhouse master, Mr Dewhurst, by two of the establishment's inmates, John McAllister and his wife, Mary. The McAllisters occupied part of a room allotted to married couples where an extra bed had been brought in. Mrs McAllister learned that it was intended for the use of an unmarried male pauper, an arrangement to which she objected, and so she complained to the governor. A similar situation had arisen on a previous

occasion when the same man had been placed in the room while she was in labour. According to Mrs McAllister, Dewhurst said he would put her in handcuffs if she did not hold her noise about the matter. She then went to find her husband, who was in the sick room, and the two of them returned to the sleeping room and removed the extra bed. Dewhurst arrived at the sick room, and pulled the bed back in. An argument ensued between the two men and the bed tick was torn, after which Dewhurst knocked Mrs McAllister to the floor with great force. He then got hold of her husband, threw him on the bed, got on him with his knees, and stuck his hands into his throat. As a result, McAllister had been spitting blood since the incident. The magistrates fined Dewhurst £5 for his undue violence. Despite this, he remained in post as governor of the workhouse.

14 NOVEMBER 1815 At Hatton Garden magistrates' court, a young woman named Ann Keen was charged by the master of the Clerkenwell workhouse, Mr Henry Turner, of assaulting and beating him. Turner claimed that the woman, an inmate of the workhouse, frequently scaled the wall to get out and returned home intoxicated with liquor, behaving in a very refractory manner. Keen was committed to prison to await trial.

1873 At the Islington workhouse today, an inquest was held on William Edwards, twenty-five, who had died after falling from a ladder. The deceased, an inmate of the imbecile wards, had been ordered to clean some windows. While about 5ft from the ground, he was leaning forward, resting on the window, when the steps toppled over and he fell on his head. He was picked up, apparently in a fit, and taken to the infirmary. After a few days, he appeared to recover and carried on as normal until a fortnight later, when he was seized with more fits and died two days later. The workhouse medical officer certified that death was the result of brain disease, but the inquest had been instigated after the coroner received an anonymous letter. A post-mortem then revealed that death had been caused by a fracture of the skull which could not have been detected externally. A verdict of accidental death was returned, but the jury recommended greater caution in employing imbeciles for dangerous work.

15 NOVEMBER 1927 John Knox, an elderly inmate of Chesterfield workhouse, was found in the road with a severe wound in his throat. He was discovered in the Clay Cross area where he had been visiting. A passing female pedestrian heard him call out, 'I have cut my throat. Send for the police.' The man was speedily taken to the workhouse infirmary.

16 NOVEMBER 1883 At a rather jovial meeting of the Conway board of guardians, the chairman, the Revd Venable Williams, observed that in the workhouse's detached infirmary, the men and women were left very much to themselves. Both he and the master had seen two men and a couple of women regularly courting at the infirmary door. (*Laughter*) One man had chucked a woman under her chin, and they were obviously enjoying themselves. (*Laughter*) On entering the infirmary they had noticed two women endeavouring to escape observation by crawling away on their hands and knees. (*Laughter*) If the building was to continue in use as an infirmary, there should be a paid nurse to superintend it. Something should be done to prevent the free intercourse between the male and female inmates. It was a nice thing for such a state of affairs to exist at any workhouse. No wonder marriages were arranged there. (*Laughter*) Yes, and elopements, too. (*More laughter*)

17 NOVEMBER 1874 John Hanson, aged sixty, and Thomas Cooper, seventy-eight, inmates of the workhouse at Brixworth, Northamptonshire, died this evening within two hours of one another. Their deaths came the day after the union surgeon, Mr Harper, had given both of them injections of morphia to help them sleep. The workhouse master, Richard Giles, told an inquest that Hanson had been in poor health for years. A few months earlier, he had fallen down from a fit and was thought to be dying. Largely confined to his bed, he had become very restless and they had to tie his hands down to stop him hurting himself and causing damage. On the evening before his death, the doctor gave him an injection and he then seemed quiet. The next morning, he appeared to be fast asleep though was breathing very hard. When he would not wake, Mr Harper was sent for but did not come until that evening. Hanson died about five o'clock. Similar evidence was given in the case of Cooper, who had died at seven. Mr Harper said he had previously given them morphia without problem and had decided to try it again, injecting it into their legs with a syringe. He had expected it to result in sleep for the night. In the morning, he was informed of the state of the men but thought it could wait until his usual round. He had called at two o'clock and on no one answering the bell, decided to call back later. On his return, Hanson had just died, his pupils appearing greatly dilated, indicating that death was not the result of narcotic poisoning. Cooper was in a coma and had contracted pupils. He was with him about two hours, and applied several remedies, but without success. In both cases, it was reasonable for him to have administered morphia. A verdict of death from natural causes was returned on both men.

18 NOVEMBER **1889** Mary McDermott and Mary Sumner, inmates of the Bolton Union workhouse, were today charged with stealing the sum of £6 from another inmate named Mary Cabanis. Cabanis had been committed to the workhouse by a magistrate, pending her removal to a lunatic asylum. At the time of her committal, she had a number of bags of gold sovereigns secreted about her clothing, amounting to a total value of £127. The woman was placed under restraint at the workhouse, and the prisoners, who assisted in the hospital wards, had charge of her. While the woman was in their care and wearing a straitjacket, the prisoners extracted a bag containing £6 from her clothing and hid it in a bathroom. The sum of £54 was found under a pillow in a way that showed Cabanis could not have placed it there. The doctor was told about the robbery by Cabanis and made further investigations, with the result that McDermott admitted the theft. Both women were committed for trial.

19 NOVEMBER **1892** A disastrous fire broke out at the workhouse in South Molton, Devon, which resulted in the death or severe injury of a number of inmates. The fire began when a petroleum lamp was knocked over and broke into two pieces. The oil escaped and caught fire, burning a tablecloth and matting laid on the floor, and within a very few minutes the lives of a dozen people were at risk. The town council fire engine soon arrived but the fire spread rapidly. It gained a good hold on the north wing which comprised the dining hall on the ground floor, sick and infirm wards on the first floor, and other apartments on the upper storey. Use of copious water from the town main and from wells on the premises prevented the fire from spreading to other parts of the building. Rescue efforts were first directed at the sleeping rooms occupied by old people, some of whom had not been out of bed for several years. One woman, Mary Fuke, an inmate for only a few weeks, could not be found and her charred remains were discovered at about nine o'clock. The death toll from the blaze eventually rose to three, with many of the old inmates sustaining severe burns.

20 NOVEMBER **1893** Reports appeared today concerning a farm labourer, aged about forty years old, who had called at the Yeovil workhouse. With much shyness, he had told the master that he was in a difficulty, for he was in a constant place of work, with a cottage and garden, but as his wife was dead, and he had no children, he had no one to keep home for him. He then asked if the master could recommend him a decent woman as housekeeper, with a view to marriage. The master told him that there were several females in the house who would probably be only too pleased to become his housekeeper, and introduced him to a widow, the mother of a boy aged ten

and a baby eleven weeks old, and who was domesticated and comely in appearance. The master told the woman the object of the man's visit, and left them in the hall together to discuss terms. Half an hour later he returned to find that wonderful progress had been made, with the man declaring that 'Lucy' was everything his heart could wish for, an affection which Lucy heartily reciprocated for George (or 'Jarge', as she called him). The couple bid each other an affectionate goodbye, and George promised to fetch Lucy and her family on the following Monday. True to his promise, he arrived at the workhouse with his employer's horse and farm wagon (having previously written Lucy a gushing love letter), and drove triumphantly away with his intended wife and her children, saying that he was going to give her all the money he earned every week, and that he was sure she would make him a comfortable home. The wedding was to take place in a fortnight's time.

21 NOVEMBER 1835 Between seven and eight this evening, a daring attempt was made to murder Mr Ellis, governor of the Abingdon Union workhouse, or some of his family, by firing through the window of his sitting room – a small apartment, which contained at the time no fewer than five persons. Miss Ellis, the sister of the governor, who had been standing at the window, had just taken a seat when the bullet passed within a few inches of her head. In the former position it could not have missed her person. The ball then passed just over the head of an aged pauper, who was standing within the door of the apartment, and it afterwards entered, for the space of an inch into a wall at the end of the passage leading from the room, whence it rebounded and fell on the floor. It appears that the shot was fired from the workhouse garden and that the distance fired was about 48 yards from the window. After the mayor and several magistrates arrived on the scene, a second gun was fired. Four or five constables patrolled the premises during that night and the two following. A reward of £200 was offered for information leading to the conviction of the offender.

22 NOVEMBER 1830 A riotous crowd gathered in the village of Selborne, Hampshire, to protest against the low wages being paid to agricultural labourers and the unemployment being caused by the mechanization of farming. The horde later attacked the Selborne workhouse, pulling down the roof, smashing the furniture and ejecting the occupants – including a man named Harrison, one of the guardians of the poor. They also intimidated the local vicar, the Revd William Cobbold, telling him that his tithes must be reduced.

The following day, similar events took place at the nearby village of Headley. A mob of up to 1,800 assembled, including some of the previous day's rioters from Selborne.

Armed with sticks, they proceeded to the parish workhouse, looted or destroyed its contents, and then pulled the building to the ground. Many of those involved received a death sentence for their actions, but these were mostly commuted and replaced by transportation to Australia.

23 NOVEMBER 1860 An inquest was held today at the Black Horse Tavern, Shoreditch, on Thomas Bates, a cabinetmaker, aged sixty-two, who had committed suicide by hanging himself. A local shopkeeper, Thomas Milton, said he had last seen the deceased on the previous Monday after Bates had been to the Shoreditch workhouse. He had come into Milton's shop and said, 'If they do not take me into the workhouse, I shall destroy myself,' and added, 'I cannot live upon one pound of bread per day.' Bates had applied several times to the board of guardians, but they would not take him into the workhouse, instead allowing him 1s 6d per week and a loaf. The Shoreditch relieving officer denied that Bates had applied for admission into the workhouse. He had previously been an inmate of the house from October 1859 until 4 August, suffering from chronic bronchitis. After being declared fit by the medical officer, he was called before the board who directed him to be discharged and given a weekly allowance. The union clerk at first said that the deceased had left the workhouse voluntarily, but afterwards admitted that the board had ordered him to leave. The jury returned a verdict that the deceased had hanged himself while in an unsound state of mind, through having been refused admission to the workhouse.

24 NOVEMBER 1893 The death occurred today of an elderly patient in the Birmingham workhouse infirmary. The man had for a considerable period been suffering from spinal disease, and though improving steadily he had become moody and taciturn. When his breakfast was served, instead of eating it, he walked out to an exercising balcony adjoining the yard and flung himself over the balustrade on to the concrete yard beneath. Death was almost instantaneous.

1896 An unusual case of suicide was inquired into today at Manchester's Crumpsall workhouse. The deceased, John Dixon, aged forty-three, had been an inmate of the workhouse infirmary for thirteen months. He was confined to bed and had partially lost the use of his limbs. A fellow patient noticed blood on Dixon's bed and it was discovered that he had stabbed himself in the abdomen and cut his throat. Mystery was lent to the affair when a witness named Mrs Dyce deposed that before his death, Dixon had whispered to her, 'I didn't do it myself. I will take it with me or he will be hung.' The jury, however, returned verdict of suicide.

25 NOVEMBER **1929** Michael Power, an elderly inmate of the Cork workhouse, was today remanded on a charge of having murdered fellow resident Thomas Coatsworth, aged forty-six. The two men were at dinner when, in the course of a quarrel, Coatsworth was struck in the left breast with a knife and died within a few minutes. Power said that he was cutting bread when Coatsworth hit him in the eye with his fist. Power returned the blow, forgetting that he had a knife in his hand when he struck him on the breast.

1860 At Worship Street magistrates court, Shoreditch, a woman named Mary Ann Fossey, seventy-three years of age, complained that, although born and bred in Shoreditch, and now afflicted with leprosy in the arms, she had vainly sought admission to the workhouse, the only excuse given to her being, 'There is not room.' She also recounted that:

> On Wednesday night last, during that pouring rain, thirteen of us laid at the back of the workhouse; it makes me shudder to think what is endured – it is a fight for life. I was born at the corner of Pitfield Street: 21 years I have been a widow, and all I have received from the parish is 6s 6d. This morning they again refused me admission, and ordered me to wait till Wednesday next, the board day; but what am I to do until then? That is the question. Week after week, morning and evening, have I applied at that door. Sometimes I have been an inmate, but of course glad to leave when there was a probability of doing something for myself. I cannot now; and do you, the magistrates, for God's sake assist me.

The magistrate, Mr Barker, directed that she should be accompanied by a police officer to the workhouse. This was done, and she was admitted forthwith.

26 NOVEMBER **1833** Today's *Morning Chronicle* reported the ongoing skirmishes between certain female inmates of the parish workhouse of St George, Hanover Square, and the master, Mr Randford. He had previously brought five healthy young girls before the Marlborough Street magistrates for being disorderly and refusing to work. Some of the girls had been sent out to different situations by the parish, but they invariably left their places and returned to the workhouse. One had been sent to five different situations, all of which she had left of her own accord.

He now brought three more girls before the Bench for having created a disturbance in the workhouse by fighting and beating another of the pauper girls. The appearance of the girls was said to be that of the lowest description of prostitutes, and the master stated that their language and behaviour was most infamous.

The justice, Mr Chambers, asked the girls their ages and was told eighteen, nineteen and twenty-two.

Mr Chambers: 'What business have these girls in a workhouse at all? How can you expect any other conduct than what you complain of will be practised, when you keep such people in idleness in a workhouse?'

Mr Randford: 'Why, what can I do with them?'

Mr Chambers: 'Turn them out, and let them get a livelihood by honest industry.'

Mr Randford: 'If I was to turn them out, I should receive an order the next morning to re-admit them. The overseers give orders to admit them out of charity.'

Mr Chambers: 'They have no business to be charitable at the expense of the parish. If they want to be charitable, let them put their hands in their own pockets. Why don't you endeavour to send these girls abroad, where they may have a chance of becoming useful members of society? The expenses would not be so much as the cost of one illegitimate child, which you are most likely to be burthened with by girls of the description of the prisoners.'

One of the girls then called out, 'I am willing to go abroad; and if the overseers won't send me, I'll soon bring a bastard for the parish to keep.'

The magistrate committed the prisoners to a month's hard labour, and suggested the master try the experiment of refusing to admit them when they came out of prison.

1881 It was reported today that two inmates of the Devizes Union workhouse had quarrelled about their places by the fire. One of the men, named Geddish, aged seventy, took a heated poker from between the bars of the grate and thrust it into the neck of the other man, named Coleman, aged seventy-seven, who died within a few minutes from the results of the injury.

27 NOVEMBER **1837** Today's *Times* gave details of the inquest at Clapham workhouse into the death of inmate Charles Morris, aged thirty-two. Morris was widely rumoured to have died while working at the mill in the workhouse, provoking allegations of cruelty by the workhouse officers. The workhouse surgeon, Mr Samuel Solly, said he had seen the deceased on 15 November when he had complained of a bad cold caught from sleeping rough in the open air. He was given some medicine and directed to the union relieving officer who gave him a loaf but refused him admission to the workhouse, telling him to attend the next day's guardians' meeting. This he did, but was again refused admission and, having nowhere to sleep that night, was given 6d by the relieving officer. He was also offered work in the workhouse labour yard on a hand-cranked flour mill. On seeing him the next day, the mill superintendent decided he was unfit to continue and gave him lighter work. Despite Morris's further repeated

applications for assistance, during which time he had been spitting blood, he was not admitted to the workhouse until three days afterwards, when he was immediately put to bed and given sherry and water. The surgeon was called the next morning but, being on his way to an appointment elsewhere, did not arrive until two hours later, when he found the deceased in a state of collapse. He ordered some warm water for Morris's feet and sent for some medicine, but the patient died soon afterwards. The inquest jury found that Morris had died from influenza, and recommended that prompter measures be taken with any future cases of a similar nature.

28 NOVEMBER 1838 An uprising occurred this evening amongst some of the female inmates of the Stepney Union workhouse at Wapping. The disturbance was led by three girls identified as Lydia Flaxman, Maria Griffiths, a cripple, and Mary O'Neale. They and several others had been rampaging in the yard. When told to do their work, they all refused and encouraged others to do the same. At nine o'clock, the matron eventually persuaded the girls to go indoors, but instead of going to their beds, they went through all the wards crying out 'Fire!', 'Murder!' and 'Starvation!' Flaxman rang a bell in a ward containing forty aged females, and spread terror amongst them all. A policeman was summoned from the adjacent station-house to restore peace. On his arrival, a number of the girls were still riotous in manner and Flaxman, the ringleader of the affray, was captured and removed to the station-house. The disorder soon resumed with Griffiths, who wielded her crutch with great dexterity, and O'Neale then also being detained and locked up. In their cell, the girls had amused themselves by singing, cursing, swearing, and kicking at the door for four hours, until they became exhausted. A magistrate later sentenced each of them to twenty-one days' hard labour in the House of Correction.

1997 An instruction was issued today to all National Health Service Trusts, putting an end to pauper burials. Patients dying in institutional care would no longer be buried in unmarked graves but would now be entitled to burial or cremation after a 'dignified' ceremony attended by staff or fellow patients, and given a memorial plaque or headstone. Hospitals would be required to do everything possible to trace the relatives of anyone dying in their care and to keep records of next of kin. Where no relatives could be traced, or the family could not afford a funeral, the hospital would have to arrange a funeral, taking account of any known cultural or religious beliefs of the deceased.

29 NOVEMBER 1869 In the Court of Exchequer today, a breach of promise action was brought by Margaret Johnstone, former assistant matron at Bethnal Green

workhouse, against Thomas Wright, one of the Bethnal Green guardians. The two had become acquainted at the union's schools at Leytonstone while Johnstone was in temporary charge and Wright was on the establishment's Visiting Committee. He had afterwards courted her and they had attended an entertainment at the workhouse together. After Wright proposed to her, they had set a date for their marriage at which time Johnstone would resign from her situation at the workhouse. Wright asked that she conceal the true reason for her resignation as he had received much teasing from his fellow guardians about the relationship. Accordingly, she cited ill health as the cause of her retirement. Wright's ardour subsequently appeared to cool and during a five-week visit to Southsea for his health, he did not communicate with her once. Following a showdown with him, in which he denied that any engagement had ever existed, she instigated legal proceedings and was awarded £300 damages.

       1895 On this day, at Old Buckenham, Norfolk, the funeral took place of George Sturman, a recently deceased inmate of the Kenninghall workhouse. A few days afterwards, a workhouse inmate was sent to clean out the mortuary and was startled to see Sturman's body. He immediately went to the workhouse master and told him that Sturman had come back again. After seeking authority from the magistrates, the grave was opened, and the coffin was found to contain nothing but sawdust. A second coffin was provided, and a second funeral was conducted the following day.

30   NOVEMBER **1889** An inquest today into the death of Rose Morris, head nurse at the Bolton Union workhouse, aroused enormous excitement and speculation. Morris, aged twenty-seven, had accused a number of the union's guardians of immorality, claiming that her charges were backed up by letters the men had written to her, and which she had subsequently handed over to the workhouse medical officer Dr Marsh. The guardians decided to suspend Dr Marsh and Nurse Morris, with Morris being told to depart from the workhouse by 30 November. Two days before this deadline, she was found dead. Several witnesses testified that Morris had been in poor health and a post-mortem had indicated the cause of death to be heart failure, accelerated by the stress of the proceedings. She was also found to have been four weeks pregnant.

A Local Government Board inquiry heard from several of those implicated by Morris. William Golding said that he had been shown several letters he was alleged to have written to her and showing an immoral relationship between them. One referred to a visit to Chester with her, something he would swear had never happened. The Mayor of Bolton, John Barrett, denounced six letters he was purported to have written to Morris as vile and wicked forgeries. Similar denials came from other guardians involved.

Dr Marsh said he had originally believed Morris's allegations, including her claim that one of the guardians had offered her £300 to go away, but he now concluded that the letters were forgeries. It was also disclosed that all the letters had been burned in the presence of Dr Marsh and his solicitor, a revelation that provoked loud hissing from many of those observing the proceedings. Marsh further swore that no improper intimacy had taken place between him and Nurse Morris.

During an adjournment of the inquiry, Marsh resigned from his post. The Local Government Board thereupon issued a letter declaring that this now resolved matters, and that the inquiry had left 'no imputation on the character of any of the guardians.' At the guardians' next meeting, the missive provoked no discussion apart from one member remarking that he hoped the letter would not be burnt.

DECEMBER

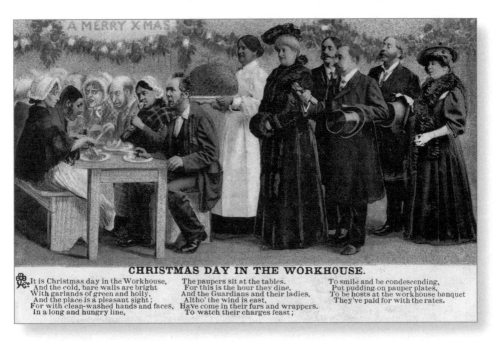

CHRISTMAS DAY IN THE WORKHOUSE.

It is Christmas day in the Workhouse,
And the cold, bare walls are bright
With garlands of green and holly,
And the place is a pleasant sight;
For with clean-washed hands and faces,
In a long and hungry line,

The paupers sit at the tables.
For this is the hour they dine,
And the Guardians and their ladies,
Altho' the wind is east,
Have come in their furs and wrappers.
To watch their charges feast;

To smile and be condescending,
Put pudding on pauper plates,
To be hosts at the workhouse banquet
They've paid for with the rates.

Christmas was a time of great celebration for most workhouse inmates, not least
because of the festive food they received – often paid for by the local well-to-do.
To some recipients, however, the gratitude they were expected to heap on 'their
betters' for such treats left an unpleasant taste in the mouth. The popular Victorian
monologue *In the Workhouse – Christmas Day* was a reflection of such attitudes.

1 DECEMBER 1765 Mark Fisher, master of the workhouse at Bluntisham, Huntingdonshire, and several of the poor under his care, were troubled with 'the itch'. In hope of providing a remedy to this painful malady, Fisher mixed a quantity of arsenic, Roman vitriol (copper sulphate), glass and soap, into an ointment, and anointed himself and five women with it. His concoction proved so disastrous that he and two of the women soon died from its effects, leaving the other three in a very serious condition.

2 DECEMBER 1862 A case of suspected arson occurred at Huddersfield's Kirkheaton workhouse. The alarm was raised at about 5.50 a.m. by an inmate who smelled burning and saw a glare of flames through her bedroom window. She roused the matron, Mrs Berry, who went downstairs and discovered the middle dayroom filled with flames. The building was soon evacuated and the fire extinguished with only relatively minor damage having been caused. Indications of arson came a few hours later when a bed in a room above the dayroom was found to be on fire in different places and had several cinders in it, despite no direct means existing for this to have arisen from the earlier blaze.

1886 At about two-thirty this afternoon, a disastrous fire broke out at Chelmsford workhouse, resulting in the destruction of nearly all the main buildings. The fire was discovered in the roof of the chapel at the centre of the building's top floor. Fire engines were summoned from the town, but by the time they arrived the chapel roof had collapsed and the flames had spread out to all four wings, creeping along the roof rafters. Men and women ran from room to room throwing bedding and furniture out of the windows. Many of the old inmates appeared paralysed by the catastrophe and children were crying at the destruction taking place. The absence of a long ladder on the premises almost resulted in the death of the master, Mr Rowe, who had returned to his private rooms to retrieve some treasured items belonging to his wife. On his return, he found his way cut off by flames. Fortunately, a ladder was just then brought on the scene and he was able to descend safely from a window. By five o'clock the fire had completely gutted the centre of the buildings. The upper wards of each wing were entirely burnt, only the bare walls standing, while the fire continued to burn below. The inmates were gathered in various detached buildings where they were given food and huddled around fires, many still in shock at the events.

3 DECEMBER 1759 Two inmates of the parish workhouse of St Andrew, Holborn, appeared for sentencing at London's Guildhall. The pair had removed a two-month-old infant from its mother, also in the workhouse, and taken it to the Foundling

Hospital, where it had died. The two were each given a fine of 40s and a month's imprisonment in the Poultry Compter.

4 DECEMBER 1890 Early this morning, a terrible fire at the Newcastle-under-Lyme workhouse resulted in the loss of six lives. The fire was discovered in the women's wing, at one end of which, on the upper floor, five old ladies had their bedroom. Just after 6 a.m., one of their number descended to the sitting room and, discovering it full of smoke, raised the alarm. Before she could be rescued she was almost suffocated. The master, Mr Edwards, and other officers were soon at the scene, where the flames had already made considerable headway. One old woman was shouting frantically from her bedroom window. With the help of one of the porters, she was brought semi-conscious down a ladder. The blinding smoke and intense heat made it impossible to enter the dormitories to rescue the other old people who probably now lay unconscious.

After the fire was extinguished, a search was conducted for the bodies of those missing. The charred remains of one of the old women was found in the corner of the staircase. The sight was a sickening one, the head being burned from the body and much of the flesh from the bones. Other remains found in the debris were burned beyond recognition, having the appearance of a mass of charcoal. In all, five women perished, together with a little boy named Willie Hood who was being nursed by one of the inmates.

5 DECEMBER 1867 Henry Pepler, aged fifty-five, was found dead in a water closet at St Luke's workhouse, City Road, where he had been an inmate for several years. The circumstances of his demise were a mystery, however. Pepler had been ill for several weeks but, declining to enter the workhouse infirmary, had been granted permission to visit an outside doctor. During the course of his illness, he had consulted doctors at three different hospitals. A post-mortem found that Pepler's stomach was a deep violet colour and contained nearly two grains of prussic acid and about ten grains of carbonate of potash. The cause of death, therefore, was poisoning by potassium cyanide. Its source, though, remained an enigma. None of the doctors consulted by Pepler had prescribed any medicine containing prussic acid. The means by which the poison had been administered were equally baffling. Although suicide was clearly a possibility, the jury at his inquest could only conclude that Pepler had died from poisoning in unknown circumstances.

6 DECEMBER 1827 A meeting of the Exeter Corporation of the Poor was held to consider alleged misconduct by the former superintendent of the Exeter workhouse,

James Gardiner, and the housekeeper of the establishment, Robert Davey. Gardiner had been discharged from his post following Davey's accusations that he had made an inmate drunk, and for other alleged misdemeanours. Gardiner now brought forth a catalogue of transgressions said to have been committed by Davey, with articles such as rolls, strong beer, sacks of malt and flour, and large amounts of beef having been illicitly removed from the workhouse under his direction, some ending up with friends of Mrs Davey. Stockings manufactured in the workhouse had been disposed of, and superfine cloth had been produced in the house for Mrs Davey's riding habit. At the end of the proceedings, members were evenly split in their views, with a motion to dismiss Davey from his post just being carried by fifteen votes to fourteen.

7   DECEMBER 1868   At Bethnal Green workhouse, a Poor Law Board inquiry began into allegations that Mrs Mary Wells, matron at the union's schools at Leytonstone, had been cruel to children in her charge. James Wells, the master of the establishment, was also accused of having been absent without leave and returning intoxicated at 1 a.m.

A few weeks earlier, four girls, all aged about fourteen, had absconded from the schools. They had been recognised by a guardian in Bethnal Green and said they had run away from the schools after being beaten. The children were then taken to the workhouse where the medical officer found marks on them that might have been made by a cane.

One of the girls, Sarah Prior, told the inquiry that the matron had only ever hit her once, a slight stroke across the hand with a small cane. She explained that the marks on her back and on the three other girls had come from being beaten with sticks by some boys they had been playing with on the day they had absconded. Another girl, Mary Jane Frogget, said she had seen the matron strike Prior four times on the back with a cane after the girl had refused to clean some brass taps in the kitchen.

Evidence against James Wells came from several of the schools' staff. He had been seen drunk on three occasions, including on his late return from a visit to Southampton. In his defence, Wells called PC Miall, the constable on duty in the vicinity at the time, who confirmed that the master had been sober. On further questioning, however, Miall admitted that he himself had recently been dismissed for drunkenness while in uniform, though off duty.

The charges against Mr Wells were found to be proved, and his immediate resignation was demanded. The charges against Mrs Wells were found not to have been substantiated, although she admitted giving the girls 'handers' contrary to the regulations. However, as her tenure of office depended on that of the master, her immediate resignation was also called for.

8 DECEMBER 1871 At Barnsley workhouse today, an ironstone miner named James Kaye was lying unconscious as a result of self-inflicted injuries. Kaye, aged forty years, had developed mental problems and entered the workhouse two days previously. He was placed under restraint in the padded room, and kept under watch during the night. The next morning his attendant left him for a short time and on returning he found that Kaye had used his teeth to unloosen a fastening on his straitjacket. Having got his hand loose, he had set about piercing his throat with the tongue of a large buckle in a very frightful manner. The effort to unfasten the straps must have been a terrible one, as nearly all his front teeth were loosened, whilst one was completely dislodged. Despite the best efforts of the house surgeon, Kaye's injuries were so serious that he died two days later.

9 DECEMBER 1835 It was reported today that considerable consternation had been caused at the Brighton workhouse by a group of female inmates who had been engaged in cleaning the men's dormitories. Taking advantage of a door left open, they had descended a flight of stairs leading to the men's dayrooms and there mingled with their partners. News of the occurrence soon reached the master and guardians, who were at that time holding their weekly meeting. They joined in the fray, resulting in men, women, guardians and governor all milling together 'pell mell'. The high constable was called in and, after a severe struggle, some of the most desperate and refractory characters were placed in the 'black hole'. The men, on showing penitence, were later released, promising in future to conduct themselves in a peaceable and orderly manner.

10 DECEMBER 1828 Today's *Times* noted the publication of a report on the condition of the workhouse at Exeter, following a number of reforms at the institution. The report's authors found that arrangements were generally now in excellent order but observed with regret and surprise that a new wine bin had been erected at the workhouse. It appeared that, despite the recent changes, there had been no end to the long-standing practice of 'the Committee of nine indulging themselves with wine, and afterwards with tea, coffee, and cream'. *The Times* wondered whether this was the clotted cream for which Devon was so celebrated. It also mused on whether the poor might, on these occasions, be eating a wholesome meal of beef and ale, with a slice of plum pudding each.

11 DECEMBER 1869 Reports appeared today of sensational revelations at the inquest on Shoreditch workhouse inmate John Presnall. The inquiry was only instigated after the body had already been buried at Colney Hatch Cemetery, when the coroner, reading a newspaper story about the matter, ordered it to be exhumed for examination. Joseph Hullett, a pauper, said he had been in the infirmary ward where Presnall was lying in bed, delirious. He was continually shouting 'Tobacco!' and to stop him, the nurse, Mrs Susannah Hart, held a handkerchief over his mouth for about two minutes. When she removed it, Presnall had shouted 'Murder!' The wardsman, named Samuel Clarke, again placed a handkerchief over his mouth. The nurse, saying 'I'll soon quiet him', fetched a bottle and poured something down his throat while Clarke held him down. After this dose had been given, Presnall had made no more noise and remained insensible until his death a day later. Mrs Hart stated that she gave the deceased some liquid provided by the dispenser, it being left to her discretion as to when she should use it. The liquid contained morphia, but she believed that half a bottle of it would have done the man no harm. Dr Whitmore, who had conducted the post-mortem, said that death had probably resulted from dropsy. The jury criticised Mrs Hart for administering morphia without the doctor's sanction and also censured Clarke and Hart for their conduct.

12 DECEMBER 1858 Today's *Observer* published details of a growing scandal at the St Pancras workhouse. It appeared that a young assistant surgeon, by the name of Muskett, had seduced several of the female inmates, one of whom had become pregnant. In attempting to effect an abortion, the man had attempted some surgical procedure. However, his actions had resulted in the woman needing to be admitted to the workhouse infirmary. Fearing the consequences of his activities coming to light, Muskett had gone into hiding from where he had made contact with the workhouse chaplain, the Revd Thomas Pugh, appealing for some spiritual aid in his time of adversity. The Revd Pugh had complied with this request and visited Muskett, whose whereabouts he subsequently refused to divulge. At their latest meeting, the St Pancras guardians had also now decided to dismiss the chaplain.

1907 On this day a gas explosion occurred at the Knighton Union workhouse, Radnorshire, causing structural damage to part of the building.

13 DECEMBER 1839 A woman named Elizabeth Searle entered the Totnes workhouse with an illegitimate child about eight months old. She was placed in the probationary ward but, being afraid to sleep alone, a workhouse inmate named Margaret Farley was allowed to sleep with her. On retiring, they partook of some penny-royal tea, and in the morning they were both found in a state of stupor and apparently dying. The child was dead, having been laid upon and smothered by them during the night. Mr Gillard, the workhouse surgeon, was immediately sent for and concluded that the two were suffering from the effects of poison. On examination, however, no trace of any

Damage caused by the explosion at Knighton workhouse.

toxic matter could be found. The tea had all been drunk, and nothing was left in the mugs. The stomach pump was applied, and other remedies administered, but without effect, and both women remained senseless. Later that day, a coroner's inquest was held on the child, and a verdict returned of 'died by suffocation'. Over the next few days, the two women gradually began to recover. Searle, aged twenty-six, apparently had two illegitimate children and was expecting a third. It was speculated that she had taken poison herself and given some to the other woman.

14 DECEMBER 1881 The Birmingham board of guardians met today to consider serious complaints against medical staff in the workhouse infirmary who, it was alleged, had administered blisters and cold showers as punishments to patients. It was said that people in the town were now terrified of entering the infirmary. A girl named Peters, after being confined to a padded room by the doctor's orders, had declared that she would not be punished for nothing, and smashed the windows with a poker, for which she was taken before magistrates and sent to prison. The chairman of the committee expressed his indignation at much of what had been revealed, declaring that some of the patients – imbeciles in particular – were unfit for punishment of any kind. Such things as padded rooms, blisters and shower-baths were cruelties, not punishments. He moved a resolution of no confidence in the senior medical officer, Dr Simpson.

Birmingham's workhouse infirmary.

A subsequent Local Government Board investigation of the matter decided, however, that there was no foundation whatsoever for the charges of cruelty. Baths and blisters had only ever been administered as remedial agents, and that if such treatments happened to follow the nurse's threats, then it was pure coincidence, although the use of such threats was in itself unwarranted. The placing of Peters in the padded room had been an 'error of judgment'. The root of the problem at the infirmary, the Board concluded, was an insufficiency of staff. In addition to all his other duties, Dr Simpson had to attend 144 bedridden and seventy convalescent patients each day, while his assistant had to prescribe for the ailments of 570 patients.

15 DECEMBER 1904 An inquest held today at Nantwich heard the distressing circumstances of the death by poisoning of the workhouse matron, Mrs Pritchard. An attendant entering Mrs Pritchard's bedroom had found her and her seven-year-old daughter lying unconscious in bed. Medical assistance was at once summoned and it was discovered that they were suffering from laudanum poisoning. Two empty bottles on a nearby washstand had contained the substance. Mrs Pritchard died soon afterwards but her daughter recovered. A sealed letter left by Mrs Pritchard was handed to the coroner's office. The inquest heard that the deceased had been in ill-health over the previous year and may have become depressed at the prospect of her daughter leaving home to be educated. Her husband had suddenly disappeared a few years earlier and had later died in

Canada. In the letter, which was addressed to a relative, Mrs Pritchard wrote that she thought she would go mad at times, her head was so bad. She added that she could not leave her little lassie behind her. The child said that her mother had drunk some medicine and had asked her to do the same.

16 DECEMBER 1879 At Doncaster workhouse, two old men, Samuel Pott and John Shirtcliffe, were seated around the fire along with other inmates, discussing the price at which firewood was being sold by the workhouse. After an argument developed between the two, they began scuffling in their seats. Pott then pulled a knife out of his pocket and stabbed Shirtcliffe in the head and face several times, inflicting a number of serious wounds. Pott was handed over to the police and later committed for trial at the Quarter Sessions.

17 DECEMBER 1886 At Lincolnshire's Boston workhouse, a twenty-year-old pauper named Matthew Herriott was scrubbing the floor of the passage of the infirmary when fellow inmate Robert Smith, eighty-five, passed through and went into the yard. When he wished to return, Herriott refused to let him pass, and pushed him with such violence that he fell into the yard. Smith was immediately taken inside, the bridge of his nose being abrased and both his eyes becoming blackened. The next day, Herriott was taken into custody charged with the assault. Smith died a week later, on Christmas Eve. After conducting a post-mortem, Dr Smith, the workhouse medical officer, told the inquest that the deceased had been a very weak and feeble man and although the assault had accelerated his demise, he could not say that it had caused it. Herriott was severely censured by the coroner and brought before magistrates for his conduct.

18 DECEMBER 1838 The *Weekly Dispatch* today reported that at a recent meeting of the Keighley guardians, a poor young woman was brought before them, charged with idleness. After a discussion as to the quantity of work that should be performed by a pauper, one of the board, a magistrate, gave his judgment that, 'You are to earn 3s a week by weaving, to nurse your own child, to wait upon your mother (who is also in the workhouse), and to wash for them as well as yourself; and if you do not do this, you shall be committed to hard labour and the silent system.' The girl, who was said to be little more than a child herself, retorted, 'Gentlemen, I will save you the trouble of condemning me to this slavery,' and, leaving the room, ran to the river, into which she was throwing herself when two of the union officers caught her, and brought her back to the board.

19   DECEMBER   1867   At Sunderland workhouse today, an inmate named John Bellwood, aged seventy-two, was eating his dinner when he began to cough. Putting his hand to his mouth to prevent the meat he was chewing from coming out, some of it became stuck in his windpipe and he died a few minutes later.

1868   Also on this day, Henry John Clark was charged at Maidstone Assizes with setting fire to the Malling Union workhouse. Clark had been in the workhouse tramp ward along with a man named Brown and his two children. Clark had brought some wood into the ward and set it alight. Brown, who was asleep, woke up and found the wood burning, with his own clothes also on the fire. Brown called out 'Fire!' whereupon Clark had threatened to knock out Brown's brains with a stick. In his defence, Clark claimed he had lit the fire to kill certain noxious insects which infested the ward, and that the guardians, instead of prosecuting him, should award him £100 for what he had done for them. Clark was sentenced to seven years' penal servitude.

20   DECEMBER   1899   Today saw the opening at London's Albert Hall of the nineteenth annual toy and doll show, organised by *Truth* magazine, and regarded as one of the most interesting features of Christmastide in the capital. On display were examples of the 25,000 or more toys donated by the magazine's readers for distribution amongst London's hospitals, workhouses, workhouse schools and infirmaries. Around 3,000 dolls, ranging in size from a few inches to more than 3ft high, had been dressed by contributors, some set in enormous tableaux illustrating fairy tales, nursery rhymes, two scenes from *Henry VIII*, and a gipsy camp containing fifty-two dolls. Each child inmate was to be the happy recipient of a separate toy for his or her own use, whilst the large and more expensive toys were presented for the general use of inmates in workhouses and hospitals. An anonymous donor had furnished a gift of 11,000 new sixpences, while Mr Tom Smith had specially made 25,000 crackers for the children.

21   DECEMBER   1816   An inquest was held at Bethnal Green workhouse following the death of an inmate, Robert Pope. Pope had been dragged from his ward into the oakum cellar by two fellow inmates, Thomas Kendall and James Saint, who then bound him by the wrists and beat him with a stave from a butter tub. The two men were angry with Pope who had reported them for climbing over the workhouse wall and taking workhouse articles with them. The following day, Pope had been black and blue, very sore, and hardly able to lie in bed. He was vomiting blood and died shortly afterwards. At Kendall and Saint's subsequent murder trial, medical evidence indicated that the attack on Pope might have accelerated his demise but was not the immediate cause of it. Accordingly, both men were acquitted.

22 DECEMBER **1875** Just before eight this morning, the training ship *Goliath*, moored on the Thames off Grays in Essex, was devastated by a fire in which many lives were lost. The ship, operated by the Forest Gate School District, was home to 480 pauper boys from East London. The fire began in the ship's lamp room when a petroleum lamp was knocked over. The blaze spread rapidly due to a strong wind blowing at the time, and all the portholes being open to dry the lower deck which had been scrubbed early in the morning. Although discipline was generally good, the screams of some of the terror-stricken youngsters were terrible to hear. It soon became clear that the vessel

Rescue efforts in progress to save boys from the blazing *Goliath*.

was doomed and all aboard tried to make their escape. Although the ship was well equipped with boats, the flames quickly burned their tackle, making them unusable. As one of the boats, filled with about thirty lads, was preparing to leave the side of the ship, another boat, the lowering gear of which had been burned through, fell on the first, killing several of those aboard. Lifelines and Jacob's ladders were burned while boys were clinging to them but most of those who dropped in the water swam until they were picked up. Few were able to leave the ship with all their clothes on and many were naked. Others just jumped into the water, although sadly not every boy in the company could swim. The eventual death toll from the disaster was twenty-three.

23 DECEMBER 1897 A terrible accident occurred this evening at the Mill Road workhouse infirmary, Liverpool. Several of the staff and their friends were rehearsing a Christmas entertainment for the inmates when a nurse at the infirmary, Edith Ellen Ashcroft, aged twenty-five, stepped across the footlights on to the stage. The muslin skirt of her costume was caught by a gas jet and she was immediately enveloped in a mass of flames. She sustained shocking injuries and died on Christmas Day. The death caused all the Christmas festivities at the establishment to be abandoned.

Liverpool's Mill Road infirmary.

1930 Also on this day it was reported that a terrible tragedy had occurred at a workhouse in Jicim, a Czechoslovakian town to the north-east of Prague. In order to destroy vermin, the workhouse had been fumigated with cyanide gas. After the rooms had been aired the inmates were allowed to return. The next morning it was discovered that the rooms had not been sufficiently ventilated, and seven people had died from cyanide-gas poisoning. Sixteen people were transferred to hospital, where three died, and the condition of the others was reported to be very serious. All the dead were between the ages of sixty and eighty.

24 DECEMBER **1844** At about six o'clock in the morning a fire broke out at the Banbury Union workhouse, Oxfordshire, in which some 275 pauper inmates were resident. The matron, Mrs Gate, up at her usual early hour, discovered the blaze amongst the oakum on the landing near the bell turret. It was started by an inmate, Mary Arnold, a girl of thirteen, falling with a lighted candle in her hand against the oakum. The sick and infirm inmates were evacuated first, and women and children could be seen running around the nearby streets wrapped in blankets and with their nightcaps. All got out safely, however. It was said that a deplorable apathy and indifference was observed amongst many of those present at the scene, some standing with their hands in their pockets and others absolutely refusing to assist.

1898 At Carlisle workhouse, Mary Beattie, fifty-five, a tramping hawker, tried to take her own life by cutting her throat with a knife. She failed in that attempt, but taking a strap from her basket, she hanged herself by the neck from a gas bracket, located just 5ft from the ground. She dropped on her knees and strangled herself.

1900 A coroner's jury today returned a verdict of 'death by misadventure' on Catherine White, an elderly inmate of the Stepney workhouse, who had died as a result of a blow on the head inflicted by another aged inmate named Wetherell. Wetherell, who had asked White to pray with her, was described as a woman of weak intellect and the coroner said that it would be ridiculous to send her for trial.

25 DECEMBER **1885** At Oxford workhouse, the usual Christmas celebrations took place. The dining hall was elaborately decorated, and outside well-wishers of the inmates assisted at the dinner, which consisted of joints of beef and legs of mutton; vegetables, potatoes and parsnips – the produce of the workhouse garden; and plum pudding. The dinner was well cooked, with the pudding having been boiled for twenty hours. The master, addressing the inmates, said it was a great

satisfaction to him to see them enjoy themselves with the good things provided for their entertainment on Christmas Day, when all was done for their comfort by the kindness and goodwill of the guardians and ratepayers. The provision for them that day had been made with the heartiest goodwill. It must be a satisfaction for them to know with what goodwill and kindly feeling their feasting had been provided. He therefore asked them to respond with even more heartiness in giving their thanks to the guardians and the visitors for the enjoyment of the day. Apples (the gift of Mr H. Pether) and oranges were then distributed, with pipes and tobacco for the men and snuff for the women. Each woman in the infirmary had a present from Mrs Spooner, and each man received a gift from Mrs Harvey. An ample tea brought the day to a close.

1835 The Christmas Day celebrations in this year at the Bishop's Stortford workhouse were marred by an outbreak of fire in the evening. However, by the prompt measures taken, the blaze was quickly subdued. Blame for starting the fire was laid upon three workhouse inmates who were later committed to Hertford Gaol.

1896 The tramps who had made the casual ward at Kingston-on-Thames workhouse their headquarters on Christmas Eve were invited to prolong their stay a few hours, in order to join in the annual Christmas Day dinner of roast beef and plum pudding, with allowances of beer, sweets, fruit and tobacco. Curiously, all of them declined the invitation.

1898 An aged pauper inmate of the male sick ward at Bath workhouse, named Foster, was found dead in a passage this morning, having fallen from a window above.

26 DECEMBER **1853** At the Plympton St Mary Union workhouse, near Plymouth, two inmates of the vagrants' ward, George Page and his son Joseph, were discovered to have lit fires in their dormitory – an action that was strictly forbidden. The fires were composed of wood and straw, one being placed in the middle of the ward and the other under a wooden sleeping crib. The two men refused to help extinguish the fires, the elder one saying that he had lit them to warm his feet, and that they would help destroy vermin. The pair were later committed to the assizes for trial.

27 DECEMBER **1864** An inquest took place at St Bartholomew's Hospital today into the death of Timothy Daley, aged twenty-eight, who had died there four days earlier.

Daley's decline into ill-health had begun in October and he had been admitted to the Holborn workhouse infirmary. According to those visiting him there, Daley said that he had never seen a doctor and was only attended by a wardsman and a female nurse. His perspiration ran through his bedclothes to the floor, and his blankets and sheets were unfit for use. Poultices on his sores went unchanged for two days. Eventually, on 14 December, he discharged himself, saying that if he stayed there another night he would be dead. He returned to his lodgings where he was visited by a doctor from the Farringdon Dispensary who found him emaciated and exhausted, and with an almost unbearable stench coming from his bedsores. The doctor organised his removal to St Bartholomew's where he received further attention but died the following day.

The Holborn medical officer, John Norton, testified that Daley had been very emaciated when admitted to the workhouse infirmary. He had often been delirious and had no control over his actions, resulting in the bedding getting very wet. The bedding had been changed every day and poultices changed two or three times a day. He had not examined the bedsores more than necessary since it could create more harm than good, the pain of moving the patient's body being excruciating.

The inquest jury found that the cause of death had been 'bedsores and exhaustion, supervening upon rheumatic fever; and that while an inmate of the Holborn Union he did not receive sufficient attention at the hands of the medical officer.' Daley's case received great publicity and added to the pressure for reform that resulted in the 1867 Metropolitan Poor Act, which brought about major improvements in the care of the capital's sick poor.

28 DECEMBER 1891 It was reported that twelve-year-old Selina Yeadon, a former inmate of the Wharfedale Union workhouse at Otley, West Yorkshire, was set to inherit a fortune from the late Major Middleton of Ilkley. Five years earlier, the lifelong bachelor had visited the workhouse in his capacity as a guardian of the union, and was particularly taken with the pretty and obviously intelligent child – so much so that he arranged for her removal from the workhouse. He had initially planned to provide for her education, so allowing her to become a governess when she grew up. Afterwards, however, with the consent of her mother, he adopted the girl as his daughter.

1903 William Johnson, aged forty-nine, an inmate of the York workhouse, today committed suicide by hanging himself. Johnson's widow told an inquest that he had suffered from delusions, the result of drink, and had left home several times believing that she was going to poison him. The doctors would not certify him as insane, but had advised him to go to the workhouse, where they thought he would soon recover. On Christmas morning she had received the following letter from him:

> Dear Lizzie, I have nothing to rite about, but you must make the best of this horrible affair. Give my love to Beaty, yourself, and all, also the children. XXXX When I went to the shop dinner there was a man who used to say two pieces which I took a lot of notice of. They was called. 'Xmas Day in the Workhouse,' and 'I am in the Asylum now.' Hoping there will be a happy New Year, and good health, from your loving WILLIAM.

The inquest also heard that Johnson's hands were tied behind his back, and on his breast was pinned an envelope, inside which was written, 'Good-bye, Sid, your mother is a vile woman. I hope God will forgive her. Good bye, my bonny Beaty.' On the outside were the words, 'To Thee, O God, I commend my spirit. Good bye, Stanley.' A verdict of 'suicide whilst temporarily insane' was returned.

29 DECEMBER 1877 At about eleven o'clock in the morning, a fire was discovered at the Auckland Union workhouse, County Durham. It was located in

The York workhouse.

the roof of the washhouse where steam machinery for washing had recently been installed. An iron chimney had overheated and ignited adjacent woodwork. The fire brigade were quickly upon the scene and soon extinguished the flames.

1930 An inquest was opened at Walthamstow today into the death of Reginald Alfred Wise, aged nine months. It was stated that on Christmas Eve his mother, Olive Kathleen Wise, aged thirty-seven and unmarried, had placed the boy into an unlit gas oven where he had died due to coal-gas poisoning. The woman, who had another child and was expecting a third, was remanded on a charge of murdering her son. It was said that she was desperately anxious not to let her children spend Christmas in the workhouse and was at her wits' end. At her subsequent trial, Wise was convicted of murder and sentenced to death, but this was later commuted to life imprisonment. She gave birth to twins in Holloway Prison and in 1932 was reprieved and released from custody.

30 DECEMBER 1892 A bizarre mystery unfolded at Newcastle-upon-Tyne today after James Murray, a patient in the workhouse infirmary, was found lying dead in his bed with a fearful gash across his throat. The bedclothes were covering his head, and it was only when these were removed that the horrible discovery was made. No blade was found beside him with which he could have committed the deed. The other men in the ward, several of whom were in their dotage, were unable to tell anything about what had happened during the night.

A woman who had known the deceased in a Newcastle lodging house claimed that on several occasions she had heard him threaten to take his life rather than suffer the misery he experienced. On further consideration, however, the initial suspicion of suicide seemed less plausible. The bedclothes above the dead man had been carefully folded back, with the exception of the upper sheet, which was pulled over his face giving the body the appearance of having been laid-out. The nature of the wound would have prevented the man pulling the sheet over his head after cutting his own throat, as all the main blood vessels were severed. On the other hand, if he had cut his throat while under this sheet, it would have been stained with the blood as it gushed from the wound. The sheet, however, was entirely free from stains, although the wall above the bed was spattered with blood. It seemed that not only was the sheet drawn over the man's face after death, but was carefully arranged to avoid contact with the wound. Although no blade was found near the bed, a knife was discovered on a windowsill near the bed of a man named Bodger. It appeared to have been recently cleaned, though some blood was still visible near the haft. Since there were no bloodstains near where the knife was found, it seemed clear that even if Murray did commit suicide, the knife must have been taken from him by another hand.

The doctors put forward their own theory of the strange crime. The position and nature of the wound suggested that it was most probably self-inflicted. However, after Murray had committed suicide, one of the other inmates must have covered the body up, taken away the knife and cleaned it, and so created the scene that had baffled the police. At the subsequent inquest, Bodger was present but apparently very ill and refusing to give evidence. The jury returned an open verdict – that there was not sufficient evidence to show whether the fatal wound was inflicted by the deceased or another person.

31 DECEMBER 1875 At today's meeting of the Garstang Union guardians, a letter was read from the Local Government Board, asking for an explanation of the alleged ill-treatment of a young inmate at the Garstang workhouse. In their letter was forwarded the copy of a report sent to them by an eyewitness who, passing by the workhouse, had heard a scream and run to investigate. On looking over the wall, he had seen an inmate throwing canfuls of cold water over another inmate, a boy, who was standing naked in the yard. Such conduct appeared to the witness as very strange and unnatural, especially on such a cold day. One of the guardians, Mr R. Jackson, stated that the lad was continually breaking out of the workhouse, and this punishment had been inflicted upon him for this offence. The lad, he said, was afterwards well wiped down, put into a bed, and some tea brought to him. He had suffered nothing serious from the treatment. The matter was given to the Visiting Committee to examine.

A depiction of the New Year's Eve celebrations at an unnamed workhouse.

1926 Also on this day it was revealed that Joseph Beeson, who died in the Hull workhouse, had directed that all his possessions should go towards placing a clock on the church tower at Benington, Lincolnshire. The clock had now been bought with the 1,100 half-crowns which it was found that he had salted away.

BIBLIOGRAPHY

Books

Anon (1732) *An Account of Several Work-Houses for Employing and Maintaining the Poor*

Anon (1885) *Indoor Paupers, by One of Them*

Ayers, G. (1971) *England's First State Hospitals 1867-1930*

Anstruther, I. (1973) *The Scandal of the Andover Workhouse*

Baxter, G.R.W. (1841) *The Book of the Bastiles*

Booth, W. (1890) *In Darkest England and the Way Out*

Crompton, F. (1997) *Workhouse Children: Infant and Child Paupers under the Worcestershire Poor Law, 1780-1871*

Crowther, M.A. (1981) *The Workhouse System, 1834-1929: The History of an English Social Institution*

Digby, A. (1978) *Pauper Palaces*

Eden, F.M.S. (1797) *The State of the Poor: Or, an History of the Labouring Classes in England*

Edsall, N.C. (1971) *The Anti-Poor Law Movement, 1834-44*

Gibson, O. (2006) *Indoor Relief: A Diary of the Life and Times of a London Workhouse*

Green, D.R. (2010) *Pauper Capital*

Greenwood, J. (1866) *A Night in a Workhouse*

Higginbotham, P. (2006) *Workhouses of the North*

Higginbotham, P. (2007) *Workhouses of the Midlands*

Higginbotham, P. (2008) *The Workhouse Cookbook*

Higginbotham, P. (2011) *Life in a Victorian Workhouse*

Higginbotham, P. (2012) *The Workhouse Encyclopedia*

Higginbotham, P. (2012) *Voices from the Workhouse*

Higgs, M. (1906) *Glimpses into the Abyss*

Higgs, M (2007) *Life in the Victorian and Edwardian Workhouse*

Hitchcock, T.V.E. (ed.) (1987) *Richard Hutton's Complaints Book: The Notebook of the Steward of the Quaker Workhouse at Clerkenwell 1711-1737*

Hitchcock, T.V.E. (2007) *Down and Out in Eighteenth-Century London*

Hodgkinson, R.G. (1967) *The Origins of the National Health Service: The Medical Services of the New Poor Law, 1834-1871*

Humphreys, R. (1995) *Sin, Organised Charity and the Poor Law in Victorian England*

Knott, J.W. (1986) *Popular Opposition to the 1834 Poor Law*

London, J. (1903) *The People of the Abyss*

Longmate, N. (1974) *The Workhouse*

Mayhew, H. (1861-2) *London Labour and the London Poor* (4 volumes)

Monnington, W. and Lampard, F.J. (1898) *Our London Poor Law Schools*

Morrison, K. (1999) *The Workhouse: A Study of Poor Law Buildings in England*

Neate, A.R. (2003) *St Marylebone Workhouse and Institution, 1730-1965*

Nicholls, G. (1854) *A History of the English Poor Law*

O'Connor, J. (1995) *The Workhouses of Ireland*

Orwell, G. (1931) *The Spike*

Powell, A. (1930) *The Metropolitan Asylums Board and Its Work, 1867-1930*

Ribton-Turner, C.J. (1887) *A History of Vagrants and Vagrancy, and Beggars and Begging*

Richardson R. (2012) *Dickens and the Workhouse*

Richardson, R. (1987) *Death, Dissection and the Destitute*

Richardson, R. and Hurwitz, B. (1997) *Joseph Rogers and the Reform of Workhouse Medicine*

Rogers, J. and Rogers, J.E.T. (1889) *Joseph Rogers, M.D.: Reminiscences of a Workhouse Medical Officer*

Stallard, J.S. (1866) *The Female Casual and Her Lodging*

Stanley, D. (ed.) (1909) *The Autobiography of Sir Henry Morton Stanley*

Twining, L. (1880) *Recollections of Workhouse Visiting and Management During Twenty-Five Years*

Williams, K. (1981) *From Pauperism to Poverty*

Wood, P. (1991) *Poverty and the Workhouse in Victorian Britain*

Websites

http://www.workhouses.org.uk/

http://www.british-history.ac.uk/

http://www.britishnewspaperarchive.co.uk/

http://www.connectedhistories.org/

http://www.historicaldirectories.org/

http://www.londonlives.org/

http://www.motco.com/

http://www.nationalarchives.gov.uk/about/living-poor-life.htm

http://www.oldbaileyonline.org/

http://www.victorianweb.org/history/sochistov.html

http://www.visionofbritain.org.uk/

INDEX OF
WORKHOUSE LOCATIONS

Bedfordshire
    Leighton Buzzard, 98
    Luton, 191
Berkshire
    Abingdon, 111, 208
    Reading, 17, 168
    Wallingford, 47
Buckinghamshire
    Chesham, 99
    Eton, 72, 89
    High Wycombe, 131
    Winslow, 98
Cambridgeshire
    Cambridge, 22, 73
    Newmarket, 137
Cheshire
    Chester, 48, 122
    Knutsford (Bucklow), 141
    Macclesfield, 117
    Nantwich, 80, 222
    Northwich, 72
    Stockport, 22
Cornwall
    Bodmin, 172
Cumberland
    Carlisle, 227
    Longtown, 176
    Penrith, 163
    Whitehaven, 114
Czechoslovakia
    Prague, 227
Derbyshire
    Ashbourne, 201
    Belper, 54, 199

Chapel-en-le-Frith, 127
Chesterfield, 116, 171, 205
Shardlow, 95
Devon
    Bideford, 77
    Devonport (Stoke Damerel), 27
    Exeter, 183, 217, 219
    Honiton, 202
    Newton Abbot, 75, 98
    Okehampton, 202
    Plymouth, 85, 128, 171
    Plympton St Mary, 192, 228
    South Molton, 207
    Tiverton, 50
    Totnes, 220
Dorset
    Cranborne, 18
    Wimborne, 18
Durham
    Auckland, 166, 230
    Bishop Auckland, 18
    Gateshead, 150
    Hartlepool, 63
    Sedgefield, 158
    Stockton-on-Tees, 112
    Sunderland, 32, 187, 224
Essex
    Braintree, 26, 82
    Brentwood, 103
    Chelmsford, 74, 216
    Colchester, 27
    Rochford, 129
    Saffron Walden, 197
    Tendring, 13

Walthamstow, 231
West Ham, 129, 139, 166, 171, 188

Gloucestershire
Barton Regis, 159
Bristol, 57, 179
Cheltenham, 204
Clifton, 68
Gloucester, 72
Stroud, 46

Hampshire
Alresford, 93
Andover, 144
Basingstoke, 125
Bishop's Waltham, 49, 76
Droxford, 49, 76
Fareham, 61, 76
Fordingbridge, 79
Gosport, 26
Headley, 208
Isle of Wight, 112
New Forest, 84
Selborrne, 208
Southampton, 158

Herefordshire
Hereford, 14
Weobley, 26

Hertfordshire
Bishop's Stortford, 228
Hatfield, 73
Hemel Hempstead, 183
Hertford, 37
St Alban's, 112

Huntingdonshire
Bluntisham, 216

Ireland
Athy, 41
Ballinasloe, 188
Ballinrobe, 99
Belfast, 107, 128, 146
Birr, 31
Carlow, 135
Castlebar, 76
Cootehill, 184
Cork, 59, 210
Drogheda, 26
Dublin, 17, 174
Fermoy, 135

Kenmare, 31
Killarney, 22, 169
Kilrush, 204
Limerick, 94
Listowel, 187
Macroom, 90, 100
New Ross, 44
Newry, 111
Parsonstown, 31
Skibbereen, 170
Sligo, 186
Swineford, 203
Youghal, 101

Kent
Canterbury, 168
Chatham (Medway), 43
Eastry, 15, 48
Greenwich, 67
Hoo, 62
Maidstone, 139
Malling, 224
Tonbridge, 92

Lancashire
Blackburn, 53, 158
Bolton, 141, 182, 207, 213
Burnley, 92
Bury, 118, 160, 199
Chorlton, 55, 118, 148, 202
Garstang, 232
Haslingden, 64
Liverpool, 18, 46, 49, 64, 67, 71, 81, 96, 132, 166, 201
Manchester, 67, 84, 89, 139, 165, 180, 209
Oldham, 23, 102, 151
Preston, 12, 31, 201
Prestwich, 164
Rochdale, 59, 71
Toxteth Park, 57, 113, 185
West Derby, 45, 49, 123, 226
Wigan, 17, 204

Leicestershire
Barrow-upon-Soar, 65, 168
Leicester, 29, 58, 71, 110, 157
Market Bosworth, 108

Lincolnshire
Boston, 175, 223
Grimsby, 209

Holbeach, 82, 170
Lincoln, 155, 179
Louth, 173
London, 224
Aldgate, 189
Bethnal Green, 44, 67, 158, 170, 213, 218, 224
Bow, 85, 150
Bradford, 157
Camberwell, 66, 95, 137
Chelsea, 64, 122
Christchurch, 81
City of London, 30, 54, 56, 124, 141
Clapham, 83, 211
Clerkenwell, 25, 30, 157, 205
Cripplegate, 36, 154
Forest Gate, 12, 225
Fulham, 177
Greenwich, 23, 181
Hackney, 67, 103, 148, 167
Hampstead, 66, 113, 148, 190
Hanwell, 102
Holborn, 229
Islington, 134, 135, 175, 205
Kensington, 64, 94
Lambeth, 19, 50, 137
Lewisham, 186
Mile End Old Town, 28, 149
Newington, 14, 50, 102
Poplar, 42, 66, 139, 147, 171
Saffron Hill, 29
Shoreditch, 45, 159, 189, 209, 210, 219
Southwark, 81
St Andrew, Holborn, 53, 216
St Ann's, Limehouse, 164
St George in the East, 200
St George, Hanover Square, 15, 210
St George-the-Martyr, 132
St Giles & St George, 35, 81, 134, 172
St Giles, Cripplegate, 154
St Luke, 217
St Margaret & St John, Westminster, 25, 62, 152, 154
St Martin-in-the-Fields, 14, 133, 195
St Marylebone, 24, 32, 111, 116, 123, 136, 175, 180
St Pancras, 36, 51, 167, 189, 191, 192, 220
St Paul, Covent Garden, 119, 182
St Saviour's, 114, 147
Stepney, 212, 227
Strand, 50, 108, 123
Tooting, 77
Training Ship Goliath, 225
Wandsworth and Clapham, 83
Wapping, 28, 212
West London, 46, 129
Westminster, 15
Whitechapel, 121, 160, 192
Middlesex
Edmonton, 63, 147
Staines, 111
Norfolk
Cromer, 172
Downham, 148
Great Yarmouth, 36
Heckingham, 82
Kenninghall (Guiltcross), 43, 132, 213
King's Lynn, 152
Loddon and Clavering, 82
Norwich, 53
St Faith's, 118, 175
Yarmouth, 117
Northamptonshire
Brixworth, 206
Kettering, 81
Northampton, 48, 73
Northumberland
Belford, 141
Longtown, 107
Newcastle-upon-Tyne, 231
Nottinghamshire
Nottingham, 40, 80, 183, 201
Retford, 13
Southwell, 200
Oxfordshire
Banbury, 227
Chipping Norton, 63
Oxford, 227
Russia
Rukovishnikoff, 154
Rutland
Oakham, 65

Scotland
    Falkirk, 72
    Glasgow, 120
    Govan, 101
    Hamilton, 163
    Montrose, 99
Shropshire
    Atcham, 57, 93, 98
    Bridgnorth, 50
Somerset
    Bath, 110, 228
    Bridgwater, 38, 101
    Chard, 158
    Yeovil, 207
Staffordshire
    Burton-on-Trent, 102, 169
    Newcastle-under-Lyme, 217
    Stafford, 95
    Walsall, 90, 112
Suffolk
    Bosmere & Claydon, Barham, 15
    Hoxne, 193
    Ipswich, 66, 181
    Thingoe, 84
Surrey
    Chertsey, 43
    Guildford, 39, 114
    Kingston-on-Thames, 128, 228
Sussex
    Brighton, 61, 74, 219
    Hastings, 152
    Horsham, 25
    Lewes, 155
    Uckfield, 134
    Westhampnett, 200
Sweden
    Oesthammar, 107
    Swerdsjo, 51
United States
    Dover, New Hampshire, 40
    Jackson, Michigan, 29
    Rochester, New York, 194
Wales
    Aberayron, 67
    Brecon, 199
    Cardiff, 93, 130
    Carmarthen, 118
    Conway, 206

    Knighton, 220
    Llandovery, 138
    Neath, 153, 181
    Newport, 48
    Pembroke, 118
    St Asaph, 195
    Swansea, 134
    Wrexham, 102
Warwickshire
    Aston, 47
    Atherstone, 56
    Birmingham, 108, 113, 141, 195, 203, 209, 221
    Coventry, 36, 56
    Nuneaton, 155
    Rugby, 22, 68
Wiltshire
    Devizes, 211
Worcestershire
    Bromsgrove, 31, 37
    Dudley, 114, 168
    Martley, 80
Yorkshire
    Barnsley, 16, 102, 219
    Bedale, 156
    Beverley, 163
    Bradford, 68, 159
    Doncaster, 223
    Driffield, 85
    East Whittton, 170
    Goole, 124
    Harrogate, 12
    Horbury, 45
    Huddersfield, 89, 91, 188, 216
    Hull, 13, 92, 96, 127, 174, 182, 233
    Keighley, 60, 71, 191, 223
    Leeds, 12, 85, 110, 130, 134, 135
    Malton, 200
    Middlesbrough, 131
    North Bierley, 59
    Pickering, 124
    Pontefract, 48, 174
    Saddleworth, 129
    Sculcoates, 114
    Sheffield, 28, 75, 112, 113, 148
    Tadcaster, 40
    Wharfedale, 229
    York, 99, 151, 229

If you enjoyed this book, you may also be interested in…

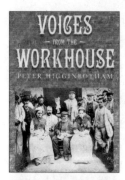

Voices from the Workhouse
PETER HIGGINBOTHAM

Voices from the Workhouse tells the inside story of the workhouse – in the words of those who experienced the institution at first hand, either as inmates or through some other connection with the institution. Using a wide variety of sources – letters, poems, graffiti, autobiography, official reports, testimony at official inquiries, and oral history, Peter Higginbotham creates a vivid portrait of what really went on behind the doors of the workhouse.

978 0 7524 6749 8

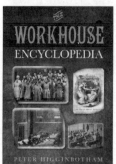

The Workhouse Encyclopedia
PETER HIGGINBOTHAM

This fascinating, fully illustrated volume is the definitive guide to every aspect of workhouse life. With hundreds of anecdotes, plus priceless information for researchers including workhouse addresses, useful websites and archive repository details, maps, plans, original workhouse publications and an extensive bibliography, it will delight family historians and general readers alike.

978 0 7524 7012 2

The Workhouse Cookbook
PETER HIGGINBOTHAM

This book is richly illustrated with over 100 photographs and covers all aspects of food in the workhouse, including full details of the diets in the prison and medical wings and the special meals available for young children. With sections on how to brew the perfect workhouse cup of tea and the menu for a typical workhouse Christmas dinner, this is a unique and shocking exploration of food in a system that has now gone for good.

978 0 7524 4730 8

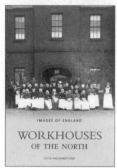

Workhouses of the North
PETER HIGGINBOTHAM

This book takes a look at both surviving and lost examples of workhouse buildings in the North of England, covering the old counties of Cumberland, Northumberland, Durham, Westmorland, Lancashire and Yorkshire. Family, local and social historians will all find it a source of useful reference and for the general reader it will provide an interesting account of an institution that few were sorry to see the end of.

978 0 7524 4001 9